D1271982

"The Mayor
Who Cleaned Up
Chicago"

William E. Dever *(Chicago Historical Society: ICHi 20811)*

"The Mayor Who Cleaned Up Chicago"

A POLITICAL BIOGRAPHY OF
WILLIAM E. DEVER

John R. Schmidt

NORTHERN ILLINOIS UNIVERSITY PRESS

DeKalb 1989

MEDIA & TECHNOLOGY SERVICES
EVANSTON TOWNSHIP HIGH SCHOOL
1600 DODGE AVE.
EVANSTON, IL 60204

© 1989 by Northern Illinois University Press
Published by the Northern Illinois University Press, DeKalb, Illinois 60115
Manufactured in the United States of America using permanent, acid-free paper.
Design by Julia Fauci

Library of Congress Cataloging-in-Publication Data

Schmidt, John R., 1947–
"The mayor who cleaned up Chicago":
a political biography of William E. Dever / John R. Schmidt.
p. cm.
Bibliography: p.
Includes index.
ISBN 0-87580-144-7
1. Dever, William E. (William Emmett), 1862–1929.
2. Mayors—Illinois—Chicago—Biography.
3. Chicago—(Ill.)—Politics and government—to 1950.
4. Corruption (in politics)—Illinois—Chicago—History—20th Century.
I. Title.
F548.5.D48S35   1989
977.3'11042'0924—dc19
[B]   89-31364
CIP

921
Dev

To Terri

Not because I'm supposed to,
but because she deserves it

Contents

Illustrations

Acknowledgments

■ One of the great pleasures of seeing a book in print is being able to thank those who helped it get there. Many persons had a part in this book.

My foremost professional debt is to Arthur Mann of the University of Chicago. He has been with this project since before the beginning, when I had only a vague idea of what I wanted to write about for my doctoral dissertation. The historical profession has long recognized Professor Mann's stature as a scholar. Those of us privileged to have been his students also know of his qualities as a mentor. His analysis is probing, his editing rigorous, his encouragement both warm and practical. The hazards of history-writing become almost manageable after working with him. Andrew Greeley probably put it best when he called Arthur Mann a "fleet admiral of history."

Much of my early research was at the Chicago Historical Society, and I am greatly indebted to the staff there, particularly to Archie Motley and the Archives and Manuscripts Department. Thanks, too, to the staffs of the University of Chicago Libraries, the Newberry Library, the Municipal Reference Library of Chicago, the Chicago Public Library, the Library of Congress, the State Historical Society of Wisconsin, the American Jewish Archives, the Boston Public Library, and the Woburn Public Library. Among the many individuals who aided me along the way, I express my particular gratitude to John Hope Franklin, Neil Harris, Barry Karl, and Paul Peterson, presently or formerly of the University of Chicago; Perry Duis, Melvin G. Holli, and the late Milton Rakove of the University of Illinois at Chicago; Paul M. Green of Governors State University; John D. Buenker of the University of

Wisconsin—Parkside; Douglas Bukowski of Rosary College; Ray Berry of Chicago-Kent College of Law; Bill Sullivan of the *Woburn Daily Times;* Dorothy Petak, my boss at Julia Ward Howe School; Howard Pollock; the late Robert E. Merriam; Studs Terkel; my mother-in-law, Angela Noncek, for help on the Polish-language translations; and my mother, Rita Schmidt, for her on-going support. My thanks to Mary Lincoln of the Northern Illinois University Press, to her staff, and to her readers, whose insights, suggestions, and constructive criticisms have helped this book reach its final form.

When I started writing about Dever, I had no children. Now I have Nicholas and Tracy. My apologies to them for being preoccupied too much of the time, and my thanks to them for keeping quiet (usually) while Daddy was in the study working.

My wife, Terri, has shared in every aspect of the development of this book over the past nine years. She has also borne two children, done more than her share of raising them, and developed a notable professional career—all while keeping her sense of humor and helping me keep my sense of perspective. Terri says she is not a Superwoman. I know better. I love her deeply, and the dedication expresses only imperfectly what I owe to her.

A.M.D.G.

Introduction

■ For the greater part of the present century, the story of politics in Chicago has been the story of the Cook County Regular Democratic Party Organization: the Chicago machine. It dominated the city's public life. To many of those growing up in the shadow of its power, the Democratic organization seemed to be almost a phenomenon of nature that one simply adapted to—like the fog in San Francisco or the flooding of the Nile. Also running through this legend of invincibility was the hint of corruption, that despite (or because) of its efficiency the machine did not really serve the cause of clean government. The knowledgeable and the cynical explained the party's resiliency by quoting the maxim of one-time alderman Paddy Bauler: "Chicago ain't ready for reform yet."

The irony of this particular view is that the Democratic machine first gained its power as an agent for reform. Sixty-odd years ago, the city's good-government activists joined with the emerging ethnic blocs to wrest control from the older rulers. They united to elect a Chicago mayor, William E. Dever. This is his story and the story of those times.

Although Dever has become an obscure figure in the history of Chicago, in his day he cut an impressive profile. He built great public works, took the public schools out of politics, cut waste, and revitalized city government, all without a trace of scandal. He also gained nationwide fame for strictly enforcing the Prohibition laws and running the gangsters out of town. He was celebrated as "the Mayor Who Cleaned up Chicago," and some men spoke of him as the next president of the United States. Dever did a lot in his one term as mayor; the record is clear, and it is enviable. Then, he lost reelection—and was forgotten.

What has also been forgotten is the significance of his elections: winning the office, then losing it. Dever's accession in 1923 was a watershed in the flow of Chicago politics. The existing courses of power were shifted. The conjunction of various disparate elements made this mayor. Likewise, Dever's defeat in 1927 represents more than an officeholder misreading the public mind. The Dever saga tells of many things.

Part of the story, of course, is about the birth of that redoubtable Democratic machine. Early Chicago political parties were loose associations of factions orbiting around various individuals. Starting about the turn of the century, certain ambitious Democratic leaders began working to deliver their party from this condition. By the early 1920s they had succeeded in bringing together all the main groups. The factional infighting was moved behind closed doors, while the party presented a unified public front. The question now was what the Democrats would do with their new-found unity. Could they take control of the local political world—and if they did achieve the upper hand, could they keep it?

Intimately associated with the development of the Democratic organization is the matter of ethnic politics. The immigrant peoples who had swelled the expanding nineteenth-century city were now, in the twentieth century, beginning to reach for a bigger share of the political spoils. The Irish politicians who ran the Democratic party were finding it advisable to make accommodations for the increasingly assertive "newer ethnics" from southern and eastern Europe. At the same time, immigrant groups of all pedigrees—old and new—were challenging White Anglo-Saxon Protestant dominance in the higher offices of the local, state, and national government. Dever's career provides important insight into these processes.

While the machine was gathering power and the ethnic groups were assimilating, Chicago's reform movement continued to evolve. The clean government forces had reached their peak during the century's first decade, then declined in number and influence. Progressivism, a great national reform movement, was awakening; and historians have long pondered what happened to it later, during the 1920s. In Chicago, at least, the reform impulse did not die out. It remained very much alive, guarded and carefully nurtured by a remarkable collection of idealistic yet politically astute individuals. How the Chicago reform movement developed and how the keepers of its spirit were able to make common cause with the new Democratic organization is another part of the story.

Bringing all these strands together is William E. Dever. In 1923 the local Democratic leaders discovered in him the perfect candidate to unite their coalition. Today, he is a perfect candidate through which to study the abstract phenomena of reform, organization development, and ethnic advancement—

because he personalizes them. The first part of his biography is a mini epic of American politics, bootstrap style. Of notable talents, though by no means extraordinarily gifted, Dever molded a successful political career on a combination of intelligence, perseverance, cunning, and geniality. When events converged to present him with his grand opportunity, he was ready. His election as mayor of Chicago, then, represents both the convergence of historical forces and the capstone of an individual's career building.

The second part of this study examines Dever's four years as mayor, and how his successes and failures in office led to his eventual defeat. The climax is the 1927 mayoral election. Though perhaps not as pivotal an election as the one four years earlier, it is significant in its own right. It steered the established Democratic organization down a particular road—and it is probably the liveliest election in the city's history. A new America was developing in the years following World War I: the country was moving toward a more urban, industrial, multicultural, multiethnic society. Chicago was changing, too; and the new Democratic machine would be successful because it would be able to service these changes. From Dever's time at least, it became established that in Chicago the machine and reform would be only the most temporary and uneasy bedfellows.

The setting for Dever's fall is in the context of the 1920s, a time everyone seems to remember, whether they lived through it or not. The images of the decade have become part of our collective unconscious. Flappers, gangsters, Gatsbyesque parties, Lindbergh showered with confetti, Babe Ruth trotting out a home run, Valentino with a burnoose, or Calvin Coolidge in a warbonnet—they overlap in the memory like a montage of sepia snapshots from a treasured old family album. Yet for all its remembered flamboyance and charm, it was a mean decade. The changes of the times produced strains and overreaction. Nativism revived on a large scale and manifest itself in various ways; in fact, mistrust of groups outside one's own sphere became widespread. In Chicago, that "most American" of American cities, these stresses were notable. The city's population grew 25 percent during the decade, and despite the spread of subdivisions, different groups began bumping into each other. Violent confrontation often resulted—most explosively when blacks and whites met but also across religious lines and when old ethnic stock fought new, and when one ethnic group disliked another. John Higham deftly captured the suspicious temper of the times when he called these years "the tribal twenties."

At the heart of this conflict was the great domestic political issue of the 1920s: Prohibition. The dry law symbolized the battle between old and new America. The older citizens valued it as a means of "Americanizing" the strange new peoples who were trying to take over their land; the newer groups saw it as something threatening their own customs and institutions and proof that they themselves were not regarded as full-fledged Americans.

Chicago, a home for many immigrants, was one of the country's "wetter" metropolises. Locally, passion over Prohibition ran high. Getting involved in the midst of such a mess presented great political risks. Yet Dever tried anyway. Why he did it, how he did it, and how he failed to pull it all off forms a rich part of our story.

Studs Terkel has referred to Dever as "the Calvin Coolidge of Chicago politics"—a Puritan in Babylon, a high-collared reformer in the Whoopee Era. It is an interesting metaphor, one that can be stretched a bit further to include two other presidents of the time. In 1923, Dever is the available man—an "honest Harding" who fits the unifying needs of his party and brings it victory. By the end of his term, he anticipates Herbert Hoover—a candidate of great promise who is overwhelmed by events in office. Analogies aside, Dever was certainly complex, even contradictory. He was a reform mayor elected by a political machine, a socialized traction zealot who made friends with the Rockefellers, an Irish immigrant's son who became the delight of WASP society, a dripping Wet who enforced Prohibition. He is one of the "marginal men" of politics, a person who could function in many environments because he fit exactly in no one place. Up to now, Dever's life and career have been sketched only in bits and pieces. I hope that I have been successful in bringing him more of the attention he deserves. Dever is worth knowing.

"The Mayor
Who Cleaned Up
Chicago"

1

Beginnings

An Inauguration

■ The crowd began to form early. Nearly two hours before the 7:30 P.M. city council meeting, hundreds of people were already streaming into Chicago's great gray City Hall. It was the evening of April 16, 1923, and they had come to see William E. Dever assume the office of mayor of Chicago.[1]

The new mayor was a straightforward, unpretentious man; he had pledged that his inauguration would be "Jeffersonian in simplicity." As a Democrat, a member of the "party of the people," he could scarcely do otherwise. But as the Republican *Chicago Tribune* wryly suggested, "it is certain that there will be many little Jeffersons and big Jeffersons and sons of Jefferson present, because the Jefferson family has been out of control of the City Hall for eight years." And so the building had been prepared for the spectacle. The banks of congratulatory flowers were carted off into anterooms to provide more space for the celebrants, and custodians were sent to bring extra folding chairs from the basement.[2]

And the crowd kept building. Not only did the political operators with their special admission tickets arrive but throngs of everyday citizens turned out. Gritty laborers in overalls, housewives with small children in hand, elderly socialites in their new spring frocks, college students jostling each other as if on the way to a football game—newspaper reporters marveled at the number and the variety of persons who wished to share in the inauguration of this new mayor.[3] It was a spontaneous outpouring of joy and optimism.

They surged past the police lines and jammed into the council chamber. The room normally seated 1200 people. On this cool spring evening, over twice that many squeezed in. They sat two on a chair; they perched on window sills; they filled the entire floor. Late arriving aldermen had to climb over the tops of desks to get to their regular places. Outside the chamber, through the corridors and stairways, and all the way out onto LaSalle Street, a mass of about 10,000 spectators had gathered, milling around in eager anticipation.[4]

At 7:29 P.M., an excited buzzing swept through the crowd: "Dever is coming!" A moment later, on the arm of outgoing mayor William Hale Thompson, the new leader appeared with his entourage. They wedged their way into the council chamber and up to the dais. A sudden hush fell on the crowd as Thompson called the council meeting to order. Some minor business was attended to, and then the new aldermen were sworn in. Thompson skipped a farewell address—he was leaving office under a cloud, and the less said the better. Instead, he called upon Dever to come forward for the oath of office. [5]

The mayor-elect was an impressive-looking man as he stepped before outgoing city clerk James Igoe. [6] Although sixty-one years old, former judge Dever still carried the powerful physique of his youth. Of medium height, his body was broad of shoulder and thick of leg, without the appearance of fat. His huge head sat atop a short neck. A fringe of iron-colored hair topped the head, and appeared again in the neatly cropped mustache under a short, square nose. The complexion was highly colored—ruddy, the *Tribune* claimed, from much smiling (for Dever had a ready grin). The eyes were soft and remarkably blue, and they twinkled with a hint of Irish merriment. Finally, there was Dever's jaw—large, jutting, and determined. It seemed to be sort of an exclamation point to the viewer, as if to reinforce one's previous impressions of the man's strength and purpose.

The audience had roared when Dever stood up. Now they hushed to listen to the rich baritone voice repeat the words that would make him the city's thirty-fourth mayor. They watched Dever deposit his bond with the council. When Thompson stepped forward again, put his hand on his successor's shoulder and announced, "A presentation of Mayor Dever, by ex-Mayor Thompson," the crowd went wild. [7]

As the spectators cheered, Dever glanced over the dais behind him and smiled. He could see many of the people who had helped him rise from a poor tanner to chief executive of the nation's second city. [8] Carter Harrison and Edward Dunne were there, both former mayors and both his political mentors. To the left was George Brennan, the "Warwick of the new administration," chief of the Cook County Democratic party. Seated on the opposite side of the platform from Brennan was a representative of Dever's other main power base—Professor Charles E. Merriam of the University of Chicago, darling of the progressive reformers. And of course, close behind Dever, as she had been for thirty-eight years, was his dearest Kate.

Dever banged his gavel. The crowd hushed again. Solemn-faced now, he told them that he had only a few things to say. He recalled his own eight years in the council and pledged to work closely with the aldermen. He promised to be a nonpartisan mayor. He told them that his office door would be open to everyone. Then Dever concluded: "I was a candidate because I wanted to be associated with something big, with something worthwhile in the history of Chicago. . . . I want my administration to be remembered for something definite in the service of the city."[9] The crowd roared its approval, and Dever smiled again. Then he banged the gavel once more, and began to go to work.

Before Chicago

In the late 1830s, the Dever family of County Donegal, in the north of Ireland, was on the move. Although the potato blight had not yet come, life was neither peaceful nor prosperous for this tribe of Catholic patriots. The Act of Union, Robert Emmett's crushed rebellion, the new Irish Poor Laws, disfranchisement and evictions, poverty and hunger— all these weighed heavily upon them. James Dever, the family patriarch, was a man of Donegal, and as a man of Donegal he was resolved to remain. But his nine sons and four daughters felt the ties to the land less strongly. They decided to immigrate to America.[10]

Between 1840 and 1855, almost the entire Dever clan left Ireland. So decisively did they abandon the old homeland that fifty years later not a trace of the family could be found in Donegal. Two of the brothers eventually settled in the coal town of Mauch Chunk (now Jim Thorpe), in eastern Pennsylvania. The rest of the Devers joined the great migration of their countrymen to Boston.[11]

Patrick Joseph Dever was one of the family making this move. He was fifteen when he came to Massachusetts in 1840. Aside from the date of his arrival, we have no record of his early career in America. Patrick had no money and no trade, so we may assume that his first work was similar to that of many a poor Irish immigrant of the day—nasty, brutish, and long.[12]

Sometime during this period Patrick met Mary Lynch. It was a fortunate acquaintance for the young man. The Lynches were one of the oldest families in the Boston Irish settlement. Mary's grandfather had been one of Emmett's rebels, fleeing Ireland for America with a price on his head in 1803.[13] Her father, Martin Lynch, was one of the community's recognized leaders. He was a successful saloonkeeper and Democratic ward politician, and—no small accomplishment—he had founded the city's first major Catholic cemetery. He also held a choice political appointment as an inspector at the federal Custom House.[14]

Patrick and Mary were wed in the spring of 1855. At some point during the next few years, Patrick Dever became a currier, a skilled worker with leather. Whether Martin Lynch arranged for him to learn the trade is unknown, though it would not have been the first time a father helped out his daughter's husband. Nor can it be determined if Martin gave the newlyweds financial aid. We do know, however, that Patrick Dever was able to buy land and open his own business in the town of Woburn, Massachusetts, in 1859.[15]

Woburn, about fifteen miles north of Boston, had been settled in 1642, only a dozen years after the Bay Colony itself was founded. For over 150 years it was just another quiet New England village. Then, in 1814, General Abijah Thompson opened a tannery. Leather-working had been carried on in the town since its earliest days, but the general's action started a boom. Other entrepreneurs soon crowded into the area. Within a generation, Woburn was the tanning center of Middlesex County, and one of the leading leather goods towns in the entire commonwealth. At the time the Devers arrived, Woburn's population had risen to over 7,000.[16]

Currying, Patrick Dever's business, involved finishing pieces of leather that had already been tanned. Patrick set up his first shop in a two-story frame building near the corner of Burlington and Sheridan streets. The Dever tannery was located on the west side of town, in a section called Cummingsville. The neighborhood is filled with ranch homes today, but in the 1860s it was largely rural. On the night of March 13, 1862, in the family quarters next door to the currying establishment, Mary Lynch Dever gave birth to the couple's third child, their first son. They named him William Emmett, the middle name commemorating the great Irish patriot.[17]

William E. Dever remembered his childhood as a "Tom Sawyer sort of life"; and looking back over a century, we can agree with him. In that pretransistor era, there was always something for a boy to do—fishing in the pond in spring, skating on it in winter; baseball from the first thaw to the first snow; hunting squirrels with rock and slingshot, and later with rifle; or just lying on the side of a grassy slope, watching the clouds drift by.[18]

When people achieve prominence, observers sift through their juvenile years for some early hint of future renown. Old friends are trotted out to reminisce. Blessed with the gift of hindsight, these childhood chums are prone to embroider matters a bit or to puff up an innocuous little memory until it takes on the dimensions of the saga of baby Hercules strangling the serpents of Hera. William Dever did not escape this fate. When he became mayor of Chicago, two stories were circulated, supposedly to demonstrate his precocious skills of oratory. In one tale, the ten-year-old Willie Dever, engaged in baling hay for twenty-five cents, passionately argues with his employer for a nickel raise. The other legend describes a slightly older Willie; he has been caught stealing watermelons and vainly tries to talk his way out of a switching. One should note, however, that in both cases, Dever's eloquence was unsuccessful.[19]

It was a good life, nonetheless. Willie attended the two-room Cummingsville Public School. We are told that he was a good student, although no record of his grades has survived. He had a voracious appetite for the printed word, and he devoured every book he could get. He favored history and biography. He particularly liked *The Autobiography of Benjamin Franklin*, the story of the original self-made man.[20]

Besides reading, Willie's other boyhood love was baseball. He became the pitcher for the neighborhood nine, and battled in numerous "big games" against other village teams. In a high point of his youth, Willie's father took him on the train to Boston so he could see Al Spalding and the Red Stockings play. Like many another boy of his day, Willie Dever dreamed of making the major league. He never did. But he continued to play baseball throughout his young manhood and remained a dedicated fan until—literally—the end of his life.[21]

As noted, William Dever's heritage was Irish Catholic. He appears to have taken genuine satisfaction from the fact. Yet certain aspects of his background were off the ethnic mainstream and would eventually set him apart from his compatriots. To begin with, there was the matter of his family. The Devers of Woburn were not the typical Irish-American family of their day. At a time when almost two-thirds of his ethnic comrades worked as laborers or domestics, Patrick Dever was a skilled artisan. He owned land and ran his own business. Eventually, his tannery would become one of the largest in Massachusetts. His wife's people, of course, were long-time "lace-curtain" Irish. So Patrick's son never had to experience the grinding poverty that the youngsters of the North End of Fort Hill endured.[22] Willie could be sure of himself, and of his place in the world. He never had to apologize for being Irish, so he could take his nationality for granted. The defensive, suspicious clannishness was not for him. His family had already overcome it.

Geography also played a part in Willie's development. Most Irish immigrants to America had settled in cities. By 1870 standards, Woburn was an urban area. But the Devers did not live in the town proper; their business and first residence were out in the country. Willie Dever's boyhood group-allegiance was geographic not ethnic. He was one of the "plain boys" as opposed to the "town boys" and the "rock boys" (from the hills). There were other Irish families in his Woburn neighborhood, and many of Willie's boyhood friends had names like Haggerty or Sullivan. But many did not.[23]

Finally, there was Willie's education. In his study of Irish-American politicians, Edward M. Levine observes that parochial schooling helped promote the cultural and social alienation of the Irish.[24] This was recognized as far back as the 1920s by such a rising Irishman as Joseph P. Kennedy, whose sent his sons to nondenominational academies to speed their assimilation. Like the Kennedys, Dever's education was not Catholic. His family had no choice in the matter, since Woburn did not have a Catholic school, but the result was the same. Public schooling helped Dever avoid a ghetto mentality. He might remain proud of his ethnic background, yet he could also cross cultural lines and take a broader view of reality. Dever recognized this advantage and used it for political currency. It is noteworthy that all of his campaign biographies point out that he was "educated in the public schools."[25]

Coming from this skewed background, it is not surpising that Dever would become something of a "marginal man" in politics. He fit nowhere exactly, so he could operate in many different situations. Such circumstances could be handy in crafting a certain type of public career, as the life of Fiorello LaGuardia illustrates.[26] Dever did not possess the spectacular combination of conflicting elements that went into making the Little Flower of New York City. His success was in his versatility—Dever would defy stereotyping, could never be relegated to a convenient niche. He would be able to get along just about anywhere, a formidable advantage in a profession of compromise that bills itself as "the art of the possible."

At the age of fourteen, with a year of high school behind him, Willie Dever entered the family business. Nourished by wartime contracts and postwar boom, the tannery had grown considerably. The Dever family had also enlarged. Five girls and three boys now crowded the little cottage in Cummingsville. The parallel growth of business and household finally caused Patrick to move the Devers to a new house near the center of Woburn sometime before 1880.[27]

Willie spent almost five years working for his father, learning what he liked to call the "2000 year old trade" of tanning and currying. By his late teens he was growing restless and determined to strike out on his own. His skilled craft gave him the mobility he wished. He worked in Boston for awhile, but that was not adventuresome enough. It was time to see the country. With another young Woburn tanner named Eddie McCafferty, Willie set out west.[28]

The two young men spent about two years on the road. They moved through upper New York state and on toward the Great Lakes. By 1884, Willie and Eddie had gotten as far as Kenosha, Wisconsin. Willie liked the Midwest and decided he would return someday. But the youthful tanners left Kenosha abruptly and headed back east. They had important business in the town of Olean, New York.[29]

Willie had first visited the little city in southwestern New York on a commercial trip for his father. While conducting business with a local merchant named Conway, he couldn't help noticing the man's pretty blonde daughter, Katherine. They began to talk and found that they liked each other. As Willie returned again and again to Olean, he began to spend more time with Kate Conway. His friend Eddie McCafferty, meanwhile, took up the courtship of the other Conway girl, Mary. Kate and Willie carried on a tender correspondence while the young leather worker roamed the country. Finally, with eight dollars in his pocket and boundless optimism in his soul, Willie proposed and Kate accepted. They were married at St. Mary's Church in Olean early in 1885.[30]

By all accounts, Kate Conway was a good spouse for William Dever. She seems to have been a warm person of loving family instincts. She often said that she was William's "worry depository," the person to whom he could pour out his frustrations. In later years the maternal aspects of her personality assumed precedence, and she appears as the typical, self-effacing statesman's wife of the early twentieth century. But as a young woman, Kate was somewhat different. She was an ardent suffragette and a keen student of politics. She took a close interest in her husband's career.[31] That William Dever became something more than a tanner is also a tribute to Kate.

The newlyweds set up housekeeping in Massachusetts. They lived in Boston while William worked in a local tannery. After a time he decided to return to work for his father, and the couple moved to Woburn.[32] The family business was thriving. Patrick was planning to open another shop in Boston. The prospect of a partnership for the eldest son could not be far around the corner. But after a few months in Woburn, William grew restless again.

One day in 1887, Kate brought a newspaper article to her husband's attention. It mentioned that tanners were in demand in Chicago, and that they were earning as much as $23 and $24 a week. William had often talked of Chicago and his fond memories of the Midwest. Perhaps this was the opportunity for which he had been looking.[33]

Dever agreed with his wife. For some reason, he had never been comfortable in the family business. Every time he returned to work for his father, he would feel the need to go out on his own all the more strongly. William was still not sure what his destiny would be. However, it evidently did not lie with Patrick Dever Company.

William and Kate made their decision. They sold their furniture and all their belongings, keeping only the two cartons of books that constituted their library. Then, after a tearful farewell at the Dever house, they made their way to the Boston South Station and boarded the night train for Chicago.[34]

Chicago in 1887

"I wish I could go to America," the German chancellor Bismarck once remarked, "if only to see that Chicago."[35] Such was the city's reputation in the late nineteenth century. Chicago was the New Metropolis of the World. It excited curiosity and even a bit of wonder. The city's vigor seemed to hum through the air like an electric current. As one writer later characterized it, Chicago was a city on the make.

The Chicago at which the Devers arrived in 1887 had existed for barely fifty years. Oldtimers could still recall the last great Indian pow-wow on the banks of the river near what was now downtown. The city looked even younger that its age, the great fire of 1871 having leveled almost everything. Chicagoans had been forced to build anew, and they had done so with characteristic zest. Within five years after the holocaust, construction was so thick that a visitor might have wondered whether there had really been a fire at all.[36]

The city was poised on the brink of great things—of that the people were sure. By 1890, Chicago would annex most of the surrounding villages and more than quadruple its land area. The census would show it to be the second most populous city in the United States. Meanwhile, work went on planning a "world size fair" to celebrate Columbus's discovery of America.[37]

Currier and Ives published an aerial lithograph of the young metropolis about this time. It is a remarkably vivid representation of Chicago's physical layout. From a congested core near the mouth of her river, the city sprawls in three directions over the flat Illinois plains. Mustered into phalanxes by the rigid gridiron street system, the brick buildings march off in uniform ranks toward the horizon, the pattern broken only by an occasional railyard or the meanderings of the Chicago River. Warehouses and grain elevators line both sides of the river. Dozens of sailing ships, with a scattering of steam craft, ply the harbor and waterways. Railroads crisscross the landscape at irregular intervals. Beyond the pale of settlement, one can distinguish the open prairie, and the farmland that gives the city life.

Chicago was the capital of an empire. Grain and lumber had been the city's first industries. Then, as its railroad lines pushed into the interior of the continent, Chicago had seized control of the livestock trade and its ally, meat packing. Money from these burgeoning businesses poured in, and the city became a financial center. Manufacturing expanded rapidly. And Chicago merchants began to develop a new kind of store, the catalogue house.[38]

The physical changes mirrored the city's population changes, for Chicago's growth was based on people. The swelling population was largely due to the coming of foreigners. Like other American urban centers, Chicago was a city of immigrants.

Chicago had a long reputation for cosmopolitan settlement. Its first non-Indian resident had been a West Indian mulatto named DuSable, and an old witticism related that "the first white man to live in Chicago was black." After formal incorporation as a city in 1837, immigration began in earnest. As early as 1850, fully 54 percent of Chicago's population was foreign-born (a percentage higher than New York's, incidentally). By 1890, at the beginning of the last wave of immigration, almost 80 percent of Chicagoans were either first- or second-generation Americans.[39]

The process was continuous but with identifiable spurts. We can also discern an order of succession among the different foreign groups arriving at the city. The Irish came first, during the 1840s. The 1850 census shows them as more than 20 percent of the total population, and about 40 percent of the foreign-born segment. During the 1850s, the city welcomed large numbers of Germans, who then became the most populous group. After a short interruption for the Civil War, fresh migration began with the Scandinavians. Finally, in the 1880s, thousands of Poles began settling in. These earliest groups would later be joined by more of their own countrymen and by Jews, Italians, Bohemians, and a multitude of others, until the gates were slammed shut in the 1920s.[40]

The immigrants stayed close together, in their own miniature national enclaves, or *ethnic neighborhoods* as they are called today. This clustering was a perfectly natural instinct, of course, the product of a desire to associate with one's own kind and the perceived need for protection against the hostile elements on the outside.[41] One latter-day journalist summed it up when he remembered his own youth: "You could always tell, even with your eyes closed, which [neighborhood] you were in by the odors of the food stores and the open kitchen windows, the sound of foreign or familiar language, and by whether a stranger hit you in the head with a rock."[42]

By 1887, Chicago already had its ethnic neighborhoods. They were not as spectacular in size as those of later years, but they were definitely recognizable. The Irish were concentrated mainly in Bridgeport, Canaryville, and other South Side areas. German settlement was beginning to creep northward up Lincoln Avenue. The Scandinavian colony was located around Goose Island, just northwest of downtown. The fledgling Polish community was already spreading out in three directions from the intersection of Milwaukee Avenue and Division Street. There were other settlements as well, peopled by these four nationalities and by other groups. These areas were merely the largest and most easily identified.[43]

There was money on the land. Great fortunes were being made by people named Pullman and McCormick, Swift and Armour, Field and Ward. But few of the immigrants ever became wealthy. And the working people of Chicago had to put up with a lot for the privilege of living in the New Metropolis of the World. Population density was high. Indoor plumbing was a luxury reserved for the squires of Prairie Avenue. In those districts bordering factories, a permanent layer of stinking smoke hovered over the streets and backyards, fouling the lungs and giving white clapboard houses a distinctive color of Chicago gray. And there were horses everywhere, polluting the streets and alleys with their manure.[44]

Work for the immigrants was usually long and hard. The ten-hour workday was normal, with many industries going for twelve or fourteen hours. Wages ranged from $2 to $25 a week. Plants were dirty and hazardous. Layoffs and firings, with no recourse of grievance, were a way of life.[45] The laborer reacted to this exploitation with periodic strikes—often long, frequently bloody. The year before the Devers arrived in Chicago, the Haymarket Riot had left seven policemen dead and four union leaders hanged in retribution. In 1893, the Pullman strike would become so protracted that the U.S. Army was finally called in.

Yet people kept coming to Chicago. They brought their skills, their tools, their money. Some brought only ambition, and the memories of places they would never see again. But all shared the vision that, somehow, this city was a promised land. From 1890 to 1920, the population of Chicago would triple. Much of the story of those years would be the story of immigrant assimilation. And though he could hardly have imagined it when he set foot in Chicago that day in 1887, in many ways William E. Dever's career would be the culmination of that process.

Setting Himself Up

The area of Chicago in which the Devers settled was located about a mile and a half west and slightly north of downtown.[46] At first, the neighborhood had been vaguely identified as part of the West Side. Later, as the city grew and pushed outward, it became known by its current name, West Town. The community was bounded by railroad tracks on the north and south, the Chicago River on the east, and the city limits at Western Avenue on the west. Milwaukee Avenue, angling through the district toward the northwest, was the principal thoroughfare and business street.

From the start West Town was a working-class community. Most of the residents held jobs in the factories clustered around the railyards and on nearby Goose Island. Today, the community is pockmarked with rubble-strewn vacant lots and scarred by the 300-foot-wide concrete right-of-way of the Kennedy Expressway. It is difficult to imagine the crowded jumble of cottages and tenements that cluttered the same area a century ago. In 1887, West Town was a thickly packed, polyglot settlement of mostly Poles, Scandinavians, and Italians. Its population density was the highest in all Chicago.

There were very few Irish in the community. The Devers were attracted to the area because of its proximity to the city's main tanning center, selecting their residence for economic rather than ethnic factors. They moved into their first Chicago flat at 239 North May Street in August 1887.[47] William quickly found work at Grey, Clark and Engel, a tannery located a half-mile away on Goose Island. The workday was the usual ten hours, from 7:00 A.M. to 6:00 P.M., with an unpaid hour off for lunch. As a skilled currier, Dever commanded top wages of $24 a week, about double the amount earned by an unskilled laborer.[48]

The work in the tannery was laborious and lengthy, but there was relief. Pick-up baseball games during the lunch hour were a popular diversion, and Dever participated with relish. Political discussions also helped pass the time. Dever was a naturally outgoing, sociable person, and he soon made many friends among his fellow workers.[49]

One such comrade was another broad-backed young Irishman named Thomas Keane. The two men became close companions during their days at Grey, Clark and Engel. Keane stayed at the tanning trade when Dever moved on to other things, but they kept in contact. Eventually, Tom Keane would also enter politics. He would become a leading Democratic powerhouse on the West Side and a staunch ally of Mayor Dever. He would also found political dynasty that remained an influential factor in Chicago government for half a century.[50]

About a year after the Devers came to Chicago, Kate once again chanced upon a newspaper item of particular significance. She read that a new night school, the Chicago College of Law, was soon to begin classes in a downtown office building. Kate clipped the article out of the paper and gave it to her husband when he came home from the tannery. William was intrigued. His long-range ambitions were vague at best, and he had shown no inclination toward a legal career. He simply did not wish to remain a tanner all his life. The opportunity to step up was at hand, so he decided to enroll in the night school courses.[51]

For the next two years Dever carried out a killing schedule. After his ten hours at the tannery, he returned home for a quick dinner before leaving for his law classes, walking the four-mile roundtrip to save the five-cent streetcar fare. He arrived back at May Street about 11:00 P.M., ate a light snack, then plunged into his studies, usually until about 2:00 or 3:00 in the morning. Then he went to bed. By 5:30 A.M. he was back up, ready to start another day's work.[52]

The curriculum at the Chicago College of Law was loosely structured. Most courses involved reading law in the chambers of local judges, with tests administered at periodic intervals.[53] Dever took most of his instruction either from state supreme court justice Joseph Bailey, or from Thomas Moran, a future appellate court magistrate. The school attracted many poor young men of large ambition. A number of them later carved out notable careers. Among Dever's classmates, for instance, were Harrison B. Riley, the future president of Chicago Title and Trust Company, and Charles A. Brown, who would one day become the city's wealthiest patent attorney.[54.]

Dever graduated with the first class at the Chicago College of Law in 1890. He was admitted to the bar, quit his currying job, and opened an office in the Chamber of Commerce building downtown. But he did not leave the tannery far behind. His first important case was in support of his friends in the 2000-year-old trade.

In 1891, the Chicago tanners went on strike for higher wages and a shorter workday. The matter eventually moved into arbitration, whereupon the tanners sought the counsel of their former colleague. Dever was retained to give the strikers' side of the issue to the state arbitration board. His forceful presentation impressed the board enough for it to rule in favor of the workers. The decision was later overturned, but Dever won praise for his efforts and began to build a local reputation.[55]

As the decade of the 1890s moved on, Dever settled into the career of a moderately successful small-time lawyer. He was a legal general practitioner, doing a little bit of everything with no real specialty. He helped settle estates,

William E. Dever, attorney-at-law. *(Chicago Historical Society: ICHi 20812)*

drew up wills, counseled small businesses on license and tax matters. He also defended persons accused of crime. Most of these cases involved minor infractions, though he did defend one man charged with murdering his wife (and won an acquittal). It was a comfortable practice.[56]

The Devers began to enjoy a measure of prosperity. After a few years, William was able to move his law office into the Ashland Block, a prestigious location on LaSalle Street. They also began to look around for a better place to live. In 1893, William and Kate moved down the block to a larger flat at 236 North May Street. They stayed at this location for about four years, then found and even finer dwelling. The Devers settled on a spacious apartment with bay windows at 225 West Chicago Avenue. This building would remain their home until William was elected to the bench in 1910.[57]

Meanwhile, the Dever household was expanding. Kate's father died, and her mother, Helen Conway, came from New York to live with them. She brought with her young Daniel McCafferty. This boy was the child of Dever's friend Eddie McCafferty and Kate's sister. For the next ten years, Daniel apparently lived with the Devers on and off (the 1900 census lists the eight-year-old boy as a "boarder"[58]). Some time later, Daniel's younger brother George also moved into the Dever house. Why the boys left their parents is not explained. Dever eventually adopted his two nephews and they became known by his family name.

If the tasks of attending to a legal practice and raising a family occupied much of Dever's energy, he also found time for recreation. He joined a number of fraternal and service organizations, most notably the Catholic Foresters and the Knights of Columbus. He actively participated in the affairs of St. Stephen's Parish. And he continued his interest in sports. He still played sandlot ball occasionally, but he was becoming a bit more sedentary now that he was in his thirties; he contented himself with watching Cap Anson's Colts. Hunting and fishing were becoming his favored pastimes. Whenever he was able to put a few free days together, Dever could usually be found tramping off into the wilds in search of either stray ducks or trout.[59]

He was also moving into community politics. Along with Joseph O'Donnell, a young ex-state legislator who lived in the same building, Dever began to wander over to the nearby Chicago Commons settlement house on Tuesday evenings. That was the night for the Free Floor Discussions. The weekly gatherings were sort of an indoor version of the Hyde Park Speaker's Corner. Neighborhood orators were given the chance to address the problems of the day, to argue over their solution, and to generally blow off steam. The meetings were topically and philosophically eclectic, and they helped to raise the political awareness of the local residents. Observers likened the Free Floor to New England town meetings, seeing them as an urban manifestation of democracy in action. Dever, for one, was fascinated by the sessions and became a regular participant.[60]

Those sessions were growing heated in the last years of the 1890s. The Seventeenth Ward, the section of West Town immediately around the settlement house, was suffering from government neglect. The long-entrenched ward politicians were of little help in securing city services for the community. They were corrupt and incompetent.

Disgusted with the situation, various reform-minded groups came together in an effort to "throw the rascals out." The old-line politicos, for their part, did not intend to give up quietly. Both sides sought allies. Dever had become a prominent figure in the community by this time, and he was courted by both factions. The reform bloc was particularly persistent. Recognizing in Dever a kindred spirit, they approached him to be their candidate for alderman in 1898.[61]

Dever refused the offer. Perhaps he thought the time had come for him to think more about security than ambition. Possibly he felt that the odds were just not right. He was not yet ready to take that first step into elective politics. For now, he would remain on the sidelines.

2

Political Apprenticeship
1900–1910

Chicago Government and Politics: 1900

■ The political world that young lawyer Dever considered entering at the century's turn was a chaotic place.[1] Government was decentralized in the extreme, with a multitude of elected officials and no fewer that eight separate taxing bodies within the city. Responsibilities overlapped and lines of authority blurred. Charles E. Merriam, a participant in the politics of the day, had an apt expression for the Chicago system: "scrambled government."

Within this jumble, two main focuses of power could be readily identified. One was the mayor of Chicago. Elected every two years by the city at large, the mayor was the chief executive officer of municipal government, charged with carrying out Chicago's laws and with the supervision of most city departments. He also had the power of appointment over the majority of patronage jobs. He presided over the city council with a veto over its legislation.

The city council stood opposite the mayor. It was made up of seventy aldermen, two from each ward. The aldermen served two-year terms, their elections staggered so that half the council faced the voters each year. The council was the city's law-making and budget-formulating body. Most of the aldermen were an individualistic sort, jealous of the prerogatives of their office. Only the strongest mayors could consistently bend the council to their will.

Then there was the rest of government. Although the mayor and the city council exerted the most authority, the existence of many rival officials and boards thwarted concentration of power. The independent taxing bodies were an example: they included the Cook County Board of Commissioners, the Chicago Board of Education, the Chicago Public Library Board, the three park boards, and the Metropolitan Sanitary District. Few everyday citizens knew precisely what these boards did, but they collected tax revenues and employed thousands. And meanwhile, other officials were elected: judges, clerks, treasurers, a county sheriff, and a state's attorney. It seemed as if there was always some election campaign going on.

The political parties reflected the diffusion and confusion of government. Both Democratic and Republican parties were hodgepodges of petty kingdoms and neighborhood despots. Central control was not to be found. In 1900, Chicago politics was a feudal system. At the head of almost every ward was one man recognized as the boss.[2] He may have been an alderman or a member of an independent government board, or he may have held no elective office at all. But his position was recognized. He ran his fief much as he wanted, and he answered to no higher authority. Like the manor lords of the Middle Ages, he built his power on personal loyalty and service to the community. The boss was the man who got you the sack of coal in the winter and the extra cake of ice in the summer. He was the man who could help your aunt obtain her first citizenship papers. He was the man who could get your kid brother out of the police lock-up. And he was the man who could find you a job.

Jobs were the main wealth of the ward boss. He was the neighborhood's best employment agency. If you wanted to work in the government bureaucracy or if you fancied a post in the police or fire departments, you went to see the boss. His letter of recommendation was needed for almost any position on the public payroll. Besides these government jobs, the ward leader also had important connections with building contractors, the street railways, the gas company, and other firms that did business with the city. Or if all else failed, the boss could give you a spot tending bar at his saloon.

In return for these favors, you and your family and friends voted for the boss's candidates. The political process was thus reduced to a simple exchange of services. It was unthinkable that you would oppose the man who had done so much for you and stood ready to do more. As Al Smith said, "Nobody shoots at Santa Claus."

Each ward boss was supreme in his own territory—but nowhere else. At the top there was a vacuum. No citywide superboss had yet appeared in Chicago. Instead, the local ward leaders battled among themselves, joining together into short-lived and constantly shifting coalitions. By 1900, however, the two parties had stabilized somewhat into a handful of major factions. Most ward chiefs found it advisable to swear fealty to one or another of these groups.

The Democratic party was split into two blocs.[3] The dominant faction was led by Mayor Carter H. Harrison II. The mayor was descended from the Kentucky branch of the distinguished family that had already produced two U.S. presidents. His father, Carter H. Harrison I, had helped revive the moribund Chicago Democratic party during the 1880s and had gone on to become five-time mayor of the the city. When the elder Harrison was slain by a disappointed job-seeker in 1893, Young Carter picked up his father's fallen banner and established new alliances with the neighborhood chieftains. Among those rallying to Harrison's call were such stalwarts as Bobbie Burke of the Cook County Democracy political club; Tom Carey, boss of the Stockyards; Jimmy ("Hot Stove") Quinn of the Near North Side; and the legendary Lords of the Levee, "Bathhouse John" Coughlin and Michael ("Hinky Dink") Kenna. Elected mayor in 1897 and reelected in 1899, Harrison was Chicago's most prominent politician. Although he himself was known to be personally honest, "Our Carter" was still able to get along quite well with some of the city's more slippery political operators.[4]

The other Democratic bloc was led by West Sider Roger Sullivan. In contrast to the patrician Harrison, Sullivan had grown up in rural poverty near Belvidere, Illinois. He moved to Chicago in his late teens and found a job in a railway machine shop. He soon became interested in politics and moved up through the patronage ranks as he widened his circle of acquaintances. In the early 1890s, when he was about thirty years old, Sullivan joined forces with influential German publisher Washington Hesing and a Hyde Park businessman-politician, John Hopkins. The three men gathered together various elements alienated by the elder Harrison and succeeded in electing Hopkins mayor in the special election following Harrison's murder. But by 1900, the Sullivanites were in temporary retreat. They had lost the mayor's office to Young Carter, and their sometime-patron, transit magnate Charles T. Yerkes, had been forced to leave town. The faction was largely Irish, though the shrewd Sullivan had begun to recruit Poles and other ethnic groups into his alliance. The Sullivanites were a force to be reckoned with.[5]

The Republicans were divided into three factions along geographic lines. The North Side bloc was captained by Fred Busse, a bulky saloonkeeper who sat in the state senate. Congressman William L. Lorimer, known as the *Blonde Boss*, controlled the West Side Republicans through an organization that had developed a reputation for efficiency and corruption. On the South Side, the Republican strongman was state's attorney Charles S. Deneen, whose faction attracted most of his party's businessmen and clean government activists.[6]

Such was the state of Chicago politics at the dawn of the twentieth century. Prohibitionists, Socialists, and other minor parties recruited a few followers, but they had little influence except in close elections. The real challenge to traditional party politics came from the forces of reform.

The Face of Reform: 1900

Reform was not new to the Chicago of 1900. There had been previous attempts to clean up the lusty young Midwestern city. At various times in history, Committees of Fifty or Committees of One Hundred, or whatever, had been formed by the self-proclaimed "best citizens" to uproot vice, lawlessness, and political corruption. All had failed. Chicagoans saw their city as a wide-open, frontier settlement: a little rough around the edges, perhaps, but otherwise vigorous and without guile. Reform was considered impractical and unnecessary. Indeed, the city's favorite politician, Old Carter Harrison, conducted his campaigns mainly on a platform of Personal Liberty, a convenient term embracing Sunday saloons and other unspecified pleasures.[7] But the tremendous growth of Chicago through the 1890s, and its graduation into a world-class metropolis, brought a fresh desire for respectability.

The impetus for the new reform movement came from a visiting British magazine editor, William T. Stead. He arrived in 1893 to write a series of articles about the World's Fair, then decided to stay on after completing his assignment. He wandered about dressed as a laborer, mingling with the natives. Stead was appalled by the social and political evils he witnessed. An idealistic young man, he decided to do something about them.[8]

Stead organized a mass meeting for November 12, 1893, at the Central Music Hall. A large crowd came out, a cross section of the city's diverse populace; one eyewitness recalled "businessmen and labor leaders, representatives of the city government and its executive clubs, preachers and saloon-keepers, gamblers and theological professors, matrons of distinguished families and 'madames' from houses of ill fame."[9] To this cosmopolitan assembly, Stead asked a simple question: "If Christ came to Chicago, what would He find?" The answer was damning: workers out of work, politicians and police on the take, the so-called best people sitting back and doing nothing useful. Stead's message was not original, but something in the young journalist's heartfelt appeal stirred the Music Hall audience. The more inspired listeners promised the speaker that they would start a new reform organization to battle the city's ills.[10]

Encouraged by this agreeable response, Stead reached for a wider audience. He put his observations together in a short book called *If Christ Came to Chicago!* It was an immediate success. Much of the book was devoted to describing the savage living conditions of the city, but public fascination centered on the chapter titled "The Boodlers and the Boodled." Here, Stead detailed the workings of politics Chicago style. Alarmed citizens read how their aldermen routinely accepted bribes ("boodle") for city favors. The readers learned much practical information: for example, a permit to build a railroad switch track for a brewery cost $2500 in bribes, while the same track for a coalyard could be obtained for only $1000. They found out how choice board of education lands had been sold for a pittance to well-connected real estate operators. They were also treated to the revealing tale of how a railway official slipped an alderman a thousand-dollar bill during the politician's derogatory speech, and how the speech suddenly became a hymn of praise for the railroad. Stead estimated that of the sixty-eight aldermen then serving in the city council, only ten were honest—"enough to have saved Sodom, but not sufficient to save City Hall from the reproach of being under the domain of King Boodle."[11]

Though the prophet of reform returned to England after his book appeared, his work went on. In 1894, the nucleus of Stead's Music Hall meeting founded the Civic Federation of Chicago, with its stated purpose "to discover and correct the abuses in municipal affairs, and to increase the interest of citizens in such affairs."[12] After about a year, some of the activists determined that another organization, devoted exclusively to politics, would achieve better results. They arranged to meet with other civic and business leaders of similar persuasion to develop such a body. On Lincoln's Birthday 1896, they proclaimed the establishment of the Municipal Voters' League (MVL).[13]

The MVL's first priority was the election of honest aldermen. Stead's book had noted that the surest source of income for the boodlers was the city streets—franchises for gas lines, electricity, telephones, and streetcar routes attracted lucrative bribes. The Sullivan-Hopkins gang had recently gained great notoriety for a particularly unsavory gas deal, while streetcar czar Yerkes was moving toward a total monopoly of the city's transit system. The Chicago City Council did nothing to stop these shady transactions; it was well known that the vast majority of its members actively encouraged them. So ravenous was the aldermanic appetite for fix money that the city's legislators were known collectively as the Gray Wolves.[14]

But the reformers meant business. Under the aggressive leadership of a bull-necked stationery-store proprietor, George Cole, the MVL launched an all-out campaign to cleanse the council at the 1896 elections. It recruited support from among the city's business and social elites. It published lists of suspected bribed votes. It hounded the council boodlers. The MVL formed local organizations in all parts of the city and backed candidates in nearly every one of the thirty-five aldermanic contests.[15]

The results gratified the activists. George Cole was able to report that twenty-seven of the thirty-five men elected to the council in 1896 were of acceptable character. The next year brought fresh reform victories. The Gray Wolves were fast becoming an endangered species, it seemed. With honest men entering the council in record numbers and many incumbent aldermen "scared straight," Chicago's legislature was undergoing a remarkable transformation. The aldermen had even become so circumspect as to refuse Yerkes's demand for new streetcar franchises, forcing him to sell off his properties and leave town.[16]

The reform movement sweeping through Chicago was not an isolated episode; it was part of a national phenomenon, the first stirrings of what would later be called *progressivism*.[17] The rapid industrialization of the country in the years after the Civil War had brought great economic and social dislocation. The 1890s were a particularly bad time, with a severe depression and increasing outbreaks of industrial violence. Many people began to wonder about the effectiveness of America's traditionally laissez-faire institutions. Perhaps a more active government was needed for the emerging urban-industrial society. The journey in this direction brought together many elements: ministers and settlement workers heeding the call of the Social Gospel, businessmen and professionals seeking more efficient government, poor people hoping for relief from the depredations of the trusts, nervous middle-class moderates looking for restraint on forces and people they could not understand—in short, as diverse a group as William T. Stead's Music Hall audience.

In analyzing the motivation and methods of these proto-Progressives, Melvin G. Holli has identified two main strands of reform.[18] The older school of American activism, with a long history predating this era, embraced the idea of structural reform. This referred to efforts to refashion the structure of municipal government, meanwhile cleaning up official corruption and promoting efficiency. Representing this philosophy were such mayors as William F. Havemeyer and Seth Low of New York and Grover Cleveland of Buffalo. In Chicago, the most notable example had been the short mayoral administration of newspaper publisher Joseph Medill. During the 1890s, a new strain of reform developed. These were the social reformers, and they concentrated on the more humanistic activities of developing a more liveable city. Unlike some of the structural reformers, who scorned the society and values of the working-class immigrants, the social reformers often made common cause with the masses. Their programs involved such things as the regulation of irresponsible public utilities, expanded parks and schools, and public relief. Hazen S. Pingree, mayor of Detroit and governor of Michigan, was the first public official to successfully implement these ideas. Although the distinction between structural reform and social reform is not conveniently hard and fast—there was much overlap—a familiarity with these different orientations is helpful in understanding what happens to reform in later years.

Certainly, the future looked promising to the reformers. They were confident of their ability to meet the problems of America and deal with them. And nowhere were the reformers more optimistic than in Chicago. In little more than five years, they had become a powerful force in the city's politics. They had their own men in key offices, and they frequently held the balance of power between contending party factions. Chicago was well on the way to shedding its image of corruption. Lincoln Steffens, the celebrated "muckraker" journalist, visited the city about this time and was pleasantly surprised: "Who was the boss of Chicago? Nobody, they said. Who owned the mayor? Nobody. Who controlled the city council? The Voters' League, a reform organization!"[19]

A new century was at hand. To many reformers, its coming had important symbolic value. Perhaps the new age of clean government and great society had arrived.

Dever for Alderman: 1900–1902

Reverend Graham Taylor needed a candidate. The 1900 aldermanic election was fast approaching, and he still had not found his man. The tide of reform was flowing through Chicago politics, and the Reverend planned to have his Seventeenth Ward at the crest of the wave.

Graham Taylor, one of the chief architects of Chicago's reform revival, was the fourth-generation clergyman of an upstate New York family. He had been born in Schenectady in 1851, studied for the Congregational ministry, and been ordained at the age of twenty-two. He spent his early career in Connecticut as a pastor and a professor at the Hartford Theological School. In the late 1880s, Taylor became interested in the social settlement movement as an active means of promoting the Christian ethic. When he accepted appointment as a faculty member at the Chicago Theological Seminary in 1891, he came west with the idea of starting his own settlement.[20]

In Chicago, Taylor became deeply involved in the fight for good government. He was one of the founders of the Civic Federation and a close friend of William T. Stead. He opened his Chicago Commons settlement in West Town in 1894; its first major activity was the formation of a nonpartisan political club, the Seventeenth Ward Council. Determined to bring reform to their neighborhood, Taylor and his associates set out to elect a proper alderman.[21]

Progress was uneven at first. The reformers could not come to terms with either the Republican or Democratic ward machines for 1895, so they ran their own man. He lost but put up a good fight. The next year they backed a Republican named Magnus Johnson, who won the election but went over to the enemy once in office. In 1896, the Ward Council prudently ran one of its own number, James Walsh, as an independent candidate. Republican ward-boss Jim Burke's organization responded by trying to count Walsh out. The Ward Council took the matter to court and got its man seated.[22]

There remained the problem of the other aldermanic seat. In 1898, Alderman Johnson was succeeded by Frank Obendorf. This sad-faced Norwegian teamster soon gained a reputation as one of the worst of the Gray Wolves, the mournful subject of numerous editorial cartoons in the popular press.[23] Clearly, the honor of the Seventeenth Ward demanded that Obendorf must go. But who would challenge him?

Such was the situation when Graham Taylor sat down to ponder candidates for 1900. Boss Burke's Republican ward organization was still potent. Taylor needed a first-rate fighter to make the rough-and-tumble battle for the alderman's seat. As his mind turned over various possibilities, Taylor's thoughts kept returning to the lantern-jawed young lawyer he knew from the settlement's Free Floor meetings: "We saw him and we sized him up when he was

Graham Taylor: minister, settlement director, and political strategist. (1897) *(Chicago Historical Society)*

just himself, when he passed by on his way to work. . . . We observed him while he thought no one was looking, we estimated him by the way he carried himself, by his work, by the company he kept, by what he enjoyed and disliked and by what he aspired to do."[24]

And so Taylor's choice fell on Bill Dever. Two years earlier, the Seventeenth Ward Council had approached Dever about running for alderman. He had declined with thanks, saying that he was too involved building his legal practice.[25] But Graham Taylor decided to try again and took the Milwaukee Avenue streetcar down to Dever's office in the Loop.

There is no record of precisely what Taylor said to Dever. Most probably, he appealed to Dever's sense of civic pride. Here was a chance to help complete the cleansing of City Hall. Step by step, reformers were replacing the crooks in the council chamber. Waste and mismanagement were being done away with. Honest, progressive government was the future of Chicago, and Dever could have a part in it.

Dever was convinced; he became the Seventeenth Ward Council's candidate for alderman. As expected, the Municipal Voters' League swiftly endorsed him. The field was crowded with two other Democrats and various minor candidates bent on unseating Alderman Obendorf.[26] But Dever soon got timely support from an unexpected source.

Mayor Carter Harrison was also looking for talent. He always needed gifted recruits in his struggle with Roger Sullivan for control of the Democratic party. Taylor and the Seventeenth Ward Council had opposed Harrison in his own campaigns, but the wily mayor knew he could learn a thing or two from the reformers. When the MVL endorsed Dever, Harrison quietly sent his agents into the ward to sound out the voters about the new man. They came back with glowing reports. The mayor then used his influence to force the other two Democrats out of the contest, leaving the way clear for Dever.[27] Although he had never met the mayor nor discussed the campaign with any of his men, what had happened was not lost on Dever.

Republican boss Burke suddenly awoke to the fact that he had to fight to save Obendorf. The mayor's intervention made Dever a formidable opponent. So the boss struck back in typical Chicago fashion. A local nonentity named Frank Bouchenville suddenly entered the aldermanic race as an independent. The reformers were wary. They suspected that Bouchenville was a tool of the Burke-Obendorf gang, thrown into the contest to divide the clean-government vote. A close examination of the Bouchenville nominating petition revealed that the names were all signed in alphabetical order—and in the same handwriting. Moreover, it turned out that this forgery was not even up to date: the petition had been used in 1898 for another campaign. The courts threw out Bouchenville's candidacy, and Boss Burke had to think up something else.[28]

Forgotten in all these maneuverings had been the Democratic ward leader, "Handsome Maurice" O'Connor. He had planned to run for alderman himself but found the ground cut from under him when the mayor announced for Dever. O'Connor was also a long-time foe of the MVL-style reform. So now the Democratic ward boss formed a tacit alliance with his Republican counterpart. It was reported that O'Connor was sending his retainers around the ward in carriages, "knocking" Dever as a "fake Democrat."[29] But to the Deverites, the campaign appeared to be running smoothly. They confidently awaited the endorsement of the voters.

What they got was a painful lesson in practical politics. The Burke organization was ready for the election. Saloons were kept open all day long, dispensing free drinks for Obendorf voters. Ballots were stolen, marked for the incumbent, then stuffed into the boxes. "Bands of hooligans" were brought into the ward, voted at a polling place, then moved on to the next one. The police stood by and allowed all manner of monkeyshines, stepping in only when violence threatened.[30] The outcome was a foregone conclusion.

Obendorf defeated Dever, 1978 to 1633. Much of the incumbent's vote was rolled up in the three "saloon" precincts under the thumb of Boss Burke; in the thirteenth precinct, for example, Obendorf won by a margin of 175 to 33. Dever carried only two of the ward's sixteen precincts, which suggests that he would have lost even had the election been honest.[31] In any event, it was over.

Or was it? Defeat in politics need not be permanent. Dever had gone down, but he was not out. He could give up, shaking his head over the 350 votes he needed to win, or he could go over the situation and plan for the next fight. The smart politician makes mistakes but learns from them. Dever was a smart politician.

Certainly, Reverend Graham Taylor was as well. No sooner had one election campaign ended than he was working on the next. He remained active in the reform movement while continuing to lobby for political renewal in his monthly paper, *The Commons*. When the boundaries of the Seventeenth Ward were shifted northward, he reached an accommodation with the redistricted alderman, Republican John Smulski. But the most significant event in Seventeenth Ward reform politics, for both Taylor and Dever, occurred in February 1901, when Raymond Robins arrived at Chicago Commons.[32]

Only thirty years old, Robins had already had enough adventure for a dozen men—"a character out of Jack London," as one writer described him. He had moved to California from his native Midwest, become a lawyer in San Francisco, then abruptly left for Alaska with the Gold Rush. In the Yukon he found both a tidy pile of gold and religious rebirth. Robins became a Congregationalist minister. He decided to invest his life in the social settlement field and moved by easy stages to Chicago. He arrived just in time to join Graham Taylor's newest assaults on political corruption.[33]

Robins took up residence at Chicago Commons. He soon convinced Taylor that he was a "past master in ward politics." At Robins's suggestion, the Seventeenth Ward Council was combined with a number of other neighborhood reform groups to form the Seventeenth Ward Community Club. Robins also worked to secure competent, honest election judges for all the ward's precincts. And he persuaded Dever to run once more for alderman.[34]

Dever had remained in ward politics. He had been mentioned as a possible candidate against Alderman Smulski in 1901 but had refused to run against another reformer. Dever was also an influential member of the new Seventeenth Ward Community Club; indeed, he was a featured speaker at its foundation dinner. He continued to build important contacts through his law office. The 1900 campaign had made Dever a household name in the Seventeeth Ward. With the addition of Robins's political savvy, he became the favorite for 1902.[35]

The new campaign was kicked off with a rally at the Chicago Commons auditorium. The members of the Seventeenth Ward Community Club marched up Milwaukee Avenue, flaming torches raised aloft, to their new building at Grand Avenue and Morgan Street. There Dever was presented to the voters as the man to lead the cleaning up of their ward.[36]

The theme of "clean up" was heavily stressed in the Dever campaign. The Community Club hit hard at Alderman Obendorf's sorry city council record, flooding the ward with pamphlets describing his activities in office. Voters were reminded that their alderman had supported a fifty-year extension of the street railway franchises. He had opposed municipal construction of sewers in favor of the subcontractor system, with all its briberies and inefficiencies. Obendorf had even voted against the public printing of proposed ordinances. The man was shown to be unfit to represent the people of the Seventeenth Ward.[37]

Nor was the Dever literature confined to the English-speaking voters. Special fliers in a variety of languages were distributed to the different nationality groups of the community. Robins was particularly sensitive to the large Polish contingent added to the ward by the 1901 redistricting. To them, Dever addressed this appeal:

To the Respected Working Citizens Living in the Seventeenth Ward:
I have accepted the nomination for alderman of our ward, depending primarily on the support of the working citizens, sympathetic to certain rules and regulations which unite me with the working people. I myself am the son of a laborer, all my young years having been spent at hard labor in a tannery. Although I sacrificed my spare time studying and achieving a lawyer's degree, I have never forgotten that I am the son of a laborer. At the time my former colleagues and co-workers went on strike many years ago defending their rights and demanding rightful pay for the sweat of their brow, then I, too, found myself in their ranks with all the counsel and advice I could possibly give, for I felt their fate was my fate.
Today, as candidate for alderman, I support all that will benefit the laborer. I would not promise anything I could not handle. But I assure you that all laborers and citizens of the Seventeeth Ward will find representation, and a determination to carry out my obligations honestly. . . .
Respected citizen-workers, my election is up to you; as a former hard-laborer, by your support I will be elected alderman.[38]

Besides the literature, campaigns require a personal touch. The style of the day was walking tours, with speeches, speeches, speeches. Dever felt that he had been somewhat lethargic in 1900 and resolved to make up for it. He crisscrossed the ward, pressing the flesh at plant gates, talking with the straphangers at the car stops, meeting as many of his neighbors as he could. Both on the street and in rented halls, he brought his message to those he wished to serve: he would end the Obendorf corruption; he would improve streetcar service; he would be the champion of the working man.

Mayor Harrison had not forgotten the man he had backed in the Seventeenth Ward two years earlier. Once again the mayor gave support to the Dever campaign. Rival Democratic hopefuls did not take the field. Even boss O'Connor was cowed: unlike 1900, there was no evidence of the Democratic ward chief "knifing" his party's candidate.

Dever's 1902 campaign concluded with a noisy rally at Aurora Turner Hall. Members of the Seventeeth Ward Community Club relit their torches and trooped the half-mile up Milwaukee Avenue from the Commons. Special squads of police were detailed to keep order at the meeting and beat back a threatened riot by Obendorf's thugs. The evening's featured speaker was John Maynard Harlan, a picturesque Republican reformer who had run for mayor against Harrison in 1897.[39]

Harlan, in fine form, spent the better part of two hours haranguing the crowd on Obendorf's misdeeds. The alderman's record was "so putrescent," he bellowed, "that I almost wish I had a head cold when I approach its discussion." Since both Obendorf and Dever claimed to have the same program, Harlan continued, the voters would have to make their decision based on the candidates' characters. And as for character, there was no doubt which man had the edge. "We all know Mr. Dever was a tanner," Harlan concluded, "so on election day, take from Obendorf his thick, tough hide, and let Dever tan it into the strong, durable leather it will make."[40]

Compared to 1900, Election Day 1902 was uneventful. The Community Club blanketed the ward with poll watchers, but there was little questionable activity to report. Dever's supporters were optimistic, though wary. Walter L. Fisher, secretary of the MVL, declared that Dever could lose only if his voters were so overconfident that they stayed home.[41]

Fisher had little cause to worry. Dever crushed Obendorf by a margin approaching three to one. He led in almost every section of the ward, with the incumbent carrying only the saloon precincts. The Polish voters came through especially strong for Dever, justifying Robins's cultivation of them.[42]

The Seventeenth Ward had a new alderman. At the age of forty, William E. Dever entered the Chicago City Council. He had started elective politics late, but he would try to make up for lost time.

Reform and the Alderman: 1902–1904

The Municipal Voters' League counted the 1902 aldermanic elections a great success. Of thirty-six candidates endorsed by the MVL, twenty-eight had won, giving the city council an "honest majority" of fifty-five to fifteen.

The results in such places as the Seventeenth Ward were encouraging, though the struggle was not yet over; there were still those fifteen Gray Wolves to be exterminated. Walter L. Fisher mused that "if other wards had done their duty like the Seventeenth, 'Bathhouse John' would have been relegated to political obscurity."[43] The fight for good government would go on, and the reformers looked forward to important contributions from freshman Alderman Dever.

The new alderman from the Seventeeth was decidedly a Democrat. He wore his party affiliation proudly. Dever recognized that his election had been engineered as much by Carter Harrison as by the MVL–Chicago Commons clique, admitting that he entered the city council in large part "through Mayor Harrison's influence."[44] Consequently, Dever joined himself with the Harrison faction of the party. He remained on warm terms with the Seventeenth Ward Community Club, the MVL, and other reform organizations; but he stayed a party regular. No matter how rough the going got in later years, Dever would not bolt to become an independent.

Advancement in party circles was swift for the alderman who had caught the mayor's eye. Three months after his election, Dever was presiding over the platform writing at the Cook County Democratic Convention. In addition, he gained a seat on the Democratic Central Committee, governing body of the county party. He also was appointed to the city council's influential Judiciary Committee.[45] He was learning the ropes quickly.

He did not always like what he learned. Although the MVL had pronounced the new city council morally upright, questionable practices still went on. Early in Dever's first term, Illinois Telephone and Telegraph sought permission to construct new cable tunnels under downtown streets. The council granted a very favorable permit on very short notice. Alderman Dever thought the permit too favorable and the notice too short. He complained to reporters: "The whole process was cut and dried. . . . I was utterly astounded at what happened. I got a copy of the ordinance within a few moments of the time the council was called together. I needed more time to study this, but my associates rammed the matter down my throat in a hurry."[46]

Dever lost that fight but was more successful in other areas. The primary task of an alderman is to provide service for his ward, and he never forgot this. Even while he was becoming one of the council's fiscal watchdogs, even later when he had become something of an "alderman-at-large" for the entire city, he still attended to the needs of the Seventeenth Ward.

One of the bigger problem's of Dever's West Town district was the lack of open space. The Seventeenth Ward had the highest population density in the city, with almost every square foot of land given over to development. The nearest uncluttered area was the shore of Lake Michigan, two miles to the east—and that was mainly swampland.

The consequence of this overcrowding was brought home to Dever in

The heart of the Seventeenth Ward, Milwaukee and Chicago Avenues, 1909. Dever's apartment was next to the building on the right. *(Chicago Historical Society: ICHi-04578)*

dramatic fashion. One night he was awakened by pounding at the back door of his Chicago Avenue flat. Three neighborhood teenagers greeted him with a plea that he come over to the local police station to save one of their friends from a beating. The alderman agreed to go with them. At the station, he found that the young man in question had been arrested for some boisterous misbehavior of a harmless nature.[47]

Dever secured the youth's release and went back home to bed. The next day he began a search for a solution to this type of affair. He soon became convinced that his neighborhood needed a public park; besides being an outlet for youthful high spirits, a park would be an oasis of greenery in an overbuilt ward. The alderman mounted a campaign to clear eight acres of shacks in the middle of the district. Through his efforts, Eckhart Park, at Chicago Avenue and Noble Street, became the first of the city's vest-pocket parks.[48]

The alderman obtained many capital improvements for his constituents. Since few of the ward's tenements had indoor plumbing, he secured construction of a public bathhouse near the new park. He also used his aldermanic influence to spur extensive renovation of the neighborhood's four public schools. Meanwhile, ward voters could hardly fail to note that the streets were now being kept clean and repaired, and that a modern electric street-lighting system was under installation.[49]

Another Dever project was the building of a major new boulevard through the ward. During his first term, the alderman proposed that a pair of diagonal streets be plotted from Union Park toward the lakefront. These five-mile-long parkways would be a speedy bypass around the Loop for traffic heading for the North or South Sides. They would also provide another avenue for commercial shopping strips, thus boosting local property values. Dever's visionary proposal made the front page of at least one newspaper, though nothing immediate was done on the project. The southeast route was never built. But in 1925, Dever—as mayor—had the pleasure of opening the northeast extension of Ogden Avenue in his old neighborhood.[50]

In sponsoring these improvements, Dever was acting the role of the new, social-reformer Progressive politician. Parks, public baths, improved streets were all ways of promoting the people's welfare. Old-line ward bosses had done this sort of thing—one reason they were so difficult to dislodge. But the bosses had concentrated on individual, one-to-one services. The patronage job, the fixed ticket, the bag of groceries were their methods. The new social-reformer officials worked on a larger landscape. They dealt in projects that would benefit the society as a whole. Give a child a ball and he may amuse himself; build a playground and all youngsters have been helped.

The Progressive impetus was particularly robust in the Seventeenth Ward. In physical appearance, Dever's ward differed little from a string of other inner-city, working-class districts. The Seventeenth was distinctive mainly in the political muscle of the Chicago Commons reformers. Graham Taylor and his Community Club consistently defeated the regular party ward organizations, reelecting Dever and a series of like-minded colleagues to the city council. This in itself was an accomplishment. An active settlement house in a neighborhood did not automatically lead to political reform—consider Jane Addams's futile attempts to rid the nearby Nineteenth Ward of boss Johnny ("De Pow") Powers. The Seventeenth Ward was a special case. The fact that ward political power was divided between both a Republican and a Democratic boss helped the reformers gain their first toehold. The ineffectiveness of these regular politicians was also important: voters were unlikely to follow a ward-boss Robin Hood unless he could deliver a suitable share of the government bounty. The Community Club activists adroitly exploited the situation. In effect, they built their own ward machine, mobilizing and bringing out the district's "decent" voters. Through their organizational skills and the conspicuous efforts of Alderman Dever, the Seventeenth became the blue-collar ward where the influence of reform was felt most strongly.[51]

There has been much discussion among historians about the motivation of the Progressives. Although an earlier generation of observers had been willing to accept the reformers' rhetoric at face value, more revisionist studies have identified a healthy dose of elitism in the movement. Samuel P. Hays, for one, saw many of the reforms as attempts to exclude the urban working-class from political power. The New-Left historian Gabriel Kolko pursued this line somewhat further, finding enough evidence of upper-class manipulation (particularly in business) to justify calling his book on the era *The Triumph of Conservatism*. Other studies of varying persuasiveness have taken this approach during the past thirty years.[52]

Certainly there was some elitism in the Progressive movement. Taking the example closest to our own study, we see that the Chicago Commons reformers exhibited it in various ways. Graham Taylor ran his community organizations the way he wanted to, with no apologies offered. The Reverend did not swear, drink, or gamble and did not allow such activities at the Commons—but he did smoke, so that was permitted. When Taylor retired from active management of the institution in 1922, succession to his office was hereditary—his daughter Lea became director. The settlements brought a brand of White Anglo-Saxon Protestant morality to the tenement districts and frequently had an uneven appreciation of the poor people's own social order. Although Reverend Taylor and the other social workers declared that they had come to be "with, not for" their neighbors, they never became totally absorbed.[53] The same thing can be said for many Progressive reformers.

Yet, they were there, and they were trying to help. The list of specific projects sponsored by "the Commons aldermen" is certainly impressive: the new schools, the bathhouse, Eckhart Park, and so on. In the Seventeenth Ward of Chicago, their social welfare accomplishments went a long way in justifying the reformers. Perhaps they were disdainful in some of their attitudes; perhaps they were merely naive. On balance, the record of the Commons activists is a positive one, and so is the general record of Progressivism.

Alderman Dever and his reform cohorts declared that they were trying to make life better for the people as a whole. In one vital area, the residents of Chicago seemed to be calling loudly for help in the early 1900s. The matter involved the state of public transportation and the question of municipal ownership. It was in the fight for this cause that Dever gained his first citywide fame.

The Transit Fight: 1904–1907

Municipal Ownership—the term holds little significance today. But at the turn of the century, this was a potent phrase. It referred to government acquisition and management of city mass transit systems. *Municipal Ownership*—M.O. for short—was a rallying cry for the disaffected who hoped to bring about urban utopia by taking over the streetcar lines. It was a serious issue, as newspaper editor Malcolm Bingay recalled:

Did a new family move into a neighborhood the first question asked was not about religious beliefs, or racial origins, or social and financial qualifications. No! It was "Where do you stand on Municipal Ownership?" Men of high and low incomes debated M.O. on street corners and swore by their gods that they would fight until death for it, as though it were a holy cause led by the Archangel Michael, and M.O. was the Holy Grail.[54]

Municipal Ownership was yet another flowering of the Progressive seed. To help the people, the Progressives knew, it was necessary to tinker with the system. Reform was especially needed in urban mass transit—*traction*, as it was known at the turn of the century. The traction companies served a public purpose, yet they were in business for private profit. They would not improve service or cut fares unless compelled to—they had demonstrated an inclination to do just the opposite. Therefore, the government must step in, seize the lines, and run them for the public good.

But all Progressives did not agree on Municipal Ownership. Some thought it was too close to socialism. A number of reformers preferred to have private companies retain title to the lines while the city managed them—municipal operation. Others questioned the wisdom of any government involvement in the transit system, aside from granting franchises and occasionally monitoring service. Reform included the eradication of political corruption and the extension of popular democracy, all Progressives acknowledged. Whether it meant taking over private property to promote public welfare, many were unsure.[55]

Dever knew where he stood. He was a true believer in the gospel of Municipal Ownership. The alderman had been elected as the candidate who would bring good streetcar service, the man who could "stand up to corporate employees making twenty-five and thirty thousand a year."[56] He had also arrived at the city council when developments in transit were approaching a critical juncture.

The city of Chicago had granted its initial street railway franchises in 1856. At first there were dozens of competing companies. Most of them quickly went under or were absorbed by larger carriers. By the time electric streetcars appeared in 1890, only a handful of transit companies were left. This was the heyday of Charles T. Yerkes and the city council "traction boodlers." Yerkes became so prosperous and powerful that at one point he controlled a majority of the Illinois state legislature.[57] Then, as we have seen, the reform wave of the late 1890s swept him away.

Municipal Ownership agitation increased with Yerkes's departure. In 1902 a Chicago M.O. referendum passed by a margin of six to one. The following year, the state legislature enacted the Mueller Law. The work of Municipal Voters' League secretary Walter L. Fisher, the law provided for a twenty-year limit on traction franchises, with the right of a municipality to hold a public referendum to buy out the companies when the franchise expired. In 1904,

Chicago voters strongly endorsed the Mueller Law and two other referenda on Municipal Ownership.[58]

Alderman Dever, meanwhile, was becoming active in the fight. He sponsored various traction reform measures in the city council, trying to get his colleagues to go on record for immediate Municipal Ownership. But the alderman ran into some unexpected resistance. Dever's political patron, Mayor Harrison, was not an M.O. zealot. The mayor favored a pragmatic approach of negotiating with the transit companies; it would be simpler to exact good service guarantees from the carriers rather than have the city bothered with running the lines. Since Municipal Ownership was a highly emotional issue, Harrison did not publicize his views.[59]

Dever was determined to smoke out the mayor. In the fall of 1904, the alderman proposed scheduling a new referendum on immediate city take-over. With the M.O. question once again on the front page, Harrison was forced to take a stand. He replied by publicly rejecting his protege's plan, explaining: "The Dever ordinance is a war measure and should, in my opinion, be withheld until all other means of settling the traction issue have failed. . . .If all negotiations with the traction companies fail, then it would be time for a war measure such as this."[60]

The mayor's opposition helped kill Dever's proposal. However, Harrison's waffling on Municipal Ownership severely hurt his personal popularity. He was already worn out from four terms of struggling with the Sullivanites; the M.O. issue was just another unwanted headache. Less than three months after Dever introduced his "war measure," Harrison announced he would not seek reelection.[61]

There was some talk that Dever might be the Democratic mayoral candidate for 1905. The *Chicago Post* reported that a coalition of ward leaders was meeting behind closed doors to organize for him. The *Tribune* further revealed that Mayor Harrison was planning to back Dever, in order to head off the candidacy of circuit court judge Edward Dunne. The latter paper was especially impressed with Dever's potential as a mayor. Calling him a "big-brained lawyer" of notable honesty, the *Tribune* reassured its readers that the alderman's flirtation with Municipal Ownership did not mean he would "commit himself to radical and impossible measures."[62]

Despite the kind words from the press, Dever lacked the votes; Judge Edward Dunne had them. The alderman withdrew in favor of the judge. Dunne managed to neutralize both the Harrison and the Sullivan blocs and was easily nominated. Running on a platform calling for immediate Municipal Ownership, he was elected mayor by a convincing margin of 24,000 votes.[63]

Dever developed a close friendship with Edward Dunne. The two men were similar in many ways. They were lawyers. They had been born in New England. They were both Irish Catholics. They were both passionate adherents to Municipal Ownership. They even looked somewhat alike. When

Mayor Dunne began his great battle for transit reform, Alderman Dever was his chief lieutenant.[64]

The new mayor unveiled his transportation package in June 1905. The proposals, known as the *Contract Plan*, called for a municipal contract with a select group of private investors, who would build and run a new transit system on behalf of the city. The trustees would enjoy a twenty-year franchise. By that time the city would have gone through the necessary procedures to acquire and operate the lines and would be able to buy out the investors.[65]

The city council was cool to Mayor Dunne's plan. Even though the voters had approved every Municipal Ownership referendum by a lopsided margin, many aldermen had doubts about the idea. Most of them favored Carter Harrison's approach of extending existing transit franchises in return for guarantees of good service. They also believed that Dunne's proposal would be too expensive. As a result, when Alderman Dever formally presented the Contract Plan to his colleagues in October, they quickly voted it down.[66]

Dunne and Dever tried again in December. This time, Dever proposed that the Contract Plan be submitted directly to the voters in a referendum; once again the council said no. But within a month, the lawmakers abruptly changed direction. Prodded by the well-organized M.O. lobby and the influential Hearst press, the city council voted to issue $75 million in bonds under the Mueller Law, for the purpose of acquiring the private transit properties. The council also authorized a public vote on the various transit plans.[67]

The referendum was inconclusive. The voters once again endorsed the principles of municipal financing and ownership. However, the proposal that the city "proceed to operate street railways" by issuing the Mueller bonds failed to win the required three-fifths vote. Faced with these results, Mayor Dunne unbent. He announced that he was willing to negotiate an agreement with the existing transit companies, although he still believed in Municipal Ownership and would oppose any long-term franchise extensions.[68]

At length, in February 1907, the city council reached agreement with the private carriers. The so-called Settlement Ordinances extended existing franchises for a term of twenty years; in return, the franchise-holders agreed to build a stated amount of track extensions each year and to pay a percentage of their profits into a city traction fund. Nothing was said about Municipal Ownership, either immediate or eventual. Predictably, Mayor Dunne denounced the agreement as a sell-out to the carriers and vetoed it. But floor-leader Dever could muster only twelve votes to sustain the mayor, as the council overrode the veto and enacted the settlement.[69]

By now the traction debate had dragged on over two years. As the 1906 referendum indicated, public opinion had shifted from hot support for immediate Municipal Ownership to a simple desire to guarantee adequate public transportation. The reform activists were split on the issue. Illustrative of this division is the case of Walter L. Fisher. Fisher, secretary of the Municipal

Voters' League, was Mayor Dunne's traction counsel. He became convinced that M.O. was an impossible dream and urged his boss to accept the Settlement Ordinances. When Dunne refused, Fisher resigned and accepted appointment as the city council's transit advisor.[70] Fisher was not alone; other reform-minded friends of the mayor thought Dunne was being too stubborn. They argued that he should endorse the settlement as the best transit solution available. But Dunne would not budge. He was determined to make his 1907 reelection campaign a plebiscite on his M.O. philosophy.[71]

Dever stayed with his mayor to the bitter end. In March the alderman wrote a series of articles opposing the settlement for the *Daily News*. They ran next to a collection of pro-settlement pieces by Alderman Charles Werno.[72] Point by point through six essays, Dever attacked the ordinances: the valuation was too high; the fare structure was unrealistic; service improvement was not effectively guaranteed; the franchises were too long. The alderman's rhetoric reached new levels as he condemned the transgressions of the traction trust:

> For a period so long that the memory of man runneth not to the contrary, these companies have consistently violated their express as well as their implied obligations. . . . The voter should not forget the lesson of history. That lesson is that the companies may be expected to use in the future, as they have in the past, every possible advantage, political, financial, legal, or technical, on their own behalf; and they cannot be expected to observe their obligations merely because these may be written down in their grants.[73]

The voters did not respond to Dever's eloquence. Mayor Dunne and his brand of transit reform were defeated by just under 13,000 votes. Into the mayor's office came fat Fred Busse, the North Side Republican wheelhorse of dubious reputation who promised relief from political confrontation and what might be termed a *return to normalcy*.[74]

Municipal Ownership appeared to be a dead issue. During Busse's tenure, the traction companies agreed to the Settlement Ordinances. They were granted twenty-year franchises, dated from the February 11, 1907, enactment of the law.[75] They had their reprieve. But in the 1920s when their licenses reached expiration, the franchise holders would again find themselves opposed by a mayor seeking immediate Municipal Ownership. This time, the mayor's name would be Dever.

Trying to Move Up

During Carter Harrison's tenure as mayor, Dever had become one of the more influential members of the Chicago City Council. The accession of Edward Dunne brought him into the council's seat of power. As the new mayor's council floor leader, the alderman from the Seventeeth Ward was recognized as one of the coming men in local politics. He was ready to make his move upward. After 1905, Dever campaigned for three major offices within three years. Each time he came close only to be defeated by unlucky circumstances.

Dever's first race was for the municipal court in 1906. This new court was a fruit of Progressive reform, replacing the archaic justice of the peace system. In the initial municipal court election, twenty-seven judges were to be chosen. Candidates were slated for two-year, four-year, or six-year terms, to provide for future staggered elections. Dever was nominated for one of the six-year terms.[76]

As is usual in Chicago politics, the judicial campaign stirred little interest. The public was busy watching the transit fight; those who paid closer attention to elections in the fall of 1906 worried about the contest for seats in congress and the legislature. An important factor in the judicial balloting was the Hearst-backed Independence League. The press lord was temporarily feuding with the Dunne Democrats and decided to run his own candidates. Third-party competition, coupled with low voter turnout, spelled disaster for the Democrats. All their main candidates went down, including the entire judicial ticket. Dever was the party's leading vote getter, with 94,380—about 20,000 behind the last Republican in the six-year field.[77]

For a while, however, it appeared that Dever might be seated on the court anyway. In the competition for two-year terms, black attorney Ferdinand L. Barnett had polled the lowest Republican total, about 90,000. Although this was better than any Democrat running for a two-year term, it was still some 4,000 votes short of Dever's tally. Now Dever's supporters came forward to claim that the three election categories were unconstitutional, and that the twenty-seven highest vote-getters should be seated on the bench, regardless of the terms for which they had run. The Dever people felt their man should challenge Barnett's election.[78]

The alderman rejected this veiled bigotry. Although not sure that the three-category arrangement was lawful, he did not believe in changing the rules once the game was over. Barnett had been harassed enough over his race during the campaign, Dever declared: "I shall not embarrass [him]. . . . I shall take no technical advantage over Mr. Barnett. I do not wish to add my mite to the prejudice already existing against him."[79]

So much for the municipal court. Dever's next chance for higher office came quite soon. Superior court judge Gary died early in 1907. With Mayor Dunne's support, the alderman received Democratic slating for the vacancy.[80] Opposing him was a Republican lawyer named William H. McSurely.

Dever decided to tie his campaign to Mayor Dunne's reelection bid. He began to talk traction. McSurely refused to discuss the issue, pointing out that the superior court might soon have to review the proposed Settlement Ordinances. Dever, however, would not be swayed—his campaign speeches continued to be filled with Municipal Ownership sloganeering. It was at this time that he wrote the six anti-settlement essays for the *Daily News*. To those who might object to a judicial candidate taking part in such a partisan debate, Dever replied that the importance of the issues outweighed all other considerations; and besides, he had agreed to write the newspaper articles before his nomination for the bench.[81] In effect, he was making the superior court contest another referendum on the mayor's transit policies.

Dunne's coattails proved to be too short. McSurely defeated Dever by about 13,000 votes out of the almost 340,000 cast. Interestingly, the results were almost identical to those of the Dunne-Busse mayoral election.[82] Once again, Dever had shown himself to be a formidable vote-getter but once again without success.

In 1908 Dever made his third attempt. He entered the spring primary as a candidate for state's attorney. Seven Democrats were competing for the party nomination. Dever was endorsed by the Dunne faction. His chief opposition came from former state's attorney J. J. Kern, the Sullivanite candidate, and young Maclay Hoyne, choice of the Harrison bloc.[83]

The daily papers described the Democratic primary fight of 1908 as "spirited." However, they carried little news of the battle. The real story that year was the Republican primary, where incumbent state's attorney Healy was being pressed by an alleged "tool of the liquor interests," John E. Wayman. Political reporters did take time out from the G.O.P. contest to predict that J. J. Kern would easily win the Democratic nomination.[84]

Kern performed as expected, topping the seven-man field with a 28 percent plurality. Dever trailed by a few thousand votes. The alderman accepted the verdict and took off on a short fishing trip to Wisconsin. Some of Dever's backers, however, suspected that he had been counted out. They observed that Healey, who had lost the Republican primary to Wayman, was preparing to contest the results. They urged Dever to return home and lead the fight. There was even some talk of Dever running as an independent.[85]

But the challenge idea died. Dever might have had right on his side, but old Judge Binnaker, who would hear all election complaints, was a Sullivan man. Former Mayor Dunne, for his part, was not encouraging. Although he told Dever that he should contest Kern's nomination if his case were good, he also advised his friend that the matter was "your decision alone."[86] Dever decided to stay on vacation.

Alderman Dever had become a well-known figure in the world of Chicago politics. Though affiliated with the Dunne faction, he was on cordial terms with both the Harrison and the Sullivan groups. Dever had risen from unknown lawyer to prominent party leader in less than ten years. He had been a candidate for three major countywide offices, had run well, and had lost by a whisker each time. There was still talk of Dever going for some higher office; yet the fact remained that he was a three-time loser. Perhaps he had reached his limit.

3

Judicial Years
1910–1922

Out of the Council

■ During his years as an alderman, Dever usually won reelection with little bother. He had been pressed only in 1906, the year he voted to raise the saloon license fee to $1000. In revenge, the ward's tavern owners had boosted the price of beer to ten cents and told their patrons that the new "Dever tax" was responsible. For awhile the alderman's prospects had appeared doubtful. But vigorous campaigning and the strong support of Mayor Dunne had neutralized the beer issue, and Dever was returned to office by a comfortable margin.[1] In 1910, however, Dever faced a challenge of far greater significance. This time the issues were not so fleeting as the high cost of lager. Rather, the concern was the basic matter of ethnic representation.

After the redistricting of 1901, the Seventeenth Ward came to include a large number of Poles. Chicago's main concentration of Polish people was located in the neighboring Sixteenth Ward, in the area commonly referred to as *Polish Downtown*. The community had been spreading outward from its core near Milwaukee Avenue and Division Street for some time. By 1910, enough Poles had drifted south into the Seventeenth Ward that they numbered an estimated 2500 of the ward's 8000 voters.[2] This development aroused the interest of Stanley Kunz.

Kunz was the Democratic boss of the Sixteenth Ward, the undisputed "King of Polish Broadway." He had entered politics with election to the state legislature in 1888. Over the next two decades, Stanley Kunz punched, clawed, and gouged his way through the rough and tumble of Chicago politics, finally grabbing the twin positions of alderman and ward committeeman.[3] He was easily the city's most powerful Polish politician. Now he moved to extend his influence into the Seventeenth Ward.

Early in 1910, Alderman Kunz announced that Stanley Walkowiak, an eminent attorney in the Polish community, would oppose Dever in the coming aldermanic primary. Kunz claimed to have no grievance with the incumbent; the Walkowiak candidacy was strictly a matter of Polish power. Since the Poles were the largest single voting bloc in the Seventeenth Ward and had been unrepresented since Alderman Smulski had resigned to become city attorney, it was only fair, Kunz declared, that the Poles of the Seventeenth once again have one of their own in the city council.[4]

Kunz's ploy startled the "better elements." Outside of the Polish neighborhoods, the Sixteenth Ward alderman had a decidedly unsavory image; he merited little respect even from his brother ward bosses. The city's newspapers thought him a menace. All the major dailies endorsed Dever for reelection, denouncing the power grab of the vulgar, tub-thumping demagogue of the Polish ghetto. That Kunz should even contemplate such a coup was outrageous to them. As the *Chicago Daily News* editorialized, it seemed "the height of absurdity . . . [to] retire one of the most effective men in the council at the dictates of the Sixteenth Ward's discredited boss."[5]

Fortified by the friendly press, Dever won the primary in a close vote, but Kunz was not yet ready to give up. He attempted to have the Republicans replace their nominee, C. J. Ryberg, with another of his Polish associates. When this effort failed, Kunz decided that the once-beaten Walkowiak would remain in the aldermanic race as an independent candidate.[6]

Dever was understandably resentful of Kunz's latest move. Ryberg and Walkowiak, his ostensible opponents, were virtually forgotten as he went into battle against the invader from the north. Dever denied that the election was a "nationality matter"—boss politics was the real issue. Kunz did not oppose him because of any ethnic consideration, Dever claimed: "his sole reason is to get me out of the council so that he can deliver the Seventeenth Ward to the next public service corporation . . . that wants a franchise." When Kunz sent feelers out to Dever, suggesting that the incumbent withdraw in return for help in the next mayoral election, Dever self-righteously exposed this attempt at a "corrupt bargain."[7]

Dever called in all his political IOUs for this campaign. The Municipal Voters' League, the Chicago Commons caucus, and the other reform groups gave him their customary staunch support. Now, in a remarkable testament to the man's personal talent for bringing together diverse elements, Dever assembled the so-called mayoral quartette. This group comprised four once-and-future rivals for the Chicago mayoralty: Carter Harrison, Edward Dunne, J. Hamilton Lewis, and John Traeger. They submerged their considerable personal and political differences to come to the aid of their friend Bill Dever. The quartette appeared arm-in-arm at mass meetings throughout the Seventeenth Ward, its members taking turns in praising their candidate and warning of the dire consequences should "Stanley the Slugger " get his way.[8]

The incumbent alderman was not without support in the Polish community. Joseph La Buy, president of the Polish Businessmen's Democratic Club,

One-half of the Mayoral Quartette: Dever's mentors Edward Dunne and Carter Harrison II. *(Douglas Bukowski Collection)*

was a prominent Dever ally. Others among the more cosmopolitan Poles, mindful of the negative image projected by Stanley Kunz, reaffirmed their acculturation by joining the Dever campaign. At least one Polish voter put this feeling into words, advising the *Chicago Tribune* that "Kunz and his gang have no right to claim support on the grounds of nationality" and that they were "Poles for revenue only." Still, Boss Kunz was a tough opponent, adept at the ways of urban electioneering. Stories began to circulate about bribes offered to Dever workers and beatings threatened to those who would not vote the Kunz ticket.[9]

Shortly before the election, Alderman Dever published an open letter listing his accomplishments. Under his leadership the ward's schools had been remodeled and their playgrounds improved. The streets had been paved. A new park had been opened, and a public bathhouse. City services in all categories had been upgraded.[10] This was a record worthy of the Seventeenth Ward's good people. Could the opposition do better?

On election day, Kunz came over from the Sixteenth Ward in his touring car to direct operations. The usual rumors of intimidation and irregularities made the rounds; but after the fury of the campaign, the voting was rather quiet. By nightfall the outcome was apparent to all. Along Chicago Avenue a man was seen riding in a wheelbarrow and banging on a drum, while being pushed by a disgruntled chap sporting a green Walkowiak ribbon. The rider was collecting his election bet. Dever had survived.[11]

Survived is an appropriate word. True, Dever's total was quite good for a three-cornered race: 2692 votes (44 percent) compared to Walkowiak with 1886 (31 percent) and Ryberg with 1483 (25 percent). But the fact remained that a majority of the ward had voted against him. Moreover, in the rapidly growing Polish precincts, Walkowiak had triumphed by margins approaching four to one.[12] Dever had obviously not disposed of the ethnic question. He was certain to face another strong challenge in 1912. And, if the opposition managed to unite behind an attractive Polish candidate the next time, Dever would enter the contest as a decided underdog.

That election was two years away. Meanwhile, there were other offices to be sought. Dever once again began to think about the mayoralty, for which the election was less than ten months away. (Starting in 1907, Chicago mayors were elected to four-year terms.) The front runners for the Democratic nomination were Carter Harrison and Edward Dunne. Dever was friendly with both former mayors. He might be just the compromise choice needed to unite the two anti-Sullivan wings of the party.

With this in mind, Raymond Robins began to organize a Dever campaign. He discussed his plans with the alderman early in May. Robins felt that his friend required greater citywide exposure. To accomplish this, he planned to have Dever speak at gatherings in all thirty-five wards by October 1, then to repeat the circuit during the winter months. While Dever was busy charming voters at business luncheons and fraternal smokers, his supporters would be quietly negotiating with the political chieftains. The alderman would thus have the jump on the other candidates; by primary time, his momentum would be unstoppable. Robins was confident that Dever's oratory and his own organizational work would combine for happy results. He told his wife Margaret that Dever was "sure to win."[13]

But before the Dever-for-Mayor bandwagon had begun to roll, a new opportunity sprang up. For many years Roger Sullivan had been laboring to build a united Democratic organization. He now proposed to put together a "harmony ticket" for the 1910 fall elections, taking a number of the rival Allies (the Harrison and Dunne groups) onto his slate. Among those to be named was Bill Dever; he would be one of six candidates for the superior court.[14]

The proposition seemed acceptable to all concerned, and the harmony ticket was widely publicized in the daily press. But the Democrats' fragile unity almost immediately began to disintegrate. The Allies felt that they were not getting a large enough share of the pie and began to back away from Sullivan's slate. Dever publicly declined his place on the ticket. He did not have anything in particular against Roger Sullivan, he told reporters. It was just that he had already made "other plans"—presumably, to run for mayor in 1911.[15]

Sullivan was determined to save the harmony ticket. A conference between the Allies and the Sullivanites was arranged at the LaSalle Hotel. The two sides met in a marathon session, finally hammering out a settlement in the wee hours of July 14. The Harrison-Dunne group returned to the fold. Besides the offices already slated for them on the original harmony ticket, they were given the additional posts of sheriff and county board president. And Alderman Dever, who had gone into the conference as one of the Allies' five negotiators, came out once again as a candidate for the superior court.[16]

Why had he taken it? It is likely that his remarks about "other plans" were merely a bargaining tactic, designed to show Sullivan that he did not need the proffered judgeship. But what of Robins's grand scheme for a citywide mayoral campaign? Probably, Dever concluded that he could not win and that the superior court slating was the best possibility open to him. The Allies were a very loose coalition, held together mainly by their shared opposition to Roger Sullivan. Dever could not count on Harrison or Dunne deferring to a third candidate; each man was something of a prima donna. They would probably rather run against each other, and risk losing to the Sullivanites, than give up another shot at the mayor's chair. Dever, meanwhile, had no wide personal following to support a mayoral bid. Even his power base in the Seventeenth Ward was eroding. His only real chance for 1911 would be as a compromise candidate. In such an event, he would be as politically well-situated on the bench as in the city council—better situated, in fact, for he would be rid of the spectre of Stanley Kunz. Dever was a pro, and he played the odds. The superior court judgeship was the surest bet he had.

And so, the Sullivanites and the Harrison-Dunne Allies marched off together to do battle against the Republican enemy. The election results confirmed the wisdom of Roger Sullivan's plans. The Democrats swept all the important offices, including the six seats on the superior court. Dever topped the judicial ticket. He ran well in all sections of the city, finishing almost 5000 votes ahead of the next-highest Democrat. Three weeks after the election, he resigned from the city council and was sworn in as a justice of the superior court.[17]

Honest Judge

The Superior Court of Cook County was an historical accident. It owed its curious existence to the Illinois Constitution of 1870. The writers of that document had noted the rapid population of growth of Chicago and had recognized that the area needed a special court system. The logical solution would have been to expand the existing Circuit Court of Cook County. But for reasons now forgotten, the statesmen of 1870 came up with a different plan. They took the Chicago Superior Court, renamed it the Superior Court of Cook County, and gave it jurisdiction over the same cases as the circuit court. Except for a few minor variations, the superior court and the circuit court were identical. In effect, they were branches of the same court.[18]

The new superior court was a court of general jurisdiction. This meant that it heard both civil and misdemeanor cases. The judges of the court also made up the bench strength of the Criminal Court of Cook County. Along with the circuit court magistrates, superior court judges were rotated over to the criminal court, where they heard felony cases. In 1910, twelve justices sat on the Superior Court of Cook County. Each was elected on a partisan ticket to a six-year term. The chambers of the court were located in the Cook County section of the new City Hall building on Clark Street.[19]

After the tempest of the city council, the superior court was an island of serenity for William E. Dever. The caseload was not heavy, the job was prestigious, and the pay was good—$11,500 a year, nearly double his previous income.[20] He was also removed from the constant pressure of politicking. Cook County judgeships are anything but nonpolitical; however, a place on the bench put Dever above the daily trench warfare. And, as Dever well knew, becoming a judge did not close off all avenues of political advancement. His old friend Edward Dunne had used his seat on the circuit court as a springboard into the mayor's office.

During this time, Dever moved out of the Seventeenth Ward. His departure was symbolic of the many changes that were overtaking the reformers in the district. The "better informed and experienced citizens" of the ward, like Dever, were making their money and leaving the neighborhood for more attractive areas. Replacing them were a steady stream of newcomers, mainly Poles and Italians. As the 1910 aldermanic election indicated, these people were more responsive to ideas such as ethnic representation than to the abstract principles of clean government or even social welfare. Reverend Taylor and the Community Club reached out to these new settlers, sought some accommodation with them, but had less and less success: after 1917, the Chicago Commons candidates for alderman were consistently defeated. Reform in the Seventeenth Ward was in decline.[21] Dever, meanwhile, was gone. Other Chicago politicians, most notably Richard J. Daley, would make a fetish of remaining in the "old neighborhood" near their roots, even as they ascended to the heights of power, but such symbolism did not interest the new justice of the superior court. Dever's political base in the Seventeenth Ward was growing weak, he was not required to live in the area anymore, he had the means to leave. So he left.

Like most Chicagoans who feel they are becoming fashionable, he sought out Lake Michigan. Early in 1911, the judge and his family found a new apartment at 708 West Buena Avenue, a half-block from the lake front, in the Uptown district. The Devers stayed there for four years. In 1915, they moved two miles up the lake shore into an even fancier area. Dever acquired a three-flat building at 5901 North Kenmore Avenue in the Edgewater community. The new brick structure was located adjacent to the mansions of Sheridan Road and only a few blocks from the recently constructed Edgewater Beach Hotel. [22] The building itself had a marble-paneled lobby and spacious enclosed sun porches. It was a fitting residence for a judge.

Dever was making a success of his life; and in the general spirit of the day, he was expressing his success by making that life more comfortable. Yet, even as he was leaving the West Town neighborhood in residence, Dever was not entirely abandoning it in spirit. He did not rush to join exclusive clubs or abandon old friends. In at least one area, he actually became closer to his ethnic roots: the struggle for Irish independence reached its peak during these years, and Dever actively supported the cause. He kept his perspective in little ways, too. On Thanksgiving Day and other holidays, he would visit orphanages in poor neighborhoods and bring a dozen or so of the children home with him for dinner. His record as a judge does not reveal any abrupt transformation from populist to plutocrat, and labor groups continued to regard him as a friend. Dever had not "gone North Shore." Becoming a judge gave him new vistas without closing off the old ones. [23]

He maintained his involvement in civic and social affairs. As a superior court justice, Dever was a prized guest at commercial and fraternal gatherings, and he garnered many invitations. He was an accomplished after-dinner speaker, with a large fund of pungent jokes and colorful yarns. The judge spoke at Italian lodge dinners, at ward businessmen's meetings, at testimonial banquets for such persons as Archbishop Mundelein—and he was at home at all of them. Some of these functions gave him particular pleasure, since they allowed him to repay old debts. When the University of Chicago dedicated a building to the Reverend Graham Taylor, Dever was on hand to honor the man who had first brought him into public life. [24]

He kept his hand in politics, too. In 1914, the quadrennial talk of a Dever-for-Mayor campaign started up again, but the judge quickly squelched it; and in truth, nobody argued with him. He did campaign for his political friends when they sought office, and he attended the usual party rallies and conventions. Dever was friendly with all factions. He continued to play the political marginal man, remaining on cordial terms with everyone, squeezing obliquely into varied places. He was identified as a Harrison-Dunne man, though he kept on the good side of Roger Sullivan's group; he even suggested that Sullivan would make a suitable running mate for President Wilson in 1916. [25] As a politician, Dever was graduating into the role of an elder statesman—and it suited him.

In the meantime, Dever was still a superior court judge. There is not much to say about his early service on the bench. None of his cases were really significant, except to the people involved. He heard his share of small damage claims, divorce petitions, and minor fraud suits. When he moved over to the criminal court, he presided at robbery and murder trials. Periodically, his actions on the bench found their way into the public press—like the time he advised a divorcing couple to go off into the wilderness for a few weeks, telling them that the beauties of nature would heal their marital wounds. But for most of his first five years at the court, Dever labored anonymously.[26]

In fact, Dever's first widely publicized trial came only at the very end of his judicial term: the Lorimer case. The "Blonde Boss" had graduated from West Side ward leader to United States senator, only to be ousted from the senate for buying his election. At home he faced more trouble as his LaSalle Street Trust and Savings Company collapsed. Lorimer and an associate were indicted for misappropriation of funds and conspiracy to defraud. They were brought to trial in Dever's court in March 1916.[27]

The case dragged on for nearly two months. The Chicago newspapers turned out reams of copy on Lorimer's courtroom adventures; Kate Dever's clippings alone fill three volumes of scrapbooks. The demands of the trial cut deeply into the time Judge Dever had planned to devote to his reelection campaign. He consoled himself with the thought that the attendant publicity might make up for it.

Lorimer was finally acquitted in early May. With only three weeks left before the judicial election, Dever let loose a flurry of campaign mailings. He even sent postcards to jurors who had sat in his court and were "familiar with my work." He never really had cause to worry, however. The Democrats recaptured six of the seven judicial seats by comfortable margins. Dever himself was knocked off his accustomed position of leading the ticket. Nevertheless, he still polled the second highest total and was easily returned to office.[28]

A few months into his second term, Judge Dever was appointed to a vacancy on the appellate court. This body heard appeals from lower court decisions. The Illinois Supreme Court selected the appellate judges from among the sitting circuit and superior court magistrates; they served three-year terms. Despite the extra work involved, an appointment to the appellate bench was highly cherished. Much of the time a trial judge performed as merely a highly paid umpire. On the appellate court that same judge might have a lasting influence on the formulation of legal precedent.[29]

The opportunities for self-expression were definitely present, though they were often subtle. Dever served two terms on the appellate court and eventually became its presiding judge. In later years, some of his friends decided to enumerate his "most important decisions." One case involved the right of the City of Chicago to require truck fenders; another concerned the insurance implications of a missing-persons matter; a third was a dispute over who would pay for a railroad-crossing project. [30] By themselves, the decisions rendered were hardly noteworthy. They are Dever's three small pieces of that vast mosaic we call *The Law*. Ironically, the one case that might have had the furthest-reaching effects came off of Dever's superior court docket. This was the matter of *Read v. Central Union Telephone*.

In the fall of 1913, William Read and various minority stockholders of Central Union Telephone (CUT) brought suit against the company in Dever's court. CUT was the principal telephone company for the state of Illinois outside the Chicago city limits. The Read group claimed that American Telephone and Telegraph, CUT's majority stockholder, was not operating the company in the best interests of all concerned. They were particularly uneasy about AT&T's plans to merge CUT with the Chicago Telephone Company. Such action was monopolistic, the Readites declared, and was against the public policy of the state of Illinois. [31]

In January 1914, Dever granted an injunction blocking the proposed merger. He also appointed six receivers to manage CUT while the case was being sorted out. After that, the long process of hearing, motion, and countermotion began. The complicated litigation ate up the better part of three years. About 16,000 pages of oral testimony were taken and 2,500 exhibits presented. The abstracts alone filled three volumes. Then, on July 10, 1917, Judge Dever issued his final decree.

Dever found for the plaintiffs. He agreed that AT&T was a monopoly, that it was trying to use the merger to suppress its competitors. The defense had argued that the Bell patents gave AT&T the right to unify the development of the telephone industry. To this, Dever responded that the "public welfare is not lost sight of in granting such exclusive privileges." And he concluded that

the peculiar circumstances of the telephone business . . . do not render it an exception to those rules of law which have been created for the protection of the public from any and all kinds of illegal exploitation. . . . The Bell system [AT&T] constitutes, and at all times since its inception has constituted, a combination in restraint of trade and commerce, both intrastate and interstate, and has at all times been attempting to monopolize the telephone business in the United States. [32]

Dever decreed that the arrangements for merging CUT with the Chicago Telephone Company were "null, void, and unenforceable." He further ruled that AT&T had sixty days to sell off its stock in Central Union Telephone. [33]

The Read decision and the reasoning behind it are a fine example of Progressive Era trustbusting. Not all the reformers believed that monopolies should be broken up or even that they were a bad thing. The centralization of business was both "inevitable and necessary" in the modern world, the Progressive party platform of 1912 had declared. Yet there were those who thought that the gathering of so much power in one place threatened free competition and, by extension, a free society. Dever was of this mind. On the bench the one-time tanner had a reputation as a "working-man's judge," who would not issue injunctions to break strikes and who would compel businesses to fulfill their labor contracts; he had not forsaken his roots. In the Read case, he spoke for the precedence of public welfare over private profits.[34]

Dever clearly believed that the entire AT&T combine should be broken up. Five years earlier, his ruling might have made the front pages of newspapers across the country. Trust-busting had received wide publicity in the high days of progressivism. But by 1917, the temper of the times had changed. America's entrance into World War I was diverting the public's attention. Even in the local press, the decision was buried inside among the ads for trusses, pushed out of the headlines by the war news. The Read group also seemed to lose interest in the case. When the telephone companies appealed Dever's ruling, the Readites entered into negotiations with AT&T. Eventually, the whole matter was settled out of court on undisclosed terms. In January 1921, the merger was announced of Central Union Telephone and the Chicago Telephone Company into Illinois Bell, an AT&T subsidiary.[35]

During the winter of 1921, Dever presided at the fraud trial of eight Chicago White Sox baseball players accused of throwing the 1919 World Series. The "Black Sox" affair created something of a national sensation, calling into question as it did the integrity of America's national pastime. Reporters from all parts of the country descended on Dever's courtroom, and the judge found himself briefly in the limelight. The case eventually moved on to another court. Once again, matters on the bench returned to their quiet routine.[36]

On March 13, 1922, William E. Dever celebrated his sixtieth birthday. He had reached the peak of his career. He was a respected jurist. He was financially independent enough to own two apartment buildings and take European vacations. He was a leader in civic affairs. He had a happy home life: a devoted wife and two fine sons who were beginning to carve out legal careers of their own. Dever had traveled a long road from the tanneries of Woburn and Goose Island. He could look back upon his life and reflect upon the paths he had taken with much satisfaction.[37]

Dever was elected to a third term on the superior court in June of that year. As usual the campaign was easy, and the Democratic judges were not seriously challenged. Dever had fallen even further from champion vote getter on the slate; in this election, he polled only the third-highest total of the five successful candidates.[38] The public had forgotten the fighting alderman of the early 1900s. Now, in the 1920s, he was sinking into that cluttered jumble of candidates whose names pop up on the ballot every few years, who are checked off by the straight-ticket voters, and who promptly fall from view again. Personally and professionally, Dever was alive and vibrant; politically, he had become a nonperson.

The Sullivan Consolidation

During the twelve years Dever spent hidden in the courts, the politics of Chicago changed significantly. If the years before 1910 were a feudal age, then the period from 1910 through 1922 was a time of evolution toward absolutism. This was the era of party consolidation. The factionalism of past days was dying out. In both parties, but particularly on the Democratic side, one group achieved the upper hand and submerged its rivals.

Feudal politics reached something of a climax in 1911. Among the Democrats, the previous year's "harmony ticket" became only a dim memory as the Harrison, Dunne, and Sullivan factions resumed their three-cornered feud. One writer has described the party's mayoral primary of 1911 as "the ultimate factional battle."[39] It certainly was a bitter struggle that saw the aging "Young Carter" eke out a narrow victory over both Dunne and the Sullivan candidate. But after the fireworks of the primary, the general election proved even more explosive. Harrison's Republican opponent was Charles Edward Merriam, a youthful University of Chicago professor who was also one of the city council's reform leaders; like Harrison, he came through the primary with a badly divided party. During the final six weeks of the campaign, formal party identification became almost meaningless. Warriors from both camps deserted sides to knife rivals and contend for control of their parties. Chicanery, fix, and counterfix ran wild. In the end, probably no one could say for sure who really won the election; but Harrison was certified the victor by 17,000 votes.[40]

From out of this chaos, something resembling order emerged. The Republican party went through a series of dramatic upheavals after the Merriam campaign. "Blonde Boss" Lorimer was expelled from the United States Senate and went into political decline. Former Mayor Busse died suddenly, splintering the North Side bloc. The Progressive party arose, helped knock Charles Deneen out of the governor's mansion, and threatened to supplant the G.O.P as one of the major political parties. Finally, the Republican party emerged as two main factions, with a half-faction floating around. Deneen's group remained the rallying point for the party's reformers. Their chief rival was the Lundin faction, a coalition of traditionalist Lorimer and Busse ward bosses directed by former congressman Fred ("Poor Swede") Lundin. The half-faction was the Brundage group. This little bloc was the creation of North Side politico Edward Brundage and Medill McCormick of the *Chicago Tribune* family; it shuttled back and forth between the two larger groups, forming alliances when convenient.[41]

The Republicans managed to combine forces on occasion and win some

Roger Sullivan: builder of the Chicago Democratic machine. *(Chicago Historical Society: DN 62, 650)*

impressive victories. However, their unity always proved temporary. By the 1920s they were battling among themselves again. The Democrats, meanwhile, successfully eliminated most factionalism and streamlined their party apparatus. Since Dever's election as mayor is the culmination of this process, it is helpful to examine the political developments of the decade from the Democrats' perspective.

The story of the Democratic party during the 1910s is the story of the triumph of Roger Sullivan. It begins with a major miscalculation by Mayor Harrison. Even after Young Carter's return to power in 1911, Sullivan had remained well situated, his faction controlling both the county and the state party machinery. Harrison had only the city government. But in the heady atmosphere of his restoration, the mayor decided it was time to be rid of Sullivan, once and for all. To accomplish this, Harrison formed an alliance with the powerful publisher William Randolph Hearst, then in his crusading reform editor phase. This latest anti-Sullivan group called itself the Progressive Democrats. It was basically the old Allies bloc of 1910, with Hearst added. Pledging themselves to a new day for the Democratic party, the Harrison-Hearstites called on all opponents of Boss Sullivan to join their offensive.[42]

They were spectacularly unsuccessful. The Progressive Democrats failed to wrest control of the state party from Sullivan hands. They challenged the regulars' delegation at the 1912 Democratic National Convention and lost there, too. Even long-time anti-Sullivanites like Edward Dunne would not help. Dunne was governor now and saw little reason to antagonize Sullivan. And, meanwhile, Harrison's own supporters were starting to break ranks. The mayor's continued fraternization with Hearst and his promotion of reform bewildered old-line ward leaders. Harrison had even ordered the Levee closed down. What would he do next? Bobbie Burke, "Hinky-Dink," "Bathhouse John," and other venerable Harrison loyalists defected. Ambitious younger men, like the Bohemian chieftain Anton Cermak, also concluded that their future lay with Sullivan's organization.[43] The mayor had apparently out-maneuvered himself.

In 1915 Sullivan was ready for a counterattack. He had engineered his own nomination for the United States Senate the previous year and surprised almost everyone by coming within 20,000 votes of victory. Now Sullivan slated popular county clerk Robert Sweitzer against the fading Harrison in the Democratic mayoral primary. Most of the mayor's allies had already deserted him, and Harrison himself ran a lackluster campaign; he later said he knew that "the game was up." Sweitzer destroyed Harrison's bid for a sixth term by a margin approaching two to one, sending Young Carter into final political oblivion.[44]

For the first time since the days of John Hopkins, the Sullivanites had the Democratic mayoral candidate. Roger Sullivan had taken a giant step toward centralized control of local politics. His faction held dominant power within the Democratic party. The pieces were in place, the stage set, everything ready. Then, unexpectedly, a new Republican star burst upon the scene—a star named Thompson.

William Hale Thompson was born in 1867. A lumbering, round-shouldered man with the face of a bereaved bloodhound and an ample expanse of belly, he was the most colorful statesman Chicago had ever produced: a political showboat. His campaign style was to yell, and when things got really rough, to yell louder. He fed his audiences a steady diet of blarney and buffoonery, and they consumed it eagerly. Thompson was the son of an old, socially prominent New England family, though he seldom mentioned his patrician pedigree. He preferred to talk about his years out West as a cowboy. "Big Bill," as he liked to call himself, had served a term in the city council and a few years on the county board. In 1915 he had been out of active politics for nearly ten years. But canny Fred Lundin knew that Thompson was a dynamic campaigner and talked him into entering the Republican mayoral primary. [45]

That was the beginning of the end for Roger Sullivan's plans to capture the mayor's office in 1915. After Thompson edged out Judge Harry Olson for his party's nomination, Fred Lundin managed to patch together a united front with the Deneen Republicans. Sullivan, on the other hand, continued to be troubled by the Harrison bloc; they were content to sulk in their tents rather than come to the aid of the party. The Democratic schism, coupled with Thompson's vigorous performance on the stump, led to a Republican landslide. [46]

After the debacle of 1915, Sullivan regrouped. Harrison was finally gone and Governor Dunne was anxious to avoid a Democratic civil war. Little opposition was left within the party as the boss quietly consolidated control. Thompson's conduct in office also helped Sullivan. The new mayor almost immediately became involved in a number of controversies that diminished his popularity and weakened his party. The result was a decisive Democratic victory in the 1916 aldermanic elections. [47] Only a year after being smashed by Thompson, the Sullivan organization had come back stronger than ever.

Roger Sullivan now took important steps to centralize power within the Democratic party. He directed that all political patronage be turned over to the newly created Democratic Managing Committee, which he and his closest associates would run. While individual ward bosses retained appointment power in their own districts, the Sullivan leadership could now monitor the distribution of jobs. [48] Most of the neighborhood bosses silently accepted this innovation. They might not like "downtown" knowing so much of what went on in their wards, but they realized their best hope for greater future spoils lay with a unified party organization. They were pragmatic. Thus, very few ward leaders objected to Sullivan's blatant power grab.

The consolidation continued. Governor Dunne lost his reelection bid in 1916, removing him as a potential rival. Meanwhile, those mavericks and unreconstructed Harrison men who could not adapt themselves to the new Democratic order were purged. The leftover anti-Sullivanites joined together in one last coalition for the 1918 primaries. Calling themselves "Allied Democracy" this time around, their slate was easily swept aside by the regular organization. [49] Now, only Thompson stood in the way.

The mayor seemed to be a pushover. He had torn the Republican party apart with a farcical run for the United States Senate in 1918, and his administration had grown notably corrupt. Moreover, his patriotism was suspect, owing to his vocal pro-Germanism in the days before American entry into the World War: "Kaiser Bill," he was being called. Sullivan gave Robert Sweitzer the job of finishing him off.

Unfortunately, factionalism continued to plague the Democrats. State's Attorney Maclay Hoyne, an old Dunne man who had never felt comfortable with Sullivan, entered the election as an independent. The situation was further confused by a fourth candidate, labor leader John Fitzpatrick. Suddenly, nothing was certain. The fight was on and Thompson jumped into it with relish. He conducted another rip-roaring campaign, shifting the offensive to his side. With the vote split four ways, Big Bill managed to squeeze back into office with 37 percent of the total.[50.]

Although Thompson had won again, the 1919 election was a Democratic landmark. It proved to be the last open mayoral battle within the party for two decades. In 1920, the recalcitrant Maclay Hoyne went down to defeat in his state's attorney race. With his removal, the public brawling ended and "organizational unity" became the watchwords. The old faction-ridden anarchy had been replaced with a well-oiled, smoothly running machine.[51]

Sullivan had succeeded through systematic planning and attention to detail. He built step by step; and although he was often forced to take a step backward, he was generally able to follow up with two steps forward. After a while, a natural momentum developed. As the Sullivanites grew stronger, more and more of the ward grandees came to appreciate the virtues of party unity and affiliated with the organization. Sullivan, too, was a practical man. He preferred to coopt his rivals rather than crush them. Like a modern Caesar in the conquest of Gaul, he took the defeated chieftains into his army and made them his lieutenants. Sullivan knew that past allegiance had little relevance for working politics. "The checkerboard is moving all the time," he one said. "The men who are strong enemies today may be friendly six months from now."[52]

It also helped that his adversaries within the party were so inept, so out of touch with reality. Carter Harrison, Sullivan's chief nemesis, is a ready example. Young Carter was an aristocrat who occasionally got his hands dirty. He liked being the august leader and playing at the game of politics; but he played on his own terms. Harrison's faction was merely a personal following. Between elections he did little to build an organization or even to keep his bloc together. When he found himself out of office, he would retreat to his California ranch and admire the orange groves. Harrison had a lofty disdain for participatory politics, observing that "a goodly share of the electorate lacks a heavy supply of gray matter above the eyebrows."[53] By the time Harrison completed his fifth term, he had alienated too many of his former companions. He did not seem to care any more. In effect, he was offering his followers a choice: personal fealty to Carter Harrison, or enlightened self-interest. Self-interest won.

Much has been written interpreting the struggle for party control as basically an ethnic competition: the Irish versus the non-Irish. There is certainly some validity in this view.[54] Roger Sullivan was Irish, and his faction had started out as a narrow, Gaelic-flavored clique. But by the 1910s Sullivan and his associates had recognized the advantages of enlisting other nationality groups. The harmony ticket of 1910 is one example. The Sullivanites played "balance the ticket" by expressly stating that certain key offices were "to be named by the Poles" or "to be named by the Bohemians." As the organization expanded, Sullivan found places for such ethnic barons as Anton Cermak, Stanley Kunz, Jacob Arvey, and others. His two-time candidate for mayor, Robert Sweitzer, was German. In any case, Sullivan held no monopoly on Irish politicians or Irish voters. Carter Harrison himself noted that the great mass of local Irish preferred to support Edward Dunne and not the Sullivan candidates. No, the Irish-against-the-world explanation is an oversimplification, springing from a generation of writers who remembered forty years of mayors name Kelly, Kennelly, and Daley.[55]

Roger Sullivan did not live to enjoy the fruits of his labor. The old boss died shortly before the Democratic National Convention of 1920. Although he had been in declining health for some time, his passing came as a shock; he had been a prominent part of the Chicago scene for so long. Sullivan's only elected office had been as a probate court clerk in the 1890s, but the citizens of his city were aware that a political giant had moved among them. They honored him in the traditional way America commemorates her dead statesmen. They named a high school after him.[56]

Yet, even with the death of its founding father, the Democratic organization scarcely missed a beat. The man dies, the machine lives on—Sullivan would have approved. His legacy had been a united, efficient Democratic party. Now his successors would have to put the capstone on his construction and realize full power.

4

The Making of the Mayor
1923

The Decline of Big Bill

■ As 1922 drew to a close, William Hale Thompson was a mayor in trouble. Chicagoans had grown weary of their rambunctious chief executive. The bright young leader who had stormed into office eight years earlier had become a familiar, middle-aged politician. Events had gotten too far out of hand for even the adroit Thompson to juggle. And, although the mayor's political demise had long been predicted, this time the afflictions appeared to be genuinely terminal.

Big Bill's misfortunes had started a few months into his second term. In July 1919, a racial fight broke out on a South Side beach. As the fighting began to spread into the neighborhoods, the mayor reacted slowly. He did not seem to grasp the seriousness of the situation. To him this was just a little scrap his police could take care of. Or perhaps, as some people suggested, he did not want to ask for help from Governor Lowden, a political adversary. So for four days, Big Bill went his own way. Then, with general anarchy threatening to overwhelm the entire city, Thompson swallowed his pride and called on Lowden. The state militia finally brought about peace, but not before thirty-eight people died.[1]

Thompson took a lot of criticism for mishandling the 1919 riot, even from his friends in the black community. There were ongoing problems as well. The mayor was accused of playing politics with the public schools and interfering in the way they were run. The school board itself was engaged in a civil war, the Thompson appointees and the holdover member battling each other with political machination and court injunction. Charges of corruption, incompetence, and partisan featherbedding were hurled back and forth. Charles E. Chadsey, a highly respected educator brought in from Detroit to be the new school superintendent, grew so disgusted that he quit after only three months. The school system had become a national disgrace.[2]

Then there was the matter of "experts' fees." The city had hired a number of engineers and other professionals to conduct a series of public works studies. Such activities are perfectly normal, of course, and generally arouse little controversy. However, in this instance, the *Chicago Tribune* rushed in crying foul. The mayor's old nemesis accused two of the consultants of bilking the city out of nearly $3 million in fraudulent fees; it also charged certain Thompson cabinet members with peddling influence and extorting kickbacks. To cap off its revelations, the newspaper filed a taxpayer's lawsuit against the mayor, two of his department heads, and two of the "experts."[3]

Politics was also proving difficult. In April 1921, Thompson's allies on the county Republican committee had taken the unusual step of refusing to reslate a number of sitting circuit court judges. Although Big Bill and his friends might have been happy to pack the court with political soulmates, the main reason for their plan was the power of the circuit court judges to appoint the members of the patronage-laden South Park Commission. It was a neat way to annex another rich little domain with little bother—nobody paid any attention to judicial elections. This time, though, Thompson had overreached himself. The public outcry was loud, echoing one theme: save the judiciary from politics.

The Democrats shrewdly slated a coalition judicial ticket that included most of the dumped Republican judges and that won wide support from newspapers, civic groups, and professional legal societies. Three times the usual number of voters turned out on election day to smash the "Thompson court-packing scheme." Nor was this merely a temporary setback for Big Bill. The Democrats continued to score convincing electoral victories through 1921 and 1922. The political balance appeared to be shifting.[4]

Thompson kept up a brave front. He went on building bridges, widening streets, and giving his opponents hell. During the summer of 1921, he launched a grand exhibition at Municipal Pier called the Pageant of Progress. Its purpose was to show off Chicago as a commercial center and, incidentally, give the hometown folks a good party. Big Bill's first pageant was an enormous success. He tried again in 1922 but ran into bad weather and a streetcar strike. To make matters worse, after the second pageant flopped, some citizens filed a new lawsuit, claiming that the fair was nothing but a political boondoggle.[5]

Yet the mayor still wanted a third term, and Thompson was one politician you could never count out. Even when he was supposed to be slipping—and Big Bill was supposed to have been slipping ever since he took office in 1915— he had always been able to turn things around and rally the masses to his side. He would not roll over and play dead. He still had considerable strengths. He controlled the city patronage army and, with Fred Lundin, the leading faction of the Republican party. The new governor of the state, Len Small, was a Thompson man. In addition, the mayor enjoyed the friendship of William Randolph Hearst and his influential newspapers; rumors even circulated that the press lord was grooming Big Bill to be his running mate on a third-party presidential ticket for 1924.[6]

So it looked as if Thompson would run again, in spite of everything. He himself was primed for the task. His troops eagerly awaited his call, anxious to leap into the fray and have at Big Bill's enemies once more. All was in readiness.

Reform Renaissance

The making of the mayor for 1923 was complicated by one of the periodic outbreaks of Chicago reform fever. The clean-government movement had been declining in the city for some time. The reformers had last mounted a credible mayoral bid with Charles E. Merriam back in 1911. Over the next decade, however, something had happened. The mighty Municipal Voters' League had lost its ginger and ceased being a decisive force in city politics. Perhaps it had grown complacent after its great early victories. Certainly, the World War and the fight to make the whole world safe for democracy had diverted attention from purely local matters. Eight years of Thompson's antics had not helped either. By the 1920s, the MVL was only a shadow of its former self.[7] Its waning was symbolic of the general ebb of the whole reform impulse.

But the reformers of Chicago were back in force for 1923, heartened by the public's disillusionment with Big Bill, and scenting victory. Late in 1922, a group of clean-government advocates gathered at the City Club for a forum on "What Are the Issues and What Kind of a Man Do We Need for Mayor?" The meeting was organized by Reverend Graham Taylor and Mrs. Kellogg Fairbank, a socially prominent novelist and political dabbler. Famed attorney Clarence Darrow was among the speakers. He clearly delineated the type of mayor the reformers wanted. "Chicago needs a mayor who has the courage to say 'no,' and say it to all his best friends," Darrow declared. "The mayor of Chicago should treat the city the way he would treat his own business. That is a popular phrase, but no one carries out the idea."[8]

What should the elected official be expected to do? The reformers were not so fuzzy minded as to expect political games playing to vanish completely. These were practical people. They found fault with the Thompson administration not so much for its partisan manipulations as for its waste and inefficiency. "Politics as usual" might not be the ideal, but it could be tolerated if the greater good were served. Big Bill's gang was simply not governing productively. The *Chicago Tribune* spoke from this vantage when it compared New York City's Tammany Hall with the Thompson machine and sadly concluded: "New York's greatness is given it by a wise political organization. Tammany levies and takes its percentage, but it gives the people a return. It built subways and a great harbor. Its public works add to the splendor of the city and ensure its future. Our [machine] levies and takes, but it does not give."[9]

Some citizens were convinced that the time had come for action. One group of business executives and clergymen assembled at the Morrison Hotel the day after Christmas. Led by Thomas D. Knight, director of the civic watchdog Better Government Association, they joined together in a concerted drive to rid the city of Big Bill and elect a businessman mayor. They called themselves by an honored Chicago reform name, the Committee of One Hundred. Most of these concerned folk were Republicans, and they aimed themselves directly at the Republican party. The Committee of One Hundred announced it would offer one candidate to the anti-Thompson Republican leaders within the next two weeks. Should the politicians reject the committee's choice, it was prepared to run its own candidate anyway. Although it would lobby only within the Republican family, the Committee of One Hundred hoped its efforts might also "stimulate" Democratic politicos to select a blue-ribbon candidate for their own party.[10]

At the City Club, meanwhile, the original band of reformers were continuing to meet informally, mapping out plans. No doubt prodded by the formation of the Committee of One Hundred, they decided to start an organization of their own. They held a public luncheon at the club on January 3, 1923. One hundred and fifty activists came, wolfed down their meals, then got down to business. The luncheon gathering formed itself into the Nonpartisan Citizens' Mayoralty Committee. A twenty-nine-member executive committee was selected to direct the new group, with Mrs. Fairbank as its head.[11]

The Nonpartisan Committee was frankly and forthrightly a lobbying body. It pledged to work for the election of a "competent, progressive, and honest mayor" who would cut government waste and protect the public schools. To accomplish this goal, the Nonpartisan Committee would seek to influence each major party to nominate in their respective primaries two "outstanding men of proved ability and integrity." It vowed not to meddle in party affairs by trying to coax crossover votes for a candidate. The Nonpartisan Committee would issue a list of five or ten persons of suitable qualifications for mayor and throw its support to whichever party accepted one of them. If neither party heeded its counsel, the Nonpartisan Committee would consider running an independent candidate.[12]

The Nonpartisan Committee took about a week to study the political situation. On January 11, amid much fanfare, it announced its selections. Seven men were named: two Republicans and five Democrats. The Republicans were Postmaster Arthur C. Lueder and Alderman A. A. McCormack. The five Democrats were attorneys Francis X. Busch, John P. McGoorty, and William H. Sexton; and superior court judges William E. Dever and Charles A. McDonald. The recommendations were listed in no particular order of preference.[13]

At a well-appointed suite in the Auditorium Hotel, a pudgy, gray-haired man with a peg-leg read over the reformers' list of candidates with great interest and chuckled softly to himself. Politics might be a game, but it was always more fun to win that game. And now he had the last piece to fit into his puzzle.

The Democrats at the Crossroads

If you met George Brennan on the street, you probably would not think he was a political boss. He did not look or act the part. Brennan was not the somber-faced, closed-mouth, backroom czar of popular legend; rather, he was a warm, outgoing man of genial disposition and genuine wit. He could discuss art and literature sensitively and was knowledgeable in history and foreign affairs. He enjoyed telling whimsical little stories to illustrate his points. Through it all, he tried to keep a proper perspective. He was serious about politics but not grim—and not overly impressed with his own importance. "I can't say I deserved Roger Sullivan's mantle," he once observed. "It just fell to me. The job of Boss was a big jackpot, and I happened to be the only man around the table with openers."[14]

Brennan was born in Port Byron, New York, in 1865.[15] He moved to Illinois as a young man, working as a mule driver. A cart accident cost him half of his right leg and his occupation. So, he went back to school and became a teacher in the coal town of Braidwood. He was later promoted to principal and, before he was thirty, had become assistant superintendent of the Joliet school district. Then, for some reason he could later never precisely determine, George Brennan decided to enter politics.

He had become acquainted with various Democratic politicians during his service as a school administrator. When the party won the 1892 state elections, Brennan went to Springfield as private secretary to the new secretary of state. He spent four years in the capital, then moved to Chicago. There, he enlisted in the Sullivan-Hopkins brigade and began to make himself useful. He quickly caught the eye of Boss Sullivan, who drew him into the inner circle and gave him some campaigns to run. Brennan did well, and the boss was impressed. He began to rely more and more on the cheerful ex-schoolmaster. By 1910, George Brennan had become Sullivan's chief lieutenant and top political manipulator.

Over the next decade, Brennan continued his studies at the old boss's knee. He learned the organization from top to bottom, from First Ward to Thirty-fifth. When Sullivan died in 1920, Brennan succeeded him as party leader. He took over easily and efficiently, holding the party together when its hereditary factionalism threatened to pull it apart. Brennan might modestly downplay the circumstances of his rise to power, but he was a shrewd and ambitious leader, and the logical man to carry on Roger Sullivan's policies.

Party unity was the new boss's immediate problem. Roger Sullivan had spent his political life trying to eliminate Democratic factionalism and had largely succeeded. In the two years following his accession as leader, Brennan kept the organization intact. He even managed to reach an accommodation with former governor Dunne and his friends during the 1922 primaries, when a new factional war seemed imminent. And yet, Brennan was still not firmly in command. The old Harrison-Dunne crowd remained somewhat wary of him; besides that, any number of power-hungry ward bosses were waiting for him to falter. Brennan needed a unifying factor to confirm his place in the center chair. Thompson's political vulnerability was the key. George Brennan was convinced he could cement his position by doing something Sullivan had never been able to do—he would elect a mayor.[16]

In the fall of 1922, Brennan and his advisors began the search for a candidate. They went into their task with no favorite choice in mind. They gave themselves plenty of time to work, three months or more until they had to find their man. They knew they must choose wisely. The Democrats had underestimated Thompson in 1919; they would not do so again.

While the party professionals sifted through the lists of would-be mayors, the newspapers went wild with speculation. It seemed as though the press had a different man nominated and elected in each edition. One day they would report that former state representative Michael Igoe had the inside track; the next day Congressman John W. Rainey was supposed to be surging; the day after that Judge Charles A. McDonald forged into the lead. Just about any Democratic politician who was under ninety and not incarcerated was considered prime mayoral timber: even that thoroughly shopworn old warhorse Carter Harrison was mentioned as a possibility.[17]

If the papers did not know who the candidate would be, it was because the politicians did not yet know either. In those pre-Gallup days, the Medium (for there was then only one) did not have the sophisticated polling techniques that bless us today. There were straw polls, to be sure; but they were crude affairs and used only for the general election, after the candidates had already been slated. No newspaper bothered to poll the citizens on what nominee they wanted; it was easier to ask the politicians whom the people would get. When the pros could not decide on one candidate, the press simply picked up any rumor they could and pushed whichever person they wanted. Let a few party warriors taking their ease at a local tap declare that Honest John Smith was a fine candidate, the next day the tabloids might report that "a real boom is on for Honest John Smith." Have Fearless Frank Jones's supporters read this and pledge that their man was the party's savior, the day after another paper might note that "Fearless Frank Jones is coming on strong as a possible candidate." This sort of reporting was not deceit: journalists were doing the best job they could. In effect, it was a kind of entertainment, a political version of baseball's "hot stove league." Until the party high priests decided on someone to anoint, all one could do was pass the time by talking politics.

This is not to say that the voter had no say in the nominating process. The smart politicians were those who could steer public opinion and party policy in the same direction. The system was simply different in those times. "Trial balloon" candidacies served a real purpose: they gave party leaders an opportunity to gauge popular and press reaction to various hopefuls. From this process, a select few strong contenders would emerge. Naturally, the wider open the race, the more possibilities to be floated. And so, for 1923, a whole fleet of Democratic mayoral candidates passed through in review.

In all, about two dozen prospective Democratic nominees were mentioned in the public press. So undecided were the party elders that they kept postponing the date of their formal slating conference, using the excuse that Brennan was recovering from surgery on his bad leg.[18] But while the leaders wrestled with the slating question and the newspapers reported the ebb and flow of various candidacies, one man remained a strong contender throughout. The press rarely recognized him as a mayor in the making. His fellow politicians, however, knew of the skills, the force of character, and the fierce ambitions of Anton J. Cermak.

Cermak had been brought to Illinois from his native Bohemia as an infant.[19]. He grew up in Braidwood at about the same time George Brennan was teaching school there, though there is no evidence Brennan was ever his teacher. After a few years in the coal mines, young Tony Cermak moved to Chicago in 1889. He settled among his fellow Bohemians on the city's West Side. Cermak soon went into Democratic politics and over the years built up a loyal following in the Pilsen and South Lawndale communities. He also helped organize and lead the United Societies for Local Self-Government, the politically potent anti-Prohibition, pro-Personal-Liberty pressure group. By 1922, at the age of forty-nine, Cermak was the recognized leader of the Czech-Bohemian voting bloc, and one of the city's most noted wet spokesmen. He consolidated his power that year by winning election as president of the Cook County Board of Commissioners.

Cermak wanted to be mayor, and he wanted it badly. He had obvious strengths—organizational ability, a large personal following, strong identification as a wet—but there were serious drawbacks as well. As a Bohemian immigrant, Cermak might be just a bit *too* ethnic for some of the city's WASPier voters. A bigger problem was the man's personal reputation. Cermak was a hustler, a wheeler-dealer. He had risen from humble origins to become a person of considerable wealth; and though nothing had ever been proven, there were suspicions of how Cermak had obtained that wealth. Finally, his anti-Prohibition stand, while an advantage in most quarters of soaking-wet Chicago, was a distinct disadvantage in others—it was simply the type of issue that was better left alone. So Cermak was out. He was just too soiled to make an effective contrast to Thompson. Brennan needed someone without a hint of impropriety, a candidate who was squeaky clean.[20]

Braidwood's gifts to the Democratic party: George Brennan and Anton Cermak. *(Chicago Historical Society: DN 80, 717)*

At about the same time Brennan was considering and rejecting a Cermak ticket, he began to think seriously about superior court justice William E. Dever. Where the idea originated cannot be determined at this date. It has been said that while defeat is an orphan, victory has a hundred fathers. Over the years, several individuals have sought or been assigned paternity of the Dever candidacy.

Harold Ickes claimed that he was the first to suggest Judge Dever to party leader Brennan. In 1922 Ickes was an attorney and former newspaperman who had been active in Progressive Republican politics. He had known the Democratic boss for over twenty years. The two men were close friends and had done each other political favors. According to Ickes's account, he knew that George needed an on-the-square candidate to run against Thompson, so he told Brennan that Judge Dever was a man whom Progressive Republicans and independents could support. Having no one better in mind, the Democratic leader accepted Ickes's suggestion.[21]

Alderman Ulysses S. Schwartz remembered events differently. According to him, the Dever boom was conceived by William L. O'Connell, a well-known attorney who was former governor Dunne's right-hand man. O'Connell supposedly approached Brennan with the themes of party and ethnic unity, telling him, "What this town needs is a really good Irishman [for mayor], and let us forget our differences now." He then unveiled Judge Dever as his choice for the office.[22] O'Connell and Dever were old comrades from Dunne's term as mayor, so the story is plausible.

However, as far as can be documented, it appears that George C. Sikes was the first person to bring Dever to the attention of the Democratic leaders. Sikes, an ex-reporter and one-time secretary of the Municipal Voters' League, was associated with the Harrison wing of the party. As early as November 11, 1922, he had written to titular party chairman Martin J. O'Brien about the judge's credentials. Sikes felt that the time had come for "a different type of mayor." He said that the people were disillusioned with politics and looked to the Democratic party for something better. He urged the party to pick a candidate who could be respected by them: William E. Dever. Sikes knew Dever to be "fundamentally honest . . . and thoroughly democratic in his instincts and point of view." He thought the judge a splendid campaigner who related well to the voters. "He understands the people of this cosmopolitan community . . . and he is trusted by them," Sikes declared. What was more, Dever could bring the party together. Sikes feared a bitter primary that might endanger Democratic electoral success. He went on:

> Mr. Dever seems to possess to an unusual degree availability as a harmony candidate. So far as factions within the Democratic Party are concerned, he is a political neutral. I am satisfied that he would not undertake to use the power of the mayor's office to destroy political leaders nor to build a political machine for himself. . . . I believe he would—if elected mayor—come nearer to giving Chicago a non-factional and non-political administration of city affairs than any man the Democratic Party is likely to nominate.

Sikes concluded by observing that Dever presented party leaders with an "unusual opportunity"—the chance to act in the public interest while promoting "the best welfare of the Democratic party."[23]

Certainly, the Democratic elders already knew of Dever's qualifications as a mayoral candidate.[24] What had to be intriguing was that the Harrison-Dunnites within the party and the Progressive Republicans on the outside were both boosting him. Ickes's support surely made Dever something special, that crusty old Bull Mooser seldom had a good word to say about anyone. And wherever Ickes was, Merriam, Robins, and that whole influential reform crowd was usually nearby.

George Brennan decided to sound out Dever firsthand. He and Mrs. Brennan arranged to have dinner with the judge and his wife. After their meal, they began to discuss the mayoral election. Neither Brennan nor Dever ever described their conversation, and accounts of it vary.[25] Most likely, the cautious Brennan did not immediately offer Dever organization support or even hint that the judge was becoming a front runner. He probably talked in generalities. But Dever was certainly smart enough to read between the lines and realize that the main chance had come. Brennan did say that he would exact only one promise if Dever became the party's candidate—that when elected, Dever would not use the patronage powers of the mayor's office to form his own private machine. Kate Dever answered for her husband. "I'm sure he would never do anything of that sort," she said. [26]

Brennan left without committing himself, but the situation was becoming clearer. Dever was a man he could work with. The party leader consulted with a number of ward committeemen and found that there was no great opposition to the judge. Meanwhile, the Nonpartisan Citizens' Mayoralty Committee had issued its list of endorsees, with Dever's name included. For Brennan, that was the last proof he needed. [27]

Very quickly now, things came together. Brennan held a meeting with William O'Connell and solidified Harrison-Dunne support behind Dever. He met with representatives of the Nonpartisan Committee to inform them he was accepting one of their candidates. The judge was told to start preparing himself for the campaign. The long-delayed Democratic slating conference finally convened, amid leaks to the press that Dever was to be the one chosen. The party chieftains met behind closed doors at the Auditorium Hotel. In a demonstration of unity, Anton Cermak was given the job of formally presenting Dever's name to the caucus. There was little debate or surface animosity as the judge was slated by a vote of forty-eight to one, with only his ancient enemy Stanley Kunz opposing him. On January 19, 1923, William E. Dever was officially announced as the regular Democratic candidate for mayor of Chicago. [28]

As George Sikes had said, Dever was the ideal candidate for Brennan's purposes. The judge could keep the party united. His background was with the Harrison-Dunne group, and those people remembered him fondly. He had also kept ties to the regular organization, demonstrating on many occasions that he was a loyal party man. Everybody liked him. Except for the erratic Kunz, who counted for nothing, Dever did not seem to have an enemy in the world.

Dever's service on the bench helped, too. It meant that the candidate did not have a long, controversial political record to defend. In fact, as a justice of the superior court, Dever could be presented as a prestige candidate, one who had been above petty partisan bickering. He certainly made a dignified appearance—though he was not stuffy, he was really a lively campaigner. True, after a dozen years at the court, Dever had little personal following. But that was fine with Brennan; it was unlikely that Dever could build enough power to seize control of the organization for himself. [29]

Finally, Dever was popular with reformers and independents. This was the deciding factor. Brennan was attempting to form a grand political coalition of diverse elements under the banner of the Democratic party. He needed a candidate who could attract new voters to the fold without alienating the party's traditional supporters. The clean-government bloc knew of Brennan's plans for party expansion. They read the political situation shrewdly and pushed forward a man with whom the regular organization could live. They sent Brennan a message that they were willing to join him. He accepted it.

So William E. Dever was to be Boss Brennan's "beau geste," his announcement to the political world that the Chicago Democratic party could nominate high-quality candidates. Such blue-ribbon slating was not uncommon for machine organizations; it usually took place when the party was in trouble and public opinion had to be soothed. But this tactic was not always a mere cynical response to voter uprisings. With the coming of progressivism, some of the smarter political operators had recognized the wisdom of running conspicuously honest, reform-minded candidates, who happened also to be loyal party men. New York's Charles T. Murphy was one of these innovators who comes readily to mind: the Tammany boss groomed such notables as Senator Robert F. Wagner, Sr., and Governor Alfred E. Smith. Closer to home, Roger Sullivan had worked with the Progressives on a variety of reform causes, most notably in promoting the direct election of U.S. senators. Dever's mayoral candidacy would be Brennan's first step along this path. [30] If successful, it might lead to all sorts of interesting possibilities. Good government could very well be good politics.

What was Dever's role in all this maneuvering? In truth, it was minor. He had been mentioned as a possible mayor at every election since 1905, but there had been little reason to think that this year the lightning would strike. His friends and admirers advanced Dever's candidacy for him, certainly with his knowledge but seemingly with little encouragement from him. He himself did nothing until it became clear that he had a serious chance for the office; then he made the necessary accommodations. Dever had built a career based on honesty, hard work, and good relations with all groups. Circumstances had combined to make a person with his qualifications the logical Democratic candidate for mayor. Events had sought the man and found him.

Campaign for Mayor

Along with Dever, the Democrats slated two running mates for the other citywide elective offices. [31] They chose former state senator Al F. Gorman to replace the retiring Clayton F. Smith as city clerk. Possibly as a sop to the disappointed Cermak, John A. Cervenka was named candidate for city treasurer. The three standard-bearers appeared together before the party caucus to urge unity. They solemnly vowed to rid Chicago of the scourge of Thompsonism and return City Hall to Democratic control. [32]

But once again Big Bill confounded his political opponents: he withdrew as a candidate for reelection. The mayor had simply been overwhelmed. Postmaster Arthur C. Lueder, who had been selected by the Committee of One Hundred and had the backing of the Brundage-McCormick-*Tribune* axis, had already entered the race against him. From the other side of his party, word reached Thompson that the ambitious state's attorney, Robert E. Crowe, was preparing new corruption indictments of Fred Lundin and assorted administration figures.[33] The mayor's only hope for survival was that the Democrats would run a weak candidate; then, Thompson might be able to squeeze through the primary and not need a unified party for the general election. The mayor actually seems to have tried to cut such a deal with Brennan and the Democratic leaders. When they named Dever, Big Bill knew that he had lost his last long shot. Less than a week after Dever's slating, Thompson bowed out.[34]

With the mayor's abdication, Arthur Lueder became the Republican front-runner. Three other candidates were also in the contest for Thompson's throne: Edward Litsinger, a protege of ex-governor Deneen, who ran in spite of his mentor's support of Lueder; Arthur Millard, a lawyer prominent in Masonic circles; and municipal court judge Bernard Barasa, whose main claim to fame was that he had been personally endorsed by Rudolph Valentino. These worthies were not expected to give Lueder much trouble, and they did not. The postmaster easily won his party's primary.[35]

The Republican nominee was cut from the classic mold of the business-man-nonpolitician. Arthur Charles Lueder had been born in Elmhurst, Illinois, in 1876, the son of a professor at the local college.[36] After serving as a sergeant in the Spanish-American War, he returned home to earn a law degree from the Chicago College of Law in 1902. He started his own real estate company and prospered financially. Lueder also got into Republican politics in an advisory and contributory role, identifying with the McCormick-Brundage wing of the party. President Harding appointed him United States Postmaster for the Chicago area in October 1921. During his fifteen months on the job, Lueder had gained a reputation as an able administrator who had increased bureau efficiency and improved employee morale. His candidacy for mayor of Chicago was his first try for elective office.

Thanks to George Brennan's careful work, Dever was unopposed for the Democratic nomination, and the party could concentrate on the general election. Thompson's surprise withdrawal had complicated the Democrats' plans. They had been preparing to wage a strong anticorruption campaign against the incumbent, contrasting Dever's clean (if obscure) record with Big Bill's well-known sins. Now that Lueder was to be the Republican nominee, they had to adjust their strategy. It would not be enough for Dever to run simply as the honest alternative candidate. The judge must now establish himself as a positive person with definite programs.

They decided to hold an open house. The Democrats set up a campaign office in the Sherman House hotel shortly after Dever's selection. Each weekday between 12:00 noon and 2:00 P.M., the candidate was on hand to greet shoppers, Loop office-workers, and anyone else who wandered in off Clark Street.[37] These receptions were informal, one-to-one affairs, designed to show off the judge's personal warmth and friendliness. The formal speeches and the hard-sell came later in the day, at the ward meetings and the public rallies.

Dever spent most evenings traveling around the city, attending as many of these events as possible. There were a great number and a great variety of functions, as can be seen from examining Dever's itinerary for just one night. At 6:30 P.M., the candidate started off in the Loop with an address to a Greek-American banquet at the Sherman House. He next journeyed to the West Side for a Chicago Commons reception at 7:15. By 8:00 he was in Uptown at Arcadia Hall, speaking before a combined Forty-eighth–Forty-ninth Wards' rally. From there, Dever headed back south for appearances at the DePaul University Auditorium and at the Forty-fifth Ward Turners' Hall. He ended his day on the near Northwest Side, with a last speech to a Polish gathering at St. Stanislaus Kostka Church.[38]

In his campaign orations, Dever usually concentrated on the same points he had made in his keynote speech, when formally accepting the organization's slating. Transit reform would be the main problem facing the new mayor, he told his audiences. He had fought for Municipal Ownership in 1907, and he was still convinced it was the best cure for the city's transit ills. The old traction trust exploitation was on the way out. The new Dever administration would bring about public ownership and operation of the lines. There would be cheaper fares, more efficient service, a unified transfer system, even a subway![39]

Dever also spoke of his concern for the public schools. He promised to appoint a first-rate school board and fight for larger education budgets. He would monitor closely the way those increased funds would be spent. He said it was appalling that "one group of experts receives $3 million, and at the same time we haven't enough money to furnish electric lights for the schoolchildren." Dever further pledged to end overcrowding in the schools by instituting a large-scale building program, freeing the youngsters who were packed together like so many sardines in a can.[40]

There was one issue Dever was careful to treat gingerly: Prohibition. Chicago was definitely opposed to the Noble Experiment; as recently as the previous November, the city had voted four to one against the dry law in a public opinion referendum. Dever, it was now recalled, had supported high saloon license fees during his city council days. Might the Democratic candidate be a closet Prohibitionist? Dever took the initiative and declared himself a full-fledged wet. He noted that he had been "raised with the people, and know some of their ideas of life." He denied that he was a "blue laws man" and promised that he would never use the police to "interfere with the private rights of citizens" and with what they did in their own homes. "I have no desire," he said, "to control the things the City of Chicago has on its tables."[41] After Dever's strong statement, the matter was dropped—and he did nothing to bring it up again.

Besides his main goals of achieving Municipal Ownership and improving public education, Dever enumerated a number of other objectives during the campaign. He vowed to conduct an economical administration. He promised to promote public works but without outlandish experts' fees. In order to foster a healthful environment, he would build beaches, parks, and other recreational facilities. Crime and vice were a growing menace, and he would suppress them. In short, Dever would work to give the people a "cleaner, better, safer, greater Chicago."[42]

It was difficult to argue with Dever's objectives, and Lueder did not try. The Democrats accused the postmaster of "building his platform with Dever planks." They had a point, for the Republican program was almost identical with the Democratic candidate's. Only on the matter of Municipal Ownership did the two men greatly differ. Whereas Dever came out boldly for city ownership and operation of the transit lines, Lueder waffled on the issue. He seemed to be in favor of government ownership, but with operation left in private hands. When pressed on the question of extending the 1907 franchises, due to expire during the next mayor's term, Lueder would only promise to "study" the matter.[43]

Lueder ran a very tight campaign. He refused repeated calls by Dever for a formal debate, though the two candidates shared the same platform on a few occasions. The postmaster gathered early support from the city's two leading newspapers, the *Tribune* and the *Daily News*. He was also very strong with the business community. Lueder spent much of his time pacifying the warring factions of the Republican party. He had some success, keeping his Brundage-McCormick and Deneen backers while winning over a number of influential members of the Thompson bloc. Big Bill himself, however, remained conspicuously silent.[44]

Lueder sought to sell himself as the nonpolitical businessman in politics. He carried this theme to most of his campaign. To those who complained that his stump style was too restrained, he replied, "Business matters are not inclined to be spectacular." Lueder asserted that his years in real estate and at the post office had prepared him to administer a major metropolis. Such experience was a more valuable apprenticeship for the city's chief executive than filling a collection of minor elective posts. "I believe that what the people want is a businessman for mayor," the postmaster told one audience. "I believe they want a man who will devote his time to his duties as mayor of Chicago, and not to building up a political machine." His job would be to set the engine of government running smoothly once more, operating at its full potential: "What this city needs is not a reformer, but a regenerator."[45]

The Republican candidate also tried to link his campaign to national politics. The G.O.P. controlled the presidency and both houses of Congress. Lueder took pains to remind voters of these facts, observing that a Republican mayor would be most effective in working with a Republican national administration. If elected, he would be able to deliver greater benefits from Washington than could a Democrat like Dever.[46] The postmaster obviously hoped for some sort of help from the Harding administration, but he was disappointed. The White House stayed out of the contest.

The Democrats conducted a masterful campaign. *Unity* was the key word for Brennan's grand alliance, as all the different factions and voting blocs rallied around the candidate. The various old-line members of the regular organization— the Coughlins, the Powerses, the Rosenbergs, and the others— could be counted on for their usual energetic support, but now the party had others to call upon.

True to their word, the Harrison and Dunne people came out enthusiastically for Dever. Carter Harrison himself was out on the stump almost from the first day of the campaign. He made dozens of speeches for his old friend, from one end of the city to the other; he even wrote a newspaper article on why he was for Dever.[47] Edward Dunne did his part, too. The old governor had been in Florida for his annual vacation at the time of Dever's slating, but he hopped the train back to Chicago and dove into the thick of the contest. Dunne saw Dever's candidacy as a new chance to achieve his old dream of Municipal Ownership. He had no use for Lueder. The postmaster had no principles, Dunne told his followers; Lueder was only a tool, "a stuffed club filled with Brundage birdshot, McCormick sand, and Crowe sawdust." Dever was the man to bring a transit renaissance and save Chicago from "the capitalist intrigue and commercial newspapers who defeated us in 1907."[48]

The Dever ticket also won the backing of the influential reform community. As Brennan had calculated, a large segment of the Progressive-Independent bloc swung to the Democratic side. The list of Dever-endorsers from this group is impressive: Mrs. Kellogg Fairbank, Colonel A. A. Sprague, Mary McDowell, Graham Taylor, Julia Lathrop, Raymond Robins, Margaret Haley, Charles E. Merriam, Harold Ickes, just to name the most prominent.[49] Many of these people had been active in the Nonpartisan Committee and had also approved Lueder as a suitable mayoral candidate. But after the party nominations, they had migrated en masse to the Dever camp. Lueder had never been particularly popular with the Nonpartisan Committee, being endorsed not so much for his own merits as for being a Republican alternative to Thompson. The postmaster had too little government experience. He was certainly not corrupt but neither was there much positive to recommend him. On the other hand, they all knew Dever's record. Lueder might one day make a fine mayor; Dever was ready now. As Harold Ickes asked: "Why waste time and go to the expense of educating a novice when the trained executive and experienced municipal statesman is already at hand?"[50] Besides that, Brennan and his organization had worked actively to forge links with the Progressives and Independents; nobody on the Republican side had even stirred. The Democrats plainly needed and wanted them.

Brennan was very astute in his use of the Progressive-Independent bloc. Instead of having all their endorsements issued at once, he had them spaced over the course of the campaign, separated for dramatic effect. In making the announcement, the distinguished citizen would usually provide a thought-ful, literate statement of why he or she had decided to support William E. Dever. This would be good for a few days' play in the newspapers, until it was time for another reform celebrity to endorse the candidate.[51] When all the notables had finished their declarations, Ickes then gathered them into the Independent Dever League (IDL). The IDL scheduled its all-stars as speakers at ward rallies throughout the city. Some friction developed with a few of the more parochial ward bosses, who doubted that their people would listen to a Robins or a Merriam. But Brennan was able to smooth things over. The "silk stockings" proved to be effective orators, in any case. They came to be in great demand and played an important role in the Democratic campaign.[52]

As the race moved on, Brennan continued to try for the widest possible support. Besides the IDL, other campaign groups were formed. The Dever Four-Minute Men, under the direction of the candidate's son Dan, specialized in talks to athletic clubs and other young men's fraternities. Colonel Sprague's Ex-Servicemen's Dever Club went after the veterans' vote. There were also organizations targeted at women, blacks, Jews, Poles, Italians, businessmen, and any other identifiable ethnic, religious, or interest bloc.[53]

While the politicos and the volunteers did their work, the candidate kept prominently in sight. When he was not shaking hands at his campaign head-quarters or making speeches in the neighborhoods, Dever was reported to be doing all sorts of newsworthy things. The Democratic publicity crew must have really stretched its imagination to plan some of his activities. One day, the daily papers ran stories on the candidate being inducted into the Elks Club. A little while later, he was shown out on the golf course, with amateur champion "Chick" Evans introducing him to the game. Next, Dever was seen inducting Jackie Coogan into the Boy Scouts and garnering the child star's endorsement. Then he was found at the Pilsen Turner Hall, cheer-ing the Judge Dever Five on to victory in the Windy City basketball tourna-ment.[54] He was having the time of his life.

He was also pulling away in the straw polls. In the early samplings, Dever and Lueder had run neck and neck. As the campaign entered its final weeks, the Democrat started to build a lead in both the *Tribune* and the *Journal* polls. The reactions of both papers were predictable. The *Tribune*, controlled by Senator McCormick's family and thus in the Lueder camp, persisted in claiming that the figures were "unreal," even as Dever's margin kept lengthening. The *Journal*, which endorsed Dever early in the campaign, placed greater faith in the reliability of its samples. When it became apparent from the polls that the Democratic candidate was the likely winner, the *Tribune* and the *Daily News* quietly shifted their allegiance to Dever.[55]

The campaign, which had been conducted on a high and somewhat dull level, ended with a descent into personality politics and mudslinging. Perhaps, it was an indication of the Republicans' desperation. Two weeks before the election, one of Lueder's advisors publicly accused Dever of having used political influence to get his son Dan a safe army assignment during the war. Dever angrily labeled the man a "damned liar." The attack was shown to be without substance and the matter died down. But, no sooner had that charge been diverted than State's Attorney Crowe announced he was considering an investigation of Judge Dever as a slumlord and rent gouger. Once again, the accusations proved to be so much political sniping, and they were quickly forgotten.[56]

A far more serious problem was the attack made on the candidate's religion. The 1920s were a time of rising nativism in the United States. The Red Scare, the revival of the Ku Klux Klan, racialist literature, restrictions on immigration, Prohibition—all these were examples of extreme reaction to the changes taking place in American society. Now that a Catholic was reaching for the highest elected office in the city of Chicago, his faith became a ready target for the local bigots. An underground whispering campaign sprang up almost from the first day of the campaign. Some of the propaganda found its way into print, as evidenced by a broadside from the so-called Committee of Public School Teachers: "Non-Catholics: If you want Rome to run our Public Schools and City Government, vote for WILLIAM E. DEVER, Democratic candidate for Mayor. He is a Roman Catholic and a member of the Knights of Columbus."[57]

At first, the Democrats did not respond to the baiting. Dever made a few general remarks about his own and his sons' public school education and hoped that would satisfy everyone. But, when the insults become too vicious to ignore, the Independent Dever League swung into action. Ickes, Merriam, and the rest were nearly all White Anglo-Saxon Protestants and could reassure some of the suspicious "100 percent Americans" that Dever's campaign was not really the vanguard of a Papist army of invasion.[58] The candidate himself, of course, was a "respectable ethnic" who had earned his reform credentials, shown himself to be something more than a parochial ward heeler. The whispers became muted; it is even possible that Dever gained a few extra votes from sympathetic Protestants and angered Catholics.

In the last week before the April 3 election, the Democrats brought their campaign to a peak. Dever and the other speakers sped around the city.

They exhorted their workers to one last effort and tried to win over the votes of any person or group they might have neglected. Seeking to spread his message further, the candidate decided to try something new, going on radio station KWY to deliver a major address. The usual last-minute batches of pamphlets were mailed and the final posters tacked on trees. The Democrats even brought out their own primitive version of a sound truck: a man on horseback galloping through the downtown streets at lunchtime, shouting "Vote for Dever" at the amused passersby.[59]

Big Jim O'Leary, the gambling king of the Stockyards, closed his election book with Dever a one to seven favorite. Big Jim knew a winner when he saw one. Dever defeated Lueder by a comfortable plurality of 105,319 votes. The totals read as follows: Dever, 390,413; Lueder, 285,094. The vote for Dever was the largest ever recorded for a Democrat in a Chicago election. His margin of victory was surpassed only by the 147,000-vote plurality Thompson had won over Sweitzer in 1915. The Democratic candidate carried thirty-two of the fifty wards.[60]

Dever's plurality was concentrated in ten inner-city wards. He came out of these wards with nearly two-thirds of that plurality, carrying them by a combined total of 66,784 votes. In each of the ten wards, his victory margin was over 5000 votes, with leads of up to eight to one. In contrast, most of Lueder's votes came from middle-class, traditionally Republican districts on the city's rim. But, even in those neighborhoods, Dever ran strongly. Lueder carried only one ward by as many as 4000 votes.[61]

Since Chicago was redistricted for the 1923 election and the former thirty-five wards converted to fifty, a ward by ward comparison with the 1919 returns is impossible; however, some trends can be sketched. In 1919, independent candidate Maclay Hoyne polled nearly 17 percent of the vote, most of it at the expense of the Democrats. John Fitzpatrick, the labor candidate, siphoned off another 8 percent. Mayor Thompson was reelected, and even his apologists conceded that the four-way split made his victory possible. Conditions were different in 1923. With the Democrats united behind Dever and the contest basically between two candidates, most of the straying votes returned to the Democratic fold. Examining the returns geographically, we notice that Dever ran about the same as had Sweitzer on the Republican North Side. On the heavily Democratic Greater West Side, which Sweitzer had carried by only 5,000 votes, Dever won by over 60,000. And on the South Side, a swing area of both Democratic and Republican enclaves that Sweitzer had lost by 20,000, Dever won by a plurality of 40,000 votes.[62]

Ethnic voting in Chicago elections has been examined in great detail. The studies indicate that most nationality groups voted according to traditional patterns in 1923. After the four-cornered election of 1919, the party shares of the various ethnic votes returned to normal. For instance, the Poles and the Italians usually went strongly Democratic in local elections. In 1923,

Election night 1923. Charles E. Merriam and Harold Ickes join the Democratic candidate in listening to the happy totals. *(Chicago Historical Society: ICHi 20809)*

each group gave Dever about 80 percent of their votes. The Germans and the Swedes, on the other hand, leaned slightly toward the Republicans—and in this election, Dever took a bit less than half of their totals.[63] Only among blacks was there a dramatic change.

According to one source, the portion of blacks voting for the Democratic mayoral candidate rose from 20 percent in 1919 to 53 percent in 1923. The shift in this vote is a special case. It did not stem from any enthusiasm for Dever but rather from mistrust of Lueder. Big Bill Thompson was one of the few white politicians of the day to cultivate the black electorate. Although he said nothing publicly, he seems to have used his influence in the black community to knife the man who supplanted him. During the campaign, some of Big Bill's black friends spread the rumor that Lueder would appoint a Ku Klux Klan member as chief of police, and Thompson associates Oscar DePriest and Louis B. Anderson worked openly for Dever. The result was a heavy Democratic vote in the Black Belt. [64]

The geographic and ethnic distribution of the election totals seems to belie a common belief that Dever was elected by a massive shift of Independent and Progressive Republican voters. The highly publicized support of the Merriam-Ickes-Robins axis did little more than dent WASP allegiance to the Republican party. Lueder ran strongly in the middle-class outer wards, and Dever could poll only about the same share of votes there as had Sweitzer. The religious issue was probably responsible for slowing any Democratic progress in these areas. At the same time, it is impossible to measure the influence that the "silk stocking" Deverites had in the ethnic wards. Robins in particular was a most effective organizer and a popular speaker in inner-city ethnic districts. And certainly, the Progressive-Independent reformer-types had gotten the ticket much favorable publicity. They gave the regular organization respectability and held out the promise that together they might achieve even more ambitious things in the future. The Democrats were glad to have them aboard.

In 1923 Dever had an appeal that crossed factional and ethnic lines. He was not closely identified with any particular section of the party; he was vaguely labeled a *reformer.* He had been the perfect standard-bearer around whom George Brennan could gather the diverse elements of his grand alliance and prevent any return to the disastrous divisiveness of 1919. He had also been an effective campaigner. He had stayed in the spotlight, presented some interesting plans for his mayoralty, yet managed to avoid any destructive controversy. Not surprisingly, he had won a great victory.

Now, he was to be mayor. He had four years in which to bring the city honest, effective, progressive government. His party was united; the newspapers were friendly; the citizens looked forward to his administration with great good will. He had all the advantages and he would use them. He would show what he could do.

5

Taking Charge

New Mayor in Town

■ "The Mayor of Chicago is the city's most impressive showpiece; he is its chief personnel agent; he is its city manager; he is its chief lawmaker; all in one; or he should be, if he did all that is expected of him. Which of these roles he will play and which the city will best enjoy, depend upon the man and the occasion."[1] So wrote Charles E. Merriam in his "intimate" account of Chicago politics during the 1920s. His analysis is quite perceptive. Although the functions and the authority of Chicago's mayor are precisely defined in the city charter, there is much latitude for individual performance and any number of ways to approach the office. To succeed, a mayor must decide what hats to wear and just how to wear them. The power is there, and the glory; but the mayor must reach for them.

Dever quickly began to put his personal stamp on city government. The congratulatory telegrams and telephone calls were still coming in when the mayor-elect called together George Brennan and the party elders for a strategy session. Tradition dictated that they hold their conference out of town. With two-score top Democrats along for company and consultation, Dever boarded a special train for the southern Indiana spa of French Lick Springs. There, amid the beauties of early spring, he mapped out his administration. [2]

He barely got back to Chicago in time for his own inauguration. Once that ceremony was completed, the new mayor began to work on the nuts and bolts of government. Much of his campaign had been directed against the scandalous excesses of the Thompson years. Dever was determined to give the city something better.

The first visible change was in the cabinet. Thompson had never given much thought to his cabinet, using it as a dumping ground for his political lackeys, working through it only when the mood struck him. Dever resolved that his cabinet would be the jewel of his administration and an effective collaborator in managing the city. He would have a strong cabinet, not merely a rubber stamp. He chose carefully and he chose well. While still respecting political considerations, Dever appointed department heads of notably high quality.

Francis X. Busch was named as corporation counsel, the chief legal advisor to the city. Busch was an eminent scholar, dean of the DePaul University Law School, and former president of the Chicago Bar Association. He had long been involved in reform causes, chiefly through the Dunne wing of the Democratic party. Busch himself was often considered mayoral timber: in the past election, he had been (along with Dever) one of the seven men endorsed by the Nonpartisan Committee.[3]

For public works commissioner, Dever picked Colonel A. A. Sprague, prominent socialite and president of the city's largest wholesale grocery firm. Sprague had earned his military title for distinguished service as an artillery officer in the past World War. During the Dever mayoral campaign, he had organized a special veterans' club for the candidate. The colonel's politics were identified with Republican reform.[4]

Mary McDowell, one of the country's best-known social workers, was appointed welfare commissioner. McDowell had directed the University of Chicago's settlement house in the Back-of-the-Yards neighborhood since the 1890s. She was also active nationally in the women's trade union movement with Margaret Dreier Robins. Politically, she had been associated with the late Progressive party.[5]

Morgan A. Collins was the mayor's selection as chief of police. Collins was a one-time medical student who switched to police work and rose through the ranks. Since 1908 he had been commander of the tough Chicago Avenue district. In a police force of dubious reputation, Collins was know as honest, firm, and fair.[6]

The positions of health commissioner and fire marshal were easily filled. The incumbent in the former office, Dr. Herman N. Bundensen, had performed conscientiously and had won the support of the city's medical establishment; Dever decided to keep him.[7] Over at the fire department, the mayor simply promoted to fire marshal the next in line, First Assistant Marshal E. J. Buckley.

For the rest of the cabinet, Dever seems to have been inclined toward more traditional factional and ethnic balancing. All segments of the party were recognized. The Harrison bloc was rewarded with the appointments of John J. Sloan as president of the Board of Local Improvements; Frank E. Doherty as building commissioner; and John Ericson as city engineer. Representing the Dunnites were Busch and the new president of the Civil Service Commission, former alderman Nicholas R. Finn. The Brennan regulars included party chairman Martin J. O'Brien as city comptroller; Thirty-ninth Ward committeeman (and prominent Pole) Leo Winiecke as public service commissioner; and Dever's old tannery chum, Thirty-fourth Ward committeeman Thomas Keane, as city collector.[8] Some of these appointments went to well-qualified individuals while others were given out as obvious patronage plums. The real art was in the mayor's ability to satisfy political necessities while putting together a solid, effective cabinet.

Dever also received the unexpected opportunity to appoint an almost entirely new board of education. School board trustees served staggered terms. Under normal circumstances it would take a mayor six years to fill the body with his own people. However, as part of one of his schemes, Mayor Thompson had once prevailed upon six of his loyal school trustees to submit letters of resignation. Big Bill then changed his plans and decided to keep the six in office. Poking through some old files one day, Dever came across those resignations; he immediately grasped the implications. He penciled in the date, then sent word to the five still-serving trustees that, somewhat tardily, he was accepting their offers to quit. The startled officials went to court, seeking an injunction against the mayor. Dever responded by dispatching a squad of police to guard the school board chambers from them. The courts eventually threw out the lawsuit and upheld the mayor.[9]

The five enforced resignations, plus two trustees whose terms were expiring and one existing vacancy, gave Dever eight places to fill on the eleven-member school board. The Mayor sought the counsel of Charles E. Merriam, Graham Taylor, and other reform-minded friends in naming the new trustees.[10] What emerged from their discussions was a board of education very different from the usual collection of wheeler-dealers and political stooges. Dever's appointments included Charles M. Moderwell, a Republican coal company owner who became the board's president; Grace Temple, past president of the Chicago Woman's Club; James Mullenbach, social worker and labor arbitrator; Julius F. Smietanka, well-known Polish attorney and former school trustee under Mayor Busse; Helen Heffernan, prominent Catholic clubwoman; Edgar N. Greenebaum, banker and leader in Jewish community affairs; William K. Fellows, architect; and Hart Hanson, educational book publisher and outgoing board member whom the mayor decided to retain.[11] This was a distinguished group, progressive, businesslike, and independent minded. Its installation served notice that Dever intended to keep his pledge to take the public schools out of politics.

The cabinet and the school board were the mayor's most visible appointments. Dever exercised similar care in lower-echelon staffing. Chicago's once renowned civil service system had suffered during the Thompson years. Big Bill had gotten around merit regulations by simply refusing to hold examinations, and then filling the vacancies with temporary workers—*sixty-day employees* they were called, because their appointments had to be renewed every two months. By the time Dever took office, about 5,500 of the city's 22,000 employees held jobs in this manner. To correct the situation, the mayor appointed a new civil service commission sympathetic to the principles of merit selection. He then began firing sixty-day employees and scheduling examinations. Within months, over 2,000 temporary workers had been discharged, to be replaced by test-certified permanent employees.[12]

Even with the reforms, there remained a large number of patronage appointments at the mayor's disposal. These included offices at subcabinet level, certain jobs for which merit examinations were considered inappropriate (such as laborer), and the remaining 3000 or so sixty-day positions that Dever had not eliminated.[13] Plenty of deserving Democrats were eager to fill these slots. With the party returning to power after eight years in the wilderness, hundreds of office-seekers besieged Dever's City Hall quarters. The mayor had promised that his door would always be open, and he saw as many of the petitioners as he could. After a month, however, the corridors of the fifth floor were still so clogged that secretaries could barely get to their desks. Dever finally decided he'd had enough. He let it be known that henceforth all job applicants would have to go through "proper channels"—meaning, their ward committeemen.[14] Dever did not like bothering with these minor patronage matters; he had more important things to do. Besides, he had told Brennan that he would not interfere.

Financial matters interested him more and demanded more of his attention. In Chicago tradition, the municipal budget was prepared by the city council and its finance committee, based on estimates submitted by various city departments. The mayor had no defined role in the process, except to approve or veto the finished budget. Although some mayors might operate behind the scenes to influence the council, others were glad to be rid of the responsibility. Thompson had been from this second school. In his later years, Big Bill had offered little financial guidance to the council or the executive departments; his philosophy seemed to be "build now, pay later." As a result, expenditures had run wild. The city had operated in the red during seven of Thompson's eight years in office. When Dever took over in the spring of 1923, the most recent budget contained a deficit of almost $6 million, and there were fears that the city would run out of payroll money before the year's end.[15]

The mayor swiftly took measures to restore immediate and long-term fiscal integrity. As for the 1923 budget, Dever was in no position to seek a tax increase; he would simply have to make the best of what money he had. His first step was to appoint a special Board of Estimate, made up of cabinet members O'Brien, Busch, Sprague, and Sloan, to coordinate all departmental estimates. Next, he called in the department heads and gave them firm orders to cut expenses to the bone. At the same time, be began to use the mayor's splendid organs of publicity to goad the politically sovereign Board of Review into more efficient tax assessment and collection. Dever even found himself helping balance the budget in an unexpectedly direct manner—his taxes on a parcel of land were discovered to be delinquent and he had to pay a $65 fine. By fall, the crisis had eased, and the administration had survived its first fiscal test.[16]

Meanwhile, the mayor had begun to assert his control over future municipal estimates. In May 1923, Dever hired the civil engineering firm of E. O. Griffenhagen and Associates to conduct a comprehensive survey of the executive departments, with an eye toward promoting efficiency and curbing spending. During the next nine months, Griffenhagen and his team became a familiar sight at City Hall as they trudged from office to office, weighted down with ledgers and slide-rules. They appear to have had some success in limiting waste—Griffenhagen reported to the mayor that at least one department head had trimmed his estimates by $400,000 after a chat with the consultant. By early 1924, the survey team had produced a virtual encyclopedia of municipal government in the form of ninety-four studies running to over 2200 pages. When the Dever Board of Estimate drew up its first executive budget that spring, it was based almost entirely on the findings of the Griffenhagen survey.[17]

While Griffenhagen worked on spending, the mayor invited the University of Chicago to do its own survey of municipal government. Funded by the university's Committee on Local Community Research, the project was not intended to be a financial study; rather, it would approach the problem of government efficiency by examining employee morale. Professor Leonard D. White's staff sifted through thousands of personnel records and conducted some five hundred interviews over a period of eighteen months. They found a system characterized by low pay, limited opportunity, lack of recognition, loss of initiative, and political interference. Their report, including numerous suggestions for stimulating employee morale, was submitted to the city council in June 1925.[18]

Crime was another issue that interested the mayor. It had been emphasized in Dever's campaign, and he took up the problem immediately upon entering office. Much of the city's difficulty stemmed from the wretched state of the Chicago Police Department. The mayor's office had simply lost control of the force. District commanders operated as they pleased, the political clout of their ward bosses backing them up. As a result, there was little coordination among districts; corruption was widespread; and the morale of honest cops at its lowest ebb.[19]

Dever put his new chief to work on restoring order. Collins's first act was to summon all district commanders to headquarters. He told the assembled captains that he was in full charge, gave them a list of instructions, warned that he would transfer or demote anyone not following orders, and sent them back to their stations. Collins next met with the press to announce his reforms. The reporters were skeptical. They had heard other new chiefs promise grand changes, with little result. When one journalist caustically asked Collins if he would seek the district commanders' opinions on his policies, the chief snapped: "They will be told what is required of them, and they will perform accordingly." The chief of police said he was going to run his own department, and he meant it. With Dever throwing the full weight of the mayor's office behind him, Collins started breaking up a number of suspected stationhouse cliques. He shifted seventeen captains to new assignments during his first six weeks in office. He also transferred 109 patrolmen.[20] The periodic shake-ups would become a Collins trademark. Whenever the department seemed to be letting down, the chief would start shuffling personnel.

Next, Collins began a series of flashy raids on the city's black-and-tan cafes, interracial nightclubs in the South Side Black Belt. The police closed scores of these establishments and arrested hundreds of people. The reasons given were that the cafes harbored prostitutes and that they promoted rowdy behavior by staying open all night. However, many black Chicagoans suspected that the raids were really aimed at stamping out public race mixing. One boarded-up proprietor even wrote to the mayor about the matter, asking for permission to reopen since "hardly five percent whites come to my place." His plea did little good. Dever publicly endorsed the raids, saying that the cabarets were sinks of corruption and "vile in the last degree." Collins accelerated his crackdown. By summer's end the black-and-tan cafes were gone, and the first crime cleanup successfully completed.[21]

Transit reform was a big topic during Dever's first months in office. He had called the transportation mess the major issue of his campaign; and with the 1907 Settlement franchises due to expire, he was eager to replace them with something better. Early in July, the mayor sent his first transit message to the city council. He called for a comprehensive, unified system of city-owned surface, elevated, and subway lines. The City of Chicago would build the new subway and other service extensions on its own, but Dever planned to purchase most of the routes and rolling stock from the existing private companies. Part of the money needed would come from the municipal traction fund: under the 1907 Settlement, 55 percent of the carriers' profits were turned over to the city. The rest of the financing would be accomplished by the sale of public utilities certificates. The city would thus restore "home rule" over its transit facilities. A municipally owned system would improve service and reduce traffic congestion, without imposing a burden on the taxpayers. All that was necessary was to reach agreement with the companies on a purchase price.[22]

Deciding on that price was a problem. Two weeks after Dever's transit message, city officials began purchase negotiations. The carrier companies put an initial price tag of $247 million on their assets and franchises. Dever thought that amount was outrageous and broke off the talks. The two sides got together again in the fall to haggle a bit more. By the end of the year, there was definitely a stalemate. The administration was pledged to Municipal Ownership but so far had not been able to do much toward getting it.[23]

The transit purchase deadlock was not typical of Dever's first months in office. Almost everything else went smoothly. In fact, one of the mayor's notable victories during this "honeymoon" period came in a transit-related area. During May, the various surface and elevated transit unions began lobbying for higher pay and better working conditions. When the Chicago Surface Lines and the four elevated companies would not budge, it appeared certain that the city would have to suffer through its fourth transit strike in five years. That is when Dever stepped in. Saying that "the time to settle this controversy is before and not after a strike is called," he announced that he was prepared to arbitrate the dispute.[24]

Chicago mayors did not normally negotiate other people's labor contracts. A few of Dever's predecessors had attempted to peacefully defuse strike situations, but such actions were unusual. Traditionally, the mayor would stand by while labor and management settled their own problems, perhaps calling out a few extra police to prevent either side from doing too much damage to the city. If municipal employees were not involved, collective bargaining was not considered the mayor's business. Dever thought differently: he would follow the example of Theodore Roosevelt in the coal strike of 1902. Like that president, Chicago's new mayor saw himself as representing the "third party" in the dispute: the public.[25]

While the unions and the transit companies bogged down in their direct negotiations, Dever began to meet separately with each group. After two weeks of this shuttle diplomacy, both sides agreed to arbitration. The mayor then appointed Corporation Counsel Busch as the "public representative" on a board with one man from labor and one man from management. During the summer the dispute was quietly settled, with terms about halfway between the two positions. Both the union and the companies seemed satisfied; and the city had avoided another crippling transit strike. Dever received the credit. He had used the power and prestige and persuasiveness of his office to get the combatants to act responsibly. The result, said the *Herald and Examiner*, was that "for once the rights of the public have prevailed."[26]

The mayor's handling of the transit dispute was well-received in the organized labor community. The transport workers' paper, *The Union Leader*, called his work "most commendable," saying that Dever had shown "courage, patience, and ability as a chief executive . . . in the best interests of the employees and the companies and the citizens of Chicago." Other unions were similarly impressed, and they demonstrated it. When the transit shop-electricians began raising their own grievances later that fall, they thought enough of Dever to postpone a threatened strike while he was away on vacation; after he returned, he got their matter into arbitration. When the gas workers considered a strike over pay raises, their union president was able to head off the action by assuring his men that Mayor Dever "has promised us a fair deal [and] the union committees have confidence in the mayor." Once again, the situation was resolved peacefully with Dever's help. Ironworkers who were ready to strike over the poor safety conditions on their construction jobs called off their action on the mayor's promise to correct the problem. The local vice-president of the International Ladies Garment Workers Union came to him about settling a seamstresses' dispute. The city's working people knew of Dever's record as a friend of the tanners, as a populist alderman, as a trust-busting judge. He was not merely a union stooge; he could react strongly when he felt labor was in the wrong. (When a wildcat tracklayers' strike endangered the transit union agreement, the mayor threatened to send in the police to restore order and worked with the other unions to get the dissidents back in line—as he had said, he did not represent either labor or management but the public.) But they trusted him as an honest broker. And so, the mayor added labor negotiations to his list of duties.[27]

As First Citizen of the city, Dever could use his prominence to promote all manner of pet projects. One of them was traffic safety. Over 200 Chicagoans a year were being killed in traffic accidents, so Dever asked the city council to appoint a special committee to investigate the matter. He also ordered the police to get tough with speeders and reckless drivers. To dramatize the situation, the mayor had the city produce a movie titled *Safety First*. This short silent film illustrated good driving techniques and traffic safety rules. It concluded with some scenes of His Honor on the steps of the Art Institute, making a speech on the proper use of the automobile.[28] Dever was one of the first city mayors to appear in such a film but certainly not the last.

That Dever had become a celebrity in a matter of months was obvious. When the mayor took up golf, reporters trooped out onto the course after him and wrote long essays on his game, much as a later generation of newspeople would do for President Dwight D. Eisenhower. When he went to the ballpark to watch his beloved Cubs, he was mobbed by the fans.[29] In July, the Devers decided to take a sentimental journey to New England. The trip took on the trappings of a royal progress. Mayor Curley of Boston presented Dever with the key to the city, and area tabloids ran feature stories on the local boy who had gone west and made good. In Woburn, old friends and neighbors turned out to fete Willie and Kate at a special townwide banquet. While the Devers were in Massachusetts, President Harding died; and Chicago's mayor went to Washington with Curley for the funeral. All this was reported back to Chicago each day by the corps of journalists who were following Dever around the country.[30]

Dever had taken power and was firmly in command. He was playing the role of mayor well, wearing his many hats and charting his new course. He was successful because he was also playing a role not mentioned by Professor Merriam, that of conciliator. Dever had gotten where he was in politics through his ability to bring people together. In the volatile Chicago of the 1920s, this was an important talent. The rapidly growing city mirrored the

As Professor Merriam observed, the mayor of Chicago wears many hats. Here Dever meets actor Tom Mix. *(Chicago Historical Society: DN 78, 892)*

problems of a changing, urbanizing America, where suspicion and mistrust on many fronts challenged attempts to develop a new national consensus. The mayor's first months in office were a triumph as he was able to practice his formidable talents winning friends and smoothing discord. Then he got involved in something else, and things were never the same.

The Beer War

Near the end of his first summer in office, Dever came face-to-face with the thorny Prohibition question. The mayor's response was his Great Beer War of 1923. Although he could not know it at the time, this was to be only the first skirmish in a four-year-long conflict that would dominate his entire administration.

Some background is in order. Soon after the coming of Prohibition in 1920, it became apparent that the law would be difficult to enforce. A number of entrepreneurs realized that large profits at low risk awaited those who could satisfy Chicago's thirst. They began operations in all parts of town, running in beer and liquor from Canada or manufacturing the beverages in their own secret factories. One of these hustlers was a young man from Brooklyn named Johnny Torrio.

Torrio had vision. The bootlegging industry as it then existed was small-time, plagued by overlapping production and petty rivalry. Like any smart businessman, Torrio knew that competition is wasteful, monopoly is efficient. He set out to bring logic and order to his chosen field. He undersold rivals, secured exclusive distribution rights, paid bribes, and exacted kickbacks. When money and persuasion did not work, he dispatched a few henchmen to intimidate by force or the threat of force. Within three years, Torrio had disposed of or absorbed most of the city's independent bootleggers. Those too powerful to eliminate, such as Dion O'Banion of the Near North Side, were joined together with Torrio in a loose federation. Each group in this new syndicate was granted its own geographical sphere of influence. The subcompanies cooperated in joint projects when it was profitable; otherwise, they stayed out of each other's way.[31]

Nevertheless, there remained a few stubborn operators who could not see the benefits of a unified syndicate and resisted being squeezed out. The three "South Side" O'Donnell brothers from the Back-of-the-Yards district were of this conviction.[32] Their recalcitrance led to violence, and brought down the wrath of city hall.

On the evening of September 7, 1923, the three O'Donnells and three retainers entered Jacob Geis's tavern at 2154 West Fifty-first Street.[33] Geis was then purchasing his beer from the Torrio syndicate and the O'Donnells suggested that he switch brands. Geis refused. Thereupon, one of the O'Donnell "salesmen" pulled him over the bar and bounced him around the room, fracturing his skull. The visitors then departed to call on five other Torrio-supplied saloons, making their sales pitch and cracking heads. One proprietor phoned the police.

After their busy tour, the O'Donnell men retired to their headquarters, a tavern at 5358 South Lincoln Street.[34] They were enjoying their leisure when in burst Daniel McFall, Torrio ally and deputy sheriff, along with three other men, all brandishing firearms. The deputy ordered the O'Donnell men to put up their hands. The O'Donnells scampered out of the side and back exits, McFall and his friends chasing after them. In the street, the two sides traded shots. One of the O'Donnell group, Jerry O'Connor, fell dead with a bullet through his heart.

The news of the gun battle touched off the mayor's fine temper. He called in Chief Collins for an immediate conference on how to deal with the beverage trade. The fact that one of the combatants was a law-enforcement officer was especially galling to Dever. Although McFall was technically an employee of the sheriff's office, his involvement still reflected badly on all the police. It mocked the mayor's efforts to reform the force. The old rumors of police villainy and venality were starting to circulate again in spite of Chief Collins's campaigns. Dever decided he must take action.

On September 12, the mayor met with the press. He announced that both he and Chief Collins had concluded that the only way to stop the shooting and restore public respect for the police was to suppress the bootlegging trade in Chicago. Illicit breweries, which until now had been allowed to operate under a policy of benign neglect, would be shut down. Dever went on to say that he felt proper regulation of the beer and liquor traffic rested with the federal government. Since Washington was not enforcing the law, the city had to step in. Dever repeated that he himself was not a Prohibitionist, that he wished that "the people might have the privilege of buying good, wholesome beer at a moderate price." But the law was the law, and it must be obeyed.[35]

At first, enforcement was easier said than done. Chief Collins posted armed guards around breweries and sent platoons of police to stop incoming beer shipments at the city limits. A few truckloads of beverage were seized, but stories circulated about police loafing on their assignments. Anonymous "insiders" bragged to reporters about how simple it was to run the Dever-Collins blockade. Despite the mayor's orders, well-connected establishments were still getting their stock and running wide open. Then, on September 17, little more than a week after the O'Connor killing, two more O'Donnell beer drummers were gunned down on the South Side.[36]

If Dever was angered by the first shooting, he was livid at this event. Halfway measures were evidently not going to be enough. Not only must the manufacturers and wholesalers be closed down, the retailers who sold the contraband liquor to the public had to be stopped as well. Once more, the mayor spoke to the press. In a ringing declaration, he vowed to wage total war on bootlegging and its violence:

Until the murderers of Jerry O'Connor and the murderers of these two men have been apprehended and punished, and the illegal traffic for control of which they battle has been suppressed, the dignity of the law and the average man's respect for it is imperiled, and every officer of the law and every enforcing agency should lay aside other duties and join the common cause—a restoration of law and order. The police will follow this case to the finish. . . . This guerrilla war between hijackers, rum runners, and illicit beer peddlers can and will be crushed. I am just as sure that this miserable traffic, with its toll on human life and morals, can be stamped out as I am that I am mayor, and I am not going to flinch for a minute.[37]

The mayor now organized a summit meeting on Prohibition enforcement with all the important police officials of city and county government. Present also were the U.S. district attorney for Northern Illinois, the Chicago corporation counsel, the Chicago city attorney, the Cook County coroner, a representative of the Illinois attorney general, and the federal Prohibition enforcement officer for the Chicago area. Plans were laid for an all-out assault against the traffic in illegal beverages. Chief Collins took responsibility for combating violations within the Chicago city limits; the sheriff of Cook County agreed to patrol the roads leading to the city and to stamp out any operations in the suburbs. With local enforcement thus spoken for, federal officials would be free to concentrate on the out-of-town breweries and distilleries that serviced Chicago. The Illinois attorney general's office promised to help by bringing swift prosecution under the state's own strict anti-bootlegging laws. The mayor was pleased with the results of the conference. For the first time, all law enforcement agencies were working together.[38]

Chief Collins began new raids. He sent out hand-picked squadrons of officers, many of them recent servicemen whose honesty and devotion to duty were unquestioned. In the Loop alone, over 200 policemen moved into action. Wholesale arrests resulted. During the first five days of the Beer War, over 800 persons were charged with Prohibition violations. Meanwhile, the chief shook up the department once again, demoting suspect district commanders and transferring their patrolmen.[39]

The raiders closed hundreds of guilty establishments, and Dever wanted them to remain closed. As the city's chief executive, the mayor controlled all business licensing. Dever now announced that he intended to use this power to revoke the license of any establishment caught dispensing alcoholic beverages. He then directed Chief Collins to proceed against the city's so-called soft drink palaces.[40]

In 1923 over 6000 soda parlors operated in Chicago. These businesses were licensed to serve nonalcoholic refreshments; most of them served stronger drinks as well, usually beer. As long as they had stayed away from hard liquor, the police had left them alone. But the new mayor and his police chief had decided to strictly enforce the Prohibition law. Within weeks of Dever's decree, hundreds of soda fountains were padlocked and hundreds more frightened into closing.[41]

The soda parlor operators were dismayed by these developments. The police had never bothered them before; everyone knew that Prohibition was only supposed to apply to whiskey, not beer. "There was an unwritten law under which the government sanctioned the sale of beer," claimed wet leader Anton Cermak; "Prohibition officers never made arrests for beer-selling, only for whiskey sales."[42] Now Mayor Dever was upsetting this gentlemen's agreement. It was totally unfair.

Unfair or not, Dever kept up the pressure. With the soft-drink parlors under control, Chief Collins was told to begin operations against drug stores, restaurants, private clubs—any place where intoxicants might be sold. The victims of these raids tried to fight back. One proprietor sought a court injunction to halt the revocation of his license, but the judge refused to hear his case. Others looked to the city council for new laws restricting the mayor's licensing power; they were unsuccessful. Still, the raids continued. By the first week of November, Dever had revoked the licenses of over 1600 businesses for Prohibition-related offenses. In addition, some 4031 saloons had been shut down by Chief Collins's zealous soldiers.[43]

That his actions might be controversial did not deter Dever. He knew that he was coming down opposite from his people and his party on one of the decade's most divisive cultural issues. Moreover, the war on bootlegging was not a rash reaction to immediate events, as it may have appeared. The whole thing was actually well thought out and planned.

The mayor had decided to move against the liquor traders from almost his first day in office. He had been shocked to discover the extent of the underground business and its malign influence on police and government. He was also distressed with the quality of the beverages the bootleggers dispensed—the stuff was near poison. Dever had instructed Corporation Counsel Busch to study the legal implications of prosecuting illegal tavern proprietors. Busch had concluded that the police had power to investigate anyone they suspected of Prohibition law violations; they did not even need a search warrant. All that was necessary was some suspicion that a banned beverage was present. If their sight or smell told them this, they could enter an establishment, seize the contraband, and make arrests. Chief Collins had been advised of Busch's legal opinion and told that a beer war would be the next phase of his general cleanup. The Back-of-the-Yards killings had merely given the mayor an excuse to call in outside authorities for help and implement a plan already in the works.[44]

Dever, then, had plenty of time to weigh the political consequences of enforcement. His reaction to these realities is revealing. In his own mind, the mayor remained a wet. His personal disagreement with the laws was very civilized. He felt that he could reconcile the warring camps, get them to agree to disagree in a calm manner. They must take themselves back to those fundamentals all good Americans believed in: that laws must be enforced, that laws must be obeyed, that bad laws will be thrown out when enough people want them changed. Dever, the marginal man in politics, had built his public career on bringing diverse elements together. He specialized in discovering sources of harmony while downplaying forces of conflict. It was natural, then, that a politician of such experience might discount the depth of opinion on an issue like Prohibition. For him, this question was no different from many others he had dealt with over the years. He would simply talk sense to the people, and they would understand.

He chose an unlikely place to defend himself, a German Day celebration at the Municipal Pier. The Germans were probably the wettest ethnic group

in the city and had been forceful advocates of Personal Liberty since the
days of the Lager Beer riots in the 1850s. But, if Dever wanted to persuade
the public that his approach was sound, he had to take up the challenge.
So he stepped before the hostile gathering and gave it to them straight. "I
have never pretended to be, and am not now, a Prohibitionist," the mayor
began. He went on:

> It is true, I am trying to make Chicago a place of law and order. I have said
> many times that I wish the people of Chicago could have good, wholesome
> beer at moderate prices; but the poison that is being sold is not beer, and
> even the price is not moderate. . . . Let us take it for granted that you and
> I do not like the Volstead Act—that we do not believe it is a good
> law. . . . There is only one way to stop it: enforce the law to the limit.
> Then, when the city and the country have been dried up, the people know
> the route to Washington. There they can find relief.[45]

Nobody in the crowd tried to lynch Dever. In fact, his remarks were
received with applause. The Germans seemed convinced (for now, at least)
that the mayor's policies would work for repeal while preserving law and
order. Certainly, Dever's party remained conspicuously behind him. Of the
organization's leaders, only Anton Cermak had publicly questioned the wisdom of the Beer War. George Brennan and the rest of the party hierarchy
were just as wet as Cermak, of course, and had been active in the repeal
movement for years.[46] But the Democrats were finally enjoying a measure
of unity, and Brennan intended to keep it that way. So all criticism of Dever's
enforcement was silenced. Despite widespread fear that the beer raids would
hurt the party ticket in the upcoming county elections, the politicos took
turns announcing their support for the mayor. They even threw a testimonial
dinner for Dever, feting him as "the best mayor in the city's history"; and
Chicagoans were treated to the spectacle of Bathhouse John and Hinky Dink
heaping praise upon the man who was nailing shut the doors of the First
Ward's saloons.[47]

The *Chicago Tribune* was not so easily won over. The city's leading newspaper
had long opposed Prohibition and did not think Dever's crusade would succeed. In a lengthy editorial on October 20, the *Tribune* reviewed the mayor's
war against the liquor traffic. The paper noted that only 18 percent of
Chicago's voters could be classified as old American stock; the rest were from
more recently arrived national groups who favored Personal Liberty. It also
pointed out that the latest local referendum on Prohibition had gone five to
one for the wets. Mayor Dever might be able to send 7000 police into the
streets in search of Volstead violators, the paper declared, but he could never
win his fight: "when a law not only does not have the support of the conscience
of the people, but when it is also regarded by them as tyrannical and unjust,

it cannot be enforced." And, the mayor himself was in for difficult times. Ignoring the fact that Dever had completed scarcely six months out of only his first year in office, the *Tribune* predicted that "if he had any political ambitions, he has sacrificed them." The editorial concluded:

> If Chicago had a recall law he might be recalled next month. When his term has expired, he will be succeeded by someone acceptable to Tony Cermak. Mr. Cermak, leading wet, will say that the man is all right and that will be enough for the majority of Chicago voters. It will probably be a very bad thing. Mr. Dever is a good mayor. His successor may be awful—but he will be wet.[48]

Others were not as skeptical of the mayor's clean-up campaign. The Hearst *Herald and Examiner* and the *Post* praised His Honor's efforts, calling on all citizens to help him vanquish the twin scourges of bootlegging crime and "green beer." Church groups invited Dever to speak to their congregations. The Kiwanis voted him a citation, as did the Teamsters' Union. Everyday citizens wrote him by the hundreds to urge his continued vigilance. Popular opinion was still with the mayor, it seemed. In spite of their anxieties over a wet backlash, the Democrats had no troubles in the county elections.[49]

While there had been some question whether the prophet was without honor in his own town, the rest of the country heartily accepted Dever. News of the remarkable happenings in Chicago spread throughout the nation. In Ohio, California, New York, Missouri—scores of states, in both metropolis and hamlet—editorial writers examined the Chicago phenomenon and the man who had brought it about.[50] The larger publications even dispatched reporters to the Windy City to observe events firsthand. Many of them were granted interviews with the mayor, who never seemed to tire of describing his struggle against the bootleggers. The *New York Times* ran a major article on Dever and his beer war. And, in December, the influential *Literary Digest* published a feature story on the "drying up of Chicago," telling its millions of readers the story of the wet mayor who was enforcing Prohibition.[51]

To answer the many requests for news about his activities, Dever wrote an essay on the clean-up and the reasons behind it.[52] The article was picked up by the wire services and ran in most major cities. The mayor began with his customary declaration, "I am not a Prohibitionist." He reviewed in great detail the chaotic conditions he had found. He told of the bootleggers' feuds, the O'Donnell gang killings, and the ensuing raids and license revocations. The mayor admitted that perhaps the police had been a bit overzealous in their early forays, arresting patrons as well as proprietors. He had curbed these excesses and did not think that his crusade would hurt the Democrats politically—on the contrary, a clean city would make his party stronger than ever. But politics was not the point. "Respect for the law had been shattered and broken down by the violators of the Prohibition law," said Dever. As mayor, he had sworn an oath to defend the law. The Eighteenth Amendment to the Constitution was part of the supreme law of the land and, no matter what his personal opinion, he was obliged to enforce it. "For any servant of the people . . . to ignore this fact," he wrote, "is a confession of cowardice and unfitness."

The mayor repeated his stand at a banquet given in his honor by the Chicago Bar Association. Speaking to over a thousand attorneys gathered at the LaSalle Hotel, Dever pronounced his beer war a success, declaring that he had made Chicago the driest metropolis in the country. He had restored the rule of law to the city. He would not flag in his efforts, no matter what the consequences. "Some newspapers say my political career is ended," he told the lawyers with a little smile. "Well, it's nearly ended anyhow—old Father Time is looking after that." He went on:

> But were I a younger man, I would do the same thing that I have done—enforce the law. . . .They have asked me to submit the matter to a referendum. I told them that I would have nothing to do with such a proposition; I would not insult the intelligence of our citizens. [But] even if there were a referendum and every single citizen voted for nonenforcement, I would still enforce the law![53]

It was clear Dever believed that control of the city had been won back from the bootleggers. A few days after the mayor's Bar Association speech, Chief Collins announced a new winter crime war. With the liquor traffic shut down, the police would concentrate on purging other forms of vice. New raids were launched, this time against gambling dens and "old men's paradises" (massage parlors).[54]

As 1923 became 1924, Dever was able to list a number of accomplishments for his first nine months in office. He reviewed these in the traditional year-end roundup in the local newspapers. In transit matters, the mayor had presented his plan for a comprehensive, municipally owned system and negotiations were in progress to make it a reality. Public works operations were running smoothly, with several important projects nearing completion. Civil service had been revitalized, and a detailed survey of all city departments begun. The city treasury held $76 million; Dever's efficiencies promised to increase that amount. Finally, the police department had been reformed, and major crime banished from the city.[55]

Dever's was a good record, one worthy of praise. He confidently looked forward to continuing his programs. Yet, there was one unsettling development for the mayor. Early in 1924, deputy Daniel McFall was acquitted of the murder of Jerry O'Connor.[56] It was a mere straw in the wind, perhaps; but it showed which way the wind was blowing.

6

The Strain of Command

The Business of Politics

■ If 1923 was a year of power consolidation for Dever, 1924 was one of fragmentation. The grand political alliance that had swept him into office began to come apart. Segments pulled in different directions. As time passed, the mayor's ability to rally a consensus declined steadily. The honeymoon was over.

Some of this was to be expected. The Democratic party of Chicago had been at war with itself for decades—unity was an unnatural state. The Democrats had come together in 1923 more because of what they were against than what they were for. With the common enemy defeated, they now faced one another to squabble over the spoils. Dever had his challenge and his opportunity. If he could minimize disaffection and limit defection, the mayor might govern effectively and plan a long tenure in office.

One continuing problem was the Harrison-Dunne faction. For years they had resisted consolidation into regular ranks. Though perennially short on funds, they had a knack for attracting attention all out of proportion to their numbers. Brennan's slating of their old comrade, Bill Dever, had temporarily placated them. They had gone all out in the mayoral campaign and expected their reward. Carter Harrison had confidently written to his one-time protege, requesting jobs for various associates. Dever gave some positions to the Harrison-Dunne bloc, but they were disappointed with what they received. With party leader Brennan left in charge of the mayor's partonage distribution, Harrison felt double-crossed.[1] In the first happy weeks after Dever's victory, rumor had it that Harrison would be the organization's next candidate for United States senator. By the end of 1923, no one was talking that way. The old mistrust was returning.[2]

The final break came early in 1924. It was a presidential election year and the Democratic National Convention was scheduled for June in New York City. George Brennan's regulars planned to enter a slate of uncommitted delegates in the spring primary. Although the organization was known to be friendly to the candidacy of New York governor Alfred E. Smith, Chicago regulars traditionally went to the convention unpledged, to allow more room for maneuvering. However, on January 11, William L. O'Connell of the Harrison-Dunnites announced that this plan was unacceptable to his associates. O'Connell gave his endorsement to William G. McAdoo, Smith's bitter rival. He also told the press that the Harrison-Dunne forces would run their own list of McAdoo delegates in the primary, as the first step toward regaining control of the party from the "Brennan machine." Once again, they were on their own.[3]

Rumblings were also heard within organization ranks. Shortly after Dever's inauguration, the Polish daily, *Dziennika Narodowego*, took the mayor to task for his appointments. Claiming that Poles deserved better representation in Dever's cabinet, the paper called for the removal of Health Commissioner Bundensen in favor of Dr. Stephen Pietrowicz, a well-known Polish physician who had served on one of Harrison's school boards.[4] When Dever chose to keep Bundensen, the focus of agitation shifted. A delegation of Polish leaders called on the mayor to discuss patronage at large. Dever was not around when they arrived at his office, so they aired their grievances to the City Hall press corps. The Poles declared that they were being shortchanged on political jobs. They produced figures showing that for 131,000 registered voters, Poles held patronage positions with combined salaries of $160,000. In contrast, 62,000 Bohemian voters were rewarded with $300,000 worth of jobs, and 32,000 Jewish voters received $450,000 in political employment.[5]

The Poles were important to any Democratic mayor; they were the city's largest ethnic group. For several years their leaders had been engaged in a "recognition drive," seeking to bring Polish power in the party into line with the Poles' voting strength. George Brennan had seen this nationalism developing and made concessions to it. In 1922 he had engineered the election of popular Polish attorney Edmund K. Jarecki as county judge. Yet, the Poles were still restless, and required careful handling. Old Stanley Kunz, by now a member of Congress, remained wary of the mayor. And, although Dever and Brennan managed to quiet the immediate patronage rumpus, the mayor's popular standing in the Polish community was balanced on a knife's edge, especially since his beer war.[6]

Prohibition continued to distress the mayor. He had thought that his bootlegging cleanup had settled the matter; he found that he had thought wrong. Disgruntled proprietors of soft drink cafes were still filing lawsuits for recovery of their licenses. In February, municipal court judge Henry Walker ruled that Dever had exceeded his powers in shutting down the soda parlors and ordered them reopened. Over the next few weeks, other judges made similar rulings. The city's bootleggers took these actions as a signal that it was safe to renew operations. By the middle of March, the *Tribune* was reporting that liquor once again flowed freely in Chicago. And once again, the tales of payoffs to police and political protection for rumrunners were heard.[7]

So Dever resumed the fight. He ordered Chief Collins to start another crackdown, closing any unlicensed establishment no matter what the courts had ruled. Collins also shook up the department again, this time shifting almost 200 patrolmen. Within weeks, the bootleggers were on the run. And in June, the state supreme court reversed the lower courts and confirmed the mayor's power over license revocation.[8]

Within the Democratic party, critics of Dever's Prohibition policy had held their peace, silent for the sake of party unity. Once the November 1923 elections were safely past, they found their voices. Anton Cermak renewed the call for a law restricting the mayor's licensing authority. He was joined by Alderman Max Adamowski of the Thirty-eighth Ward, whom Dever had alienated on a personal political matter.[9] Other opposition was more subtle. Democratic aldermen began attacking the Dever Board of Estimate's recently prepared city budget, claiming that the administration was cutting needed jobs while wasting a fortune on useless studies. There was talk that the budget would be held hostage until the mayor loosened up on Prohibition.[10]

The Cermak-Adamowski ordinance went no further than the pages of the daily newspapers. On the budget, Dever was forced to compromise. He restored most of the jobs and suspended his plans for sweeping fiscal reform.[11] Of course, the city council did not resist budget-reform just to protest Dever's handling of Prohibition. Many aldermen felt that the mayor was usurping their powers by presenting an executive budget; others simply wanted to preserve their patronage. However, the continuing debate over Prohibition enforcement was sapping the mayor's political influence. It legitimatized opposition to him within his own party. Quite a few Democratic politicians felt Dever was out of step with popular opinion on the drink question. If he had misread the minds of the people on this important issue, might not he be wrong on other points? Erosion of Dever's credibility as a political leader had begun.

Yet, despite these difficulties, Dever still had his strengths. The Progressive-Independent reformers who had helped elect him—Ickes, Merriam, Taylor, and the rest—remained loyal, pleased with the mayor's efforts for a clean, financially sound government. His tough law-and-order stand also attracted support from those "upper-class businessmen" reformers (such as Julius Rosenwald) who had been neutral in the 1923 election.[12] He still had the power of the mayor's office, the power to lead and to publicize, to reward and to punish. And he still had George Brennan.

The party leader was stronger than ever. His entire 1924 slate of candidates had been summarily endorsed by the party hierarchy, even though it included a confirmed dry for governor (Norman Jones) and a converted Republican for U.S. senator (Colonel Sprague). The primaries that followed were another

MEDIA & TECHNOLOGY SERVICES
EVANSTON TOWNSHIP HIGH SCHOOL
1600 DODGE AVE.
EVANSTON, IL 60204

Brennan triumph: the organization slate easily won selection as national convention delegates, completely shutting out the Harrison-Dunne ticket.[13] There was no mistaking who controlled the party machinery. A few regulars might snipe at Dever and party solidarity might be cracked, but the boss was still for the mayor. That counted for much.

The relationship between Dever and Brennan was complex, and many interpretations of it have been advanced.[14] Some observers have pictured the mayor as a simple front-man, a stooge who took orders from the power behind the throne while presenting a fine profile and clean image to the public. Others have suggested that once Brennan elected Dever to office, the mayor went off on his own quixotic way, and the party leader was forced to follow grudgingly to cut losses. Still another scenario portrays the mayor as a dedicated reformer who contracted a devil's alliance with the evil machine, then found he could not control it.

All these analyses contain some elements of truth; yet, they do a disservice to both men. Certainly, both Brennan and Dever were intelligent enough to consider all the implications when they joined forces. Brennan was no narrow, parochial dictator. If he had been, he would not have selected Dever, who was well known to have a mind of his own. The party leader realized that with this man he had that rare opportunity to unite his party and give the city good government as well. Brennan did not need a puppet in the mayor's office to help him loot the municipal treasury. The patronage jobs Dever left in his care were sufficient power. The income that came in through political influence ("honest graft," Senator Plunkitt had called it) was also substantial; it was estimated that Brennan earned $40,000 a year just from bonding city officials. The arrangement was more than satisfactory. If the mayor's actions sometimes stirred up controversy, well, that was the way politics operated. New coalitions could be formed. Brennan felt that he had found a winner in Dever. All evidence indicates that the party leader sincerely admired the mayor and liked him personally. For Dever's part, the feeling was mutual.[15]

Brennan, in fact, seemed to be grooming Dever for higher office. In the first flush months of the new administration, political insiders began to whisper that Dever would be the party's nominee for governor in 1924. The mayor's bootlegging clean-up and the national publicity given to it upped the stakes. Now Brennan started hinting about Dever as a possible vice-presidential or even presidential candidate. The mayor merely smiled at such talk and said that he was happy in his present job—and allowed the speculation to continue.[16]

For a prospective national candidate, Dever was well situated. He was a big-city mayor at a time when urban voters were becoming increasingly important. His honest administration offered a favorable contrast to the recent Harding scandals. True, Dever's Catholic faith weighed against him; but his position on Prohibition might balance that. Although the mayor was a declared wet, he had gained renown through earnest enforcement of the dry law. He was thus a viable possibility as a compromise candidate if the convention deadlocked along wet-dry lines. And if a Prohibitionist such as McAdoo captured the presidential nomination, Dever would still be a good choice for second place: he might be able to attract wet voters to the ticket without alienating the dry ones.[17]

Dever's undeclared candidacy remained under consideration in the local papers as the convention approached. Presumably, George Brennan would have preferred his own man on the national ticket, but the party leader was a realist and knew that Al Smith was the favorite of urban-wet-Catholic voters. With the sudden death of Tammany chieftain Charles F. Murphy, Brennan inherited the role of the party's leading "big city boss." So he put Dever on the back burner. He took over Smith's campaign and started organizing for the showdown.[18]

The Democratic National Convention of 1924 was held in New York City's Madison Square Garden. This was the famous 103-ballot convention. Smith and McAdoo deadlocked the balloting for over two weeks, until the exhausted delegates agreed on an obscure West Virginia lawyer named John W. Davis. Dever attended the political carnival as one of Illinois's delegates. He got some ink as a compromise candidate and a few token votes on the roll calls, however, the mayor's religion evidently made him unacceptable to those same elements that opposed Al Smith. He was never seriously considered.[19]

Second place was another matter. After his nomination, candidate Davis met with Brennan and the other Smith leaders to discuss the vice-presidency. Davis reportedly offered to take Dever as his running mate. But by this time Brennan had changed his mind. He told Davis that the Catholics who backed Al Smith for the top spot would feel insulted to be offered only the second prize. Brennan suggested instead that Charles W. Bryan, the brother of William Jennings Bryan, would be the best man to run with Davis, and the nominee agreed. Bryan it was.[20]

Brennan's reasoning in rejecting a Dever vice-presidency makes sense. It is also likely that the canny boss was looking beyond the current election, to 1928. The marathon convention had torn the Democratic party apart. Davis already looked like a loser. Any Catholic on the ticket with him would be blamed for the defeat because of his religion. Such a debacle could finish Catholics as credible national candidates for a generation to come. Better to steer clear and save Dever for another day.

The Problems of a Great City

Shortly before leaving for the New York convention, Dever was called upon to make the commencement address at the University of Chicago. As mayor he was often asked to preside at ceremonial functions, and he frankly enjoyed them. He readily accepted the university's invitation. He spoke on a topic with which he was well-acquainted: "The Problems of a Great City."

Dever began by reviewing the growth of American cities. They had burst forth so quickly that state governments could not handle them. Power and responsibility were becoming blurred, the mayor felt, and the situation would get worse before it got better. Dever offered no solutions to these difficulties; instead, he spoke of the particular problems involved in governing the city of Chicago. By now, everyone expected the mayor to make some sort of statement about his clean-up crusade. He did not disappoint his audience, repeating his pledge to fully enforce all laws. But the major portion of Dever's address dealt with "the great physical problems of the city" and his plans for solving them. Public works were on his mind.[21]

Dever had a tough act to follow. During the preceding eight years, Mayor Thompson had initiated so much construction that he had become known as "Big Bill the Builder." Even today, it is difficult to travel the city without stumbling onto some bridge or tunnel or public building bearing a plaque inscribed "William Hale Thompson, Mayor."[22] In this area at least, the two mayors thought alike. Dever shared the booster spirit of his predecessor. He believed that public construction programs showed the vigor of a city and helped improve the lives of its citizens. He also knew that he could do the job cheaper than Thompson.

Among American cities Chicago was the leader in public planning and construction. It had stepped out in front as early as 1906, when a group of local businessmen had commissioned a special study of the city's physical conditions. What had developed was architect Daniel Burnham's famous Plan of Chicago. The Burnham Plan proved to be more that a simple inventory of existing concrete and cobblestones. It was a comprehensive blueprint for urban development, and it caught the fancy of Chicago's citizens. They endorsed the Burnham Plan at a special referendum in 1910. At that time, the Chicago Plan Commission was established as a public body to aid in implementing Burnham's proposals.[23]

"Aid" it did. Charles H. Wacker, a wealthy brewer and one of the planners of the 1893 World's Fair, became chairman of the Plan Commission. Under his dynamic leadership, civic and financial dignitaries were enlisted in the commission's cause. Publicity releases, stereopticon lectures, movies, and other devices were used to promote the gospel of public works. The Plan Commission even produced a textbook on the Burnham Plan for use in the city's schools. Whenever a funding referendum was scheduled, Wacker and his cohorts would bombard the voters with even more breathless literature through the mails. And without exception, the electorate endorsed the commission's programs.[24]

When Dever assumed office, many of Burnham's projects were already in place. A number of others, such as the new Union Station and the extension of Ogden Avenue, were nearing completion. For his own contribution to the building boom, the mayor decided to press forward on two new programs.

The first of these was the Near South Terminal project. This ambitious plan involved the revitalization of the entire area directly south of the Loop, almost an entire square mile in the heart of the city. The land was ripe for development. From State Street west to the Chicago River lay a jungle of ancient train yards and freight terminals. Fourteen different rail lines passed through on their way to Dearborn, LaSalle, and Grand Central stations. The tracks were a blight on the landscape and a barrier to motor traffic coming into downtown from the south. A nasty double bend in the river just below Roosevelt Road added to the confusion.[25]

The area had definite possibilities. Once the river was straightened, the railroads would be able to pull up their superfluous track and consolidate operations. This would free considerable acreage, allowing the southward extension of LaSalle, Wells, and Franklin streets. Commercial construction might then begin both on land reclaimed from the yards and on air rights over the remaining tracks. Something along the order of New York City's Grand Central Terminal project was envisioned. In the decade since the Manhattan facility had opened, millions of dollars in hotel, office, and mercantile development had sprung up in the surrounding neighborhood. The Chicago planners were confident they would enjoy similar success. They talked of spending upwards of $100 million on renewing the Near South land parcel, and building the greatest railroad terminal in the world. [26]

Dever began his campaign for the project on March 6, 1924. He met that day with representatives of the Near South Side's fourteen railroads. The companies had often talked of combining their facilities, but the high costs involved had kept them from reaching an agreement. Now the mayor told them it was time to act. Either the companies would get moving on consolidation, or the city would condemn their excess trackage, build a new terminal, and present them with the bill. Under those circumstances, the railroads found it advisable to establish the Railroad Terminal Commission to actively pursue unification.[27]

The next stage in the program was straightening the river. Since the Chicago River was a major waterway, the work required federal approval. The mayor dispatched Corporation Counsel Busch to Washington to lobby for the project. After securing endorsement from the Army Corps of Engineers, Busch was able to gain congressional consent in short order. Dredging started in March 1925.[28]

Meanwhile, the Railroad Terminal Commission assembled under the chairmanship of Rock Island Line president Gorman. It was soon apparent there would be no quick agreement among the railroads; negotiations continued to drag. Dever kept up the pressure, kept threatening the companies with a city take-over. But by the time the river improvement was finished in 1929, a new mayor was in office. The Great Depression of the 1930s halted most public works construction, and the terminal project was never completed. All the city got out of the episode was a straight river. Not until the 1970s, when declining rail traffic closed Dearborn and Grand Central stations, was the Near South Side land opened to development.[29]

Dever's other great public works project was the South Water Street improvement. Here he had more success. Running along the south bank of the Chicago River from Michigan Avenue to Market Street, South Water Street was the city's produce market. The half-mile had a long and colorful history. The earliest settlers had built their cabins along the right-of-way, making South Water the town's first residential street. As Chicago grew into a commerical metropolis, the street evolved into a warehousing and food distribution district. Lake vessels sailed into the river and docked at convenient wharves located behind South Water's buildings, while out in front, carts, wagons, and trucks jammed the narrow cobblestone pavement. It was a noisy, dirty, smelly thoroughfare located only two blocks from City Hall, a "silly old street for a great city."[30]

The Burnham plan called for moving the produce market to an outlying location and modernizing South Water Street. The planners proposed building a monumental boulevard in the style of the Champs Élysées, but they would go the Parisians one better—they would construct a double-decked street. Commercial traffic would be relegated to the lower, river level, while the upper deck would carry pleasure vehicles and the promenade[31] As Daniel Burnham was fond of saying, in Chicago they made "no little plans."

The South Water Street improvement was authorized by the Plan Commission in 1918, with funding approved by the voters shortly thereafter. Yet nothing happened for the next five years. A number of local property owners, satisfied with things as they were, brought lawsuits to halt the project. Mayor Thompson did not press the issue, so matters remained in limbo. In the meantime, the Sanitation Department was spending a fortune keeping the street clean. Businesses were in a bind, too; since no one knew what the city was going to do, they had to operate with short-term, six-month leases. Early in 1924, Dever's corporation counsel reviewed the situation with him and advised the mayor to either start the project immediately or abandon it forever.[32]

Dever decided to go forward with the plan. He obtained $10 million from the city council to start demolition work, and scheduled another referendum for additional funds. Nuisance lawsuits still plagued the project. Dever had no use for such obstructionism. He thought the property owners were being too greedy and publicly warned that "we'll see them in hell before we permit the city to be sandbagged into unreasonable agreements."[33] The mayor put Corporation Counsel Busch to work cajoling and twisting the arms of reluctant landlords. In June the bond issue passed by the usual lopsided margin. The site for a new produce market on the Southwest Side was acquired and construction begun. Over the summer the last of the lawsuits were settled. Wholesalers began vacating South Water Street, looking for temporary quarters until the new market was finished.

Demolition of the old market began that fall. By now the project was officially known as Wacker Drive, named after the Plan Commission's long-time chairman. As the work progressed, the mayor developed more elaborate plans for the street. He organized a property owners' league, to ensure that new buildings would be of a suitable magnificence for the city's front drive. Ornate lighting standards, massive concrete benches, and other specially designed street furniture were deployed along the wide sidewalks. Dever also talked of constructing a similar boulevard on the north bank of the river. He even gave thought to extending the riverfront drives as far as Division Street on the north and Roosevelt Road on the south.[34]

Wacker Drive was opened to traffic amid gigantic public celebration on October 20, 1926. It never quite became the American Champs Élysées, but it did provide the city with a decorative ceremonial drive along its riverfront. For years, local guidebooks proudly boasted of it as "the world's only double-decked street." Wacker Drive was eventually extended in both directions. Today it runs over a mile from Lake Shore Drive west and south to Harrison Street, and is Mayor Dever's most notable material monument.[35]

The Dever administration engaged in other activities besides public works. Welfare Commissioner Mary McDowell was particularly active. On taking office, McDowell had brought together representatives from the city's social welfare organizations and asked for suggestions on the programs she should undertake. The agencies decided that unemployed, friendless men were Chicago's most serious social problem. As a result, the city established the Men's Service Station on the West Side "Skid Row." The station served as a combination employment agency and soup kitchen. When severe cold weather hit the Midwest in January 1924, McDowell's department arranged lodging for the homeless. Altogether, about 20,000 indigent men were cared for during the first four months of the year.[36]

Helping the needy was recognized as a legitimate function of government, and the mayor dutifully detailed the Welfare Department's work in his annual reports. But it was not an exciting business, was not the sort of thing that stirred voter's souls. Old progressives like Dever worked hard for political and economic reform: rooting out bribery in government, smashing evil traction trusts, and so forth. Great building projects could promote the public welfare in many ways, and that also appealed to them. Direct relief frequently received less attention, even though a product of the same social reform impulse. Voluntarism, not government intervention, was the American tradition in this area. The churches and the private settlement houses were still

Part of the grand parade celebrating the opening of Wacker Drive: October 20, 1926. (*Chicago Historical Society: DN 82, 361*)

operating. And there was always present the suspicion that anyone who could not achieve success in the Land of Opportunity had somehow caused his or her own problems. So while bridge and highway improvements got millions, the public lodging house periodically had to shut down for lack of funds.

This preference for brick and mortar over flesh and blood was not as crass as it might seem. These were simply different times. The cities of America were enjoying a period of boom. The booster spirit was ascendant. The city showed the world its importance by erecting skyscrapers, by digging subways, by laying out parks, by opening railroad terminals. The whole population benefited from these improvements, not just a small, impoverished segment;

and the citizens got something that would last.[37] Dever's city was reveling in the sunshine of youth. Like a young person, it gloried in its vitality and thought mainly of its growth. When the infirmities of older age took hold, it could worry about more mundane problems.

Black Chicago

While the boosters went about their boosting, great social changes were overtaking Dever's city and the cities of America. Most apparent to the contemporary observers was the rise of the newer ethnic groups. In Chicago, an event of a more long-rang consequence was the emergence of a significant black community. Although less important in the immediate context, the patterns of race relations developed during the era would affect the city for nearly a half-century to come.

Relatively few blacks had lived in Chicago or in any of the North until the First World War. Then, starting about 1915, thousands of southern blacks began the massive northward movement know as the *Great Migration*. The vast majority of these people were from rural backgrounds, and the promise of greater employment opportunities in industry was a powerful attraction to them; so was the prospect of less discrimination. Many of the migrants came north, settled, and found better jobs. As for discrimination, the North proved to be no utopia. The new settlers discovered that they had to face a more subtle brand of racism, often just as unyielding as the bigotry they had left.[38]

Symptomatic and symbolic of the obstacles they met was the basic matter of housing. The problem in Chicago was acute. The area open to black residence was a narrow half-mile wide corridor starting below Roosevelt Road on the Near South Side. Upwards of 50,000 new residents poured into this district during the first four years of the migration. When the "Black Belt" started to push south into white neighborhoods, violent racial confrontations resulted. Property-bombing incidents averaged one a month. Tempers flared and tensions mounted, eventually erupting in the great race riot of 1919. After that blowup, an uneasy peace settled on the city, though sporadic incidents continued.[39]

Dealing with the racial complexities of this new era was a problem most politicians were happy to duck. Like the general white population, Chicago's political leaders showed little concern over what happened to blacks. At best, they were indifferent; at worst, they were unashamedly racist. The wisdom of the time declared that the Negro had his place and that place was definitely subservient to the white's. Of all the city's white officials, probably William Hale Thompson showed the most sensitivity toward blacks. Big Bill had been an alderman in the racially mixed Second Ward, and he knew a good deal about black life firsthand. As mayor he made numerous political appointments in the black community and practiced a racial understanding rarely seen in those days. With good reason, he was the most popular white politician in the Black Belt.[40]

When Dever was elected in 1923, there was little indication how the new mayor would act in race-related matters. The issue had not come up during the campaign, except when some of Thompson's black friends had accused the Republican candidate Lueder of racism. Many of the city's blacks had sat out the election. While the black population of Chicago was continuing its steady rise, the total black vote declined by one-third compared to the 1919 election. From what was left, Dever attracted about 53 percent.[41]

Dever tried to give blacks a fair deal when he took office. Although not nearly as liberal with jobs as Big Bill had been, he did leave some patronage to the black Thompsonites who had supported his election. As was the established tradition with Democratic mayors, he appointed two black assistant corporation counsels, Earl B. Dickerson and William L. Offord. The mayor also made sure that the new Chicago Housing Commission had black representation, naming civil engineer Charles S. Duke and Urban League secretary A. L. Foster to that body in 1926. Dever's most publicized black appointee was undoubtedly Dr. George Cleveland Hall: the well-respected surgeon was the first member of his race to serve on the Chicago Public Library Board.[42]

However, everyday discrimination continued, despite fancy City Hall jobs for the few. The housing market remained limited by custom and covenant, opening a bit only when new subdivisions allowed whites to flee from the "changing" neighborhoods. Black workers were still the "last hired, first fired." Public facilities, places of entertainment, and indeed, much of the Loop itself remained alien territory for the mass of black citizens. Chicago racism went on, and Chicago's mayor did little to affect it in either direction. Dever took what was then considered a middle road. He stood up against the harassment of black students who had transferred into white schools. He met with black civic delegations and posed with them for newspaper pictures. He proclaimed his belief in the American traditions of justice and fair play. And that was about it.[43]

Dever's racial record is similar to that of most white Chicagoans of the period: mixed, with a good deal of unconscious racism. His closing of the black-and-tan cabarets is one example. Much of the public fascination with the raids stemmed from white horror of "race mixing" between members of opposite sexes. And yet, Dever entirely overlooked this aspect of the affair. None of his statements was racially inflammatory, and he seems to have been concerned only with the public nuisance matters involved; to him, the racial overtones were minor. During Dever's administration, other incidents tinged with racism also appear to have resulted from insensitivity rather than from any definite pattern or policy of race baiting.

In his personal life, Dever seems to have known few black people. He grew up in a section of the country where blacks were seldom seen, and he never made a point of reminiscing about any black friends or acquaintances he may have made along his way. He could perform small acts of racial understanding, as in his treatment of Ferdinand Barnett during the 1906 judicial election. Then again, he could go the other way: after he left office, for instance, Dever lent his efforts to securing racially restrictive real estate covenants in the Uptown neighborhood.[44] If anyone had brought the contradictions of these actions to his attention, the irony would probably have been lost on him.

For their part, the city's black population appeared neutral toward the mayor. Racially charged incidents such as the cabaret raids did not make Dever a permanent ogre in the Black Belt. Among black journalists, Claude A. Barnett of the Associated Negro Press remained a staunch advocate of the mayor, and the *Broad-Ax* newspaper was generally favorable. (The *Chicago Defender*, which leaned more toward Big Bill and the Republicans, found more to criticize in Dever.) Julius Rosenwald's support of Dever probably helped the mayor's standing in the black wards: Rosenwald was a white businessman who had devoted much of his considerable philanthropy toward black causes. Whatever the reasons, the black community became actively hostile toward Dever only when he ran against Thompson, and the Democrats mounted a racist campaign. Until that happened, black Chicagoans generally took Dever as he took them—at a distance.[45]

So for the years of the Dever administration, the blacks of Chicago stayed stuck in their bleak limbo. To borrow Ralph Ellison's phrase, the Negro voter was the "invisible man" of the city's politics, at least when the Democrats counted up the votes. Blacks had traditionally supported Republicans as the party of Lincoln. In Chicago, that support was reinforced by the presence of Thompson, whom many blacks called the *second Lincoln*. It took the Depression and the New Deal to shatter this rock-bound alliance, and whether Chicago Democrats could have cracked it during the 1920s is doubtful. They made no more than a token effort, satisfied that blacks made up less than a tenth of the city's population. The Brennan organization believed that it was more vital to cultivate the white ethnic groups and stray WASPs.[46] Mayor Dever did what he felt he had to do, in justice's sake, for the black people of Chicago; but he would go no further in search of real racial understanding. He would leave that for a future, more enlightened generation.

The Problems of a Great City's Mayor

When Dever returned home from the 1924 convention, he immediately threw himself back into work. It was a peaceful summer. He could concentrate on his building projects and on those many little ceremonial duties he loved. The political wrangling that had vexed him earlier in the year had settled down. But it was to be only a temporary respite. By autumn, the school system had become the mayor's newest headache.

This must have been an unpleasant surprise to Dever. He had kept his campaign pledge to take public education out of politics: he had appointed a "clean" school board, then left it alone. And for the first year, matters had run smoothly. The trouble started when the board hired a new superintendent.

William McAndrew was the man they picked. Although he was brought in from the outside, McAndrew was no stranger to the Chicago schools. Forty years earlier, he had been one of the original teachers at Hyde Park High School, and later had become its principal. At Hyde Park he demonstrated both his high integrity and his disdain for political influence. When the son of a local politician flunked out, the boy's father sent word that his son had best be reinstated. Principal McAndrew refused and promptly found himself out of a job. He spent a year as a railway clerk in St. Paul, then went to work in the New York City public schools. He held a variety of administrative jobs in the New York system, finally rising to associate superintendent of schools. He was in that position when called back to Chicago in January 1924.[47]

McAndrew's appointment received wide praise at first. Here was the man to bring Chicago superior schools and put up with no nonsense while doing it. But McAndrew's greatest strength was also his biggest weakness. His idealism made him unwilling to compromise. His straightforward, direct approach to problems frequently became brusqueness; he had no political or diplomatic skills. McAndrew believed that he merely had to issue orders and they would be obeyed without question. After all, *he* was the general superintendent of schools and knew what was best. He would have no debate.[48]

The new superintendent was quick to stir up controversy. Without taking any consultation, McAndrew abruptly announced a comprehensive restructuring of the city's educational system. Among his reforms would be the institution of two-platoon schedules at overcrowded schools, a network of junior high schools, and intelligence testing for all students. These were fine plans on paper but not very savvy of Chicago's social and political sensitivities. For many in the working classes, McAndrew's innovations were threatening. The new programs seemed to represent that same type of unresponsive elitism that had saddled the country with Prohibition and cut-off free immigration. Vocational education and IQ-testing could lead to a caste system in the city schools; the children of working people would be denied equal educational opportunity and forever consigned to lower-paying manual jobs. Labor leaders loudly denounced the McAndrew reforms, while thousands of protest letters poured into the board of education and the city council scheduled special hearings. In his zeal to modernize public education overnight, the superintendent had made the Chicago schools one more arena in the cultural warfare of the "tribal twenties."[49]

McAndrew then alienated the teaching staff with his decision to curb the teacher councils. These informal assemblies met every five weeks during class hours to provide faculty advice in the running of individual schools. Some of them had been operating for nearly twenty years. McAndrew, however, saw the teacher councils as a rival to administrative power, with the potential to hinder his reforms. He suggested that the teachers should hold their meetings after regular dismissal time. The chief faculty union, the Chicago Teachers Federation, responded by obtaining a city council resolution endorsing the good work of the teacher councils and supporting their right to meet during school hours. Just as affairs were reaching a climax, summer vacation put everything on hold. When classes resumed in September, McAndrew had convinced a majority of the school board to back him. The board of education formally ended the practice of closing schools for the teacher councils. It also reaffirmed the superintendent's discretion over calling meetings of the citywide General Teacher Council. McAndrew had apparently won.[50]

Margaret Haley, leader of the Chicago Teachers Federation, was undaunted. Her union had fought a long, difficult struggle to secure recognition, and she did not intend to have a rookie superintendent ride roughshod over it. She decided to take her case directly to the mayor. This put Dever in an awkward position, since Haley and the teachers' union had been among his staunchest supporters. Still, he wanted to stay out of internal school board business. During the summer vacation, Dever had issued a statement endorsing the teacher councils and their school-hour meetings. That was enough for him. He told Haley that he would keep his hands off the dispute and repeated to all parties his hope that "cooler heads" would prevail.[51]

But tempers remained hot. While Superintendent McAndrew made the rounds of the business and civic luncheons to describe his programs, Margaret Haley organized a series of rival meetings. To the thousands of teachers who attended, she brought warning that the gutting of their councils was merely the first step in busting the unions. Soon McAndrew and his school board would be cutting salaries and laying off teachers, she claimed; they must stay united. Labor and political chieftains, leaders of the opposition to the other McAndrew schemes, turned out at the Haley meetings in great number, pledging solidarity with the teachers. The unions sent Dever repeated invitations to address their rallies, but he adamantly refused to get involved.[52]

On October 3, Haley turned her guns on the mayor. She announced that the public school system was teetering on the brink of bankruptcy because the Dever administration was lax in collecting taxes. According to Haley, out of $40 billion in taxable property, only $4 billion was being collected. Candidate Dever had promised to bring the tax-dodgers to justice; however, Haley claimed, Corporation Counsel Busch had told her that the administration had to "go slow" on its prosecution of the delinquents. If the mayor attempted a tax crackdown, the property-owning interests had vowed to retaliate by helping scuttle Dever's pending transit ordinance.[53]

Dever once again disavowed any responsibility. He denied that he had pussyfooted on gathering taxes because of political considerations. He acknowledged that some school taxes were going uncollected but refused to shoulder the blame for the situation. The board of education was an independent taxing body, the mayor reminded his critics. It was up to the board to ensure that the schools were receiving all entitled revenues. He trusted that he had clarified matters sufficiently, and that he could move on to other business.[54]

So the mayor continued to remain aloof from the school wars. He intervened in a minor dispute over some junior high school transfers but that was the exception to his rule. He would not rescue the teacher councils, and they died. Dever did recognize that McAndrew's glacial personality was at the root of many problems, and he privately enlisted Professor Merriam to talk to the superintendent about diplomacy, public relations, and other useful arts. Unfortunately, the dour little man would not take the hint, and indicated that he intended to continue on the course he had set. After that, the mayor would do no more. Dever the marginal man, the deethnicized Irish Catholic, could stay as true to his principles as any WASP. The price he paid in this instance was the friendship of Margaret Haley and the city's teachers. By not acting for them, they felt that he had acted against them. The mayor had lost another ally.[55]

And then Prohibition emerged—again! No matter how many times Dever thought he had laid the problem to rest, it would not stay buried. Its specter continued to haunt him. True, he had cleaned up the city and banished the bootleggers. But Chicago was only a part of the picture. The suburbs were quite a different matter.

Chicago had become a dry island in a sea of booze. Syndicate kingpin Johnny Torrio had realized that he could not work with the current city administration. Chief Collins had turned down bribes of up to $100,000 per month, and Dever's Beer War had made the situation all too clear:[56] the heat was on. As long as this mayor and his police chief stayed in power, the heat would stay on. So Torrio simply moved his operations out of their reach. He decided to relocate in Cicero, a gritty Bohemian factory town eight miles west of the Loop. Torrio arranged an accommodation with one of the suburb's political factions, then sent his chief enforcer, a young tough named Al Capone, against the rival parties. Within a month, Cicero had become a syndicate duchy. From this secure base, Torrio mounted forays into other villages. Soon hundreds of taverns and roadhouses were operating openly just outside the Chicago city limits.[57]

It seemed that other politicians did not take the Volstead Act as seriously as did Chicago's mayor. County and suburban leaders had promised Dever full cooperation in his liquor crackdown—and they had not followed through. Cook County government had three major elected officials: an unlikelier set of allies for Dever's Beer War would have been difficult to find. The state's attorney was the officer charged with investigating and prosecuting criminal cases in Cook County. The incumbent was Robert E. Crowe, an ambitious Republican politician who specialized in brave speeches and showy arrests but never seemed able to convict anyone. Sheriff Peter B. Hoffman, rumored to be on Torrio's payroll, was a model of ineptitude, in any case. (A few years later, Chicago reporters Ben Hecht and Charles MacArthur would write a play, *The Front Page*, featuring a dimwitted Cook County sheriff named Peter B. Hartman.) Finally, the president of the county board, the chief executive of Cook County government, was Anton Cermak, the wettest politician in the state. So Prohibition enforcement stopped at the city line.[58] In a bizarre preview of the 1950s, bootlegging had become the first industry to flee the central city for the suburbs.

To understand the persistence of the resistance to Dever's Beer War, events should be viewed in their greater context. The dry dispute was not just a local phenomenon. By the mid-1920s, Prohibition had become the country's number-one political issue. What made the debate particularly heated was the spectre of nativism looming behind Prohibition. Some dry advocates went beyond the moral arguments for temperance and presented their laws as a method of social engineering. They saw Prohibition as a way to remove the new immigrant groups from their dependence on saloon society, making these people good, upright, thrifty, sober Americans in the process. The Eighteenth Amendment and the Volstead Act to enforce it had been advanced during the war as patriotic sacrifices for the national effort and thus enacted. When the war fever ended, the country was left with Prohibition. Throughout the 1920s, then, the question of what to do with the law took on the trappings of a full-blown cultural conflict. The drys were determined to keep Prohibition as a means of promoting traditional American values. The wets were just as determined to be rid of a law that challenged their own deeply held customs and beliefs. Although there were other aspects of the wet/dry debate, the clash of cultures aroused the most passion.[59]

In Chicago, meanwhile, the wet struggle against Prohibition had become caught up in the drive to unite the Democratic party. Mutual mistrust among the ethnic groups was still strong, despite the best efforts of Sullivan and Brennan. Yet, the wet movement was something that could cross nationality lines. Here was an area where Irishman, Pole, Italian, and German might come together—along with Greek, Jew, Bohemian, and Balt. For such people the Volstead Act was a symbol of all who did not consider them worthy of first-class citizenship. If older America insisted on lumping them together in the generic category of inferior beings, then the ethnic outsiders would take it from there, would answer their adversaries with one voice. Some

issues meant more than petty rivalries. And so the voters of Chicago churned
out increasingly large votes against Prohibition in three separate referenda.[60]

The anomaly of Dever's administration continuing to enforce a hostile law
was not lost on some members of his party. The breach in the organization
continued to widen as time passed. Dever's detractors were positive that the
Beer War had been a total failure. They felt that the party had stood behind
the mayor, had given him his chance. Enforcement simply did not work.
The time had come for Dever to back off. If he remained committed to his
strange crusade, he would drag the whole party down with him.

The Democrats' family quarrel finally broke into public on October 6,
1924. The party was holding a testimonial dinner for Cermak, who had
recently returned from an extended trip to Europe. A large contingent
gathered at the Sherman House to honor the popular organization wheelhorse,
and they suffered through the usual tasteless food and flowery political oratory.
The mayor spoke near the end of the program. After the expected words of
praise for the guest of honor, Dever felt called upon to address the topic that
was on everyone's mind. He defended his treatment of Prohibition. He repeated his declaration that he was actually a wet. He said his job was to
enforce the law, and he was just doing his duty. "If you're not fond of the
law tell your troubles to the men in Congress," Dever advised his audience.
"Ask them to make some revision. Don't put the blame on me." He sat down
to a polite smattering of applause.[61]

Clarence Darrow was the next speaker. The great lawyer dabbled in Democratic politics, at one time serving a term in the state legislature. He had
recently defended the killers Leopold and Loeb in the sensational Bobby
Franks murder case, and was at the height of his fame. Speaking in his
familiar courtroom growl, Darrow started to talk about Prohibition. The law
was very hard on him, he claimed. "I can't get a drink without going to
bootleggers—and I frequently want a drink." The audience chuckled and
Darrow went on. He told his listeners that Tony Cermak was his kind of
politician. Cermak was wet and proud of it. Looking directly at the mayor
now, Darrow concluded: "[Cermak] doesn't grab a foolish law and hide behind
it. He doesn't say he enforces the laws because they're on the books. He says
he dislikes the law and makes no more excuses. . . . I like Tony Cermak
because he's wet, and because he doesn't make excuses."[62]

Dever sat red faced and tight lipped during Darrow's attack. When the
attorney finished his remarks, there was a long silence, then thunderous
clapping, then an excited hubbub throughout the room. The mayor merely
turned and started talking to the man seated next to him.

Darrow's blast of Dever was the hot topic of conversation along the corridors
of City Hall for days thereafter. The story was picked up nationally and ran
in newspapers all over the country. Local dailies analyzed the significance
of the event in great detail. Informed opinion held that the organization was

seeking to distance itself from Dever's unpopular Prohibition policies. The Democrats saw trouble ahead in the November elections. The party pros did not care much about the national ticket; they never did. Their concern was with saving local and state candidates. So it was necessary that Dever be publicly flogged. Some observers suggested that Darrow's speech was part of a carefully orchestrated theatrical stunt, that Dever had been warned he would come under attack at the banquet and had agreed to quietly endure it like a good party man.[63]

Whatever the background or the reasons for Darrow's speech, the elections went the way the organization had feared. The Republicans won a smashing victory in the Chicago area. President Coolidge carried the city with 60 percent of the vote; Davis was far behind with 22 percent, only slightly better than the third-party candidate, Senator LaFollette. More important, the Democrats also took a drubbing in the local contests. In fact, the lopsided election totals enabled the Republican party to gain control of all the major patronage-bearing offices except mayor of Chicago and president of the county board.[64]

The grand alliance that had carried Dever into the mayor's chair was in pieces. The Harrison-Dunne bloc was plotting new wars; the teachers' unions looked upon the mayor with mistrust; and many of his other friends in organized labor had become wary of him. The Democratic organization was in confusion and disarray; whether the election debacle signaled its total collapse, no one yet knew. The mayor faced the future with uncertain support, just at the time he was embarking on the most important task of his administration—the final resolution of Chicago's transit problem.[65]

7

Showdown on Transit

Chicago Transit: 1924

■ Transportation was a problem in the Chicago of 1924. This was nothing new; to many hardened residents it seemed that poor transit was a fact of urban life, as unavoidable as dirty air or noisy streets. You might complain about it to your next-door neighbor or others on the job, but it was something you accepted. Yes, it had always been bad. Now, it was becoming worse.

In 1924 two private companies controlled public transportation in Chicago. The Chicago Surface Lines ruled the city's streets. CSL had been founded in 1914 as a merger of the North Side's Chicago Railway Company with the South Side's Chicago City Railway Company and two minor carriers. These four companies had been the survivors of a half-century of traction wars dating back to the days of the first "animal railway." The Surface Lines now operated a fleet of more than 3000 crimson and cream streetcars on 172 routes over 1060 miles of track. Each day it took in 3.6 million fares. It was the largest street railway system in the world.[1]

The Chicago Rapid Transit company (CRT) ran the elevated lines. Like CSL, it was a child of merger. There had originally been four elevated companies: South Side, Metropolitan, Northwestern, and Lake Street. These systems had joined together in a loose association in 1913 and became completely unified as CRT in 1924. The new conglomerate ran nearly 2000 electric cars over 91 miles of routes. It had no subway, operating either on steel elevated structures or at ground level. All the major trunk lines funneled into the Loop, the double-tracked viaduct circling downtown. Trains from three sides of the city moved around the Loop elevated in a counterclockwise direction and spun back onto their own tracks. The Chicago rapid transit system was not as elaborate as those of New York, London, or even Boston. But it did possess its own superlative: the northwest corner of the Loop, at Lake and Wells streets, was said to be the busiest railway junction on earth.[2]

Other transit systems served Chicago. Steam railroads carried commuters to downtown from the suburbs and satellite towns. A small collection of electric interurban lines skirted the city limits to connect with the local routes. There was even a new company, the Chicago Motor Coach, which thought that gasoline busses could replace streetcars, and was running a few dozen of the dinky little vehicles on the city's boulevards.[3] But, from a practical standpoint, CSL and CRT had a monopoly on Chicago public transportation.

The word *public* was important. When a person had to travel about the city, he took the trolley or the "L" (elevated train). Automobiles were gaining in popularity and had become numerous enough for the city council to institute "No Parking" zones in the downtown area. More and more people were driving their own cars, but any significant shift to auto travel would be in the future, probably the far-distant future. Urban dwellers had depended on mass transit ever since the cities had grown too large to cross on foot. Public transportation was the lifeblood of the city.[4]

Unfortunately, Chicago's mass transit truly *was* in a worse state than ever before. Many of CSL's 3000 streetcars were in sorry condition. Some of them were converted horsecars, trundling along with over thirty years' service. Another batch of cars was nothing more than narrow boxes, with two benches set lengthwise down either side; the passengers called them *bowling alleys*. The company had a few newer cars running, but these were greatly outnumbered by the deteriorating wrecks. And the tracks were nothing special. Maintenance was hit-or-miss, and riders of the Riverview Park roller coasters might be more than a bit justified when they claimed they enjoyed a smoother ride within the amusement park than on their way to or from it.[5]

CRT's operations were somewhat better. The rapid transit company had hundreds of modern all-steel cars running alongside its older wooden coaches, and its tracks were in reasonable repair. The problem with the "L" was overcrowding, a situation derived from local circumstances. Unlike other American cities, Chicago elevated lines did not run over city streets. Once out of downtown, all routes (except Lake Street) went through alleys. The first Chicago "L" builders had been in a hurry. State law and hostile public opinion had promised long delays for their construction plans, so the entrepreneurs had convinced friendly aldermen to let them put their structures in the alleys behind major streets. When a building stood in the way, they simply curved their tracks around it. Thus the Chicago elevated lines were built with a series of curves, double-curves, sways, and dips. These logistics slowed operating speeds and limited trains to forty-eight feet.[6] Other cities could move their commuters in ten-car trains of seventy feet each on arrow-straight express tracks; Chicago had to cram its passengers into miniature coaches that swerved around buildings at something under thirty miles per hour. And if a train got caught in one of the frequent jam-ups at the Lake-Wells junction, the average speed became even slower.

Just getting to a streetcar or an elevated line was a chore. Service was frequent enough, with headways that might make a later generation blink in amazement. But the lines did not go everywhere. Once the city had been compact, almost every point being a block or two from some transit route. When the city grew, however, it outgrew its transportation system, and the carriers had not kept up. CSL was required by its franchise to construct twenty-three miles of track extensions each year; it had never reached that figure. The elevated lines did not have even these limited guidelines to follow. They had stopped building trunk lines in 1908. So families moving into new subdivisions on the outer fringes of the city found themselves isolated from reliable public transport.[7]

Any commuter wishing to travel the twelve miles downtown from a new settlement like Portage Park had to undertake a major expedition.[8] For example, if a man started from a bungalow near Montrose and Austin avenues, he was forced to walk a half-mile to the nearest streetcar line, Irving Park Boulevard. He then boarded the Irving Park car and rode six miles east to the Ravenswood "L" line. At Ravenswood he paid another fare and got on a train that took a circuitous route to the Loop. This was the quickest way downtown, taking about one-and-a-half hours. However, if the traveler wanted to save the ten-cent elevated fare, to buy a cup of coffee and a piece of pie for lunch, he could leave the Irving Park car at Milwaukee Avenue and take the CSL line all the way to the Loop. On a good day, this journey took just under two hours.

Crosstown trips were more involved. To travel to the Southwest Side, say, to Austin and Sixty-third Street, the Portage Park resident was obliged to ride almost five miles east to Western Avenue, change to a southbound car, then backtrack the five miles on Sixty-third Street. And since all rapid transit routes radiated from the Loop, crosstown elevated trips also included long detours. A patron deciding to take the "L" from Douglas Park to Englewood, both places only a few miles apart on the Southwest Side, would have to travel by way of downtown.

For this shoddy service, in cramped cars on a snail's schedule over truncated routes, the city's transit riders had to pay ever higher prices. Five cents had been the traditional carfare in Chicago. But the carriers had grumbled that they could not do business at that price, so now CSL was getting seven cents, and the "L" company a dime. And still they were not satisfied; there was talk of even more outrageous fares, perhaps even fifteen or twenty cents.[9] Progress had its price, everyone knew. But was this progress? And at what price?

So the straphangers waited. They endured the inconveniences and the high fares, praying for deliverance, calling for someone to show them the solution to the mass transit mess. It was a task worthy of a sage and a statesman. The man who could accomplish it would be the hero to 3 million people.

The Dever Transit Plan

William E. Dever thought he had the answer to the traction question: Municipal Ownership. The passing years had not cooled his ardor for the noble plan. He could vividly recall the time when he had stood with Edward Dunne in the fight against the 1907 Settlement—he and eleven other staunch aldermen had voted to sustain the mayor's veto of that nefarious scheme. The traction magnates and their lackeys had mocked them as the Savior and his Twelve Apostles.[10] The forces of darkness had triumphed then; the people had been betrayed as franchise extensions were rammed through. But the day of reckoning, so long delayed, had finally arrived. Dever was ready: government for the people would find a way out from the chaos that private greed had created.

The Municipal Ownership idea had not been forgotten for years, to be conjured up only when Dever took charge of the mayor's office. The chronic shabbiness of the city's public transit had stimulated many plans for government rescue. Two of these should be mentioned.

The first effort originated in the city council early in 1916. Prodded into action by irate commuters, the council established the Chicago Traction and Subway Commission, a body of three engineers who were told to survey the system and plan improvements. The commissioners returned in ten months with an elaborate, 446-page report. This was the first comprehensive overview of Chicago mass transit, and it did not skimp. It included plans for $275 million in service expansion; 58 miles of subways, 157 miles of new elevated lines, and 529 miles of streetcar extensions. The report concluded with the suggestion that the city council create a municipally run transit corporation to buy out private carriers and implement the new projects.[11]

The aldermen did not get around to acting on the commission's report for nearly two years. Then, in August 1918, the city council set up the Chicago Local Transportation Company as the city's new transit authority. The CLTC was charged with consolidating all surface and elevated operations under one management and starting work on the proposed extensions. Meanwhile, the City of Chicago was to tap its transit fund to build a downtown subway, which the CLTC would then rent. To ensure that the new transit corporation would operate in the public interest, the city council would appoint the members of the CLTC board. Mayor Thompson opposed the plan and vetoed the ordinance. But the aldermen overrode him, setting the stage for a public referendum.[12]

At first the CLTC plan seemed certain to pass. Most of the city council, five of the six daily newspapers, and almost all of the business community supported it. But opposition developed—and quite surprisingly, it came from some of the more zealous proponents of city-owned transit. For them, the plan was not pure enough, was not truly Municipal Ownership. There was no guarantee that the city could retain control over the CLTC board, they claimed. Furthermore, the purchase price for the existing lines was much too high: $149 million for CSL, $71 million for the elevated. Fares would have to be raised, services cut. The plan was plainly a sell-out to the Interests. An antiordinance coalition formed, led by such luminaries as Edward Dunne and Carter Harrison. Labor unions joined in, and even a few business groups. What had been a sure thing in August became a near thing by October. And, on November 5, 1918, the voters rejected the CLTC ordinance by a 53 to 47 percent margin.[13]

Mayor Thompson tried next. Big Bill came up with a novel approach to Municipal Ownership in 1921 with his Metropolitan Transit District Plan. The proposed district would include all surface transportation lines in the city and inner suburbs (rapid transit was not part of the plan). As an independent public authority, the Metropolitan Transit District would be yet another of Chicago's little governments. It would have the power to borrow money for operations and service extensions, and could levy taxes on the residents within its boundaries.[14]

During the 1960s and 1970s, scores of regional transportation authorities were created along the lines envisioned by Mayor Thompson in the early 1920s. Big Bill's Metropolitan Transit District plan was decades ahead of its time, and perhaps that was the problem. Thompson needed the state legislature's approval of the enabling acts to establish his transit district; but he could not get it, and his plan died.[15]

That was the situation when Dever became mayor. Various other traction relief programs were being bandied about, though nothing concrete was under consideration.[16] It remained for the new mayor to take the initiative. Dever had run on a platform of transit reform. He considered his election a mandate for action. Since the CLTC and the Metropolitan Transit District proposals had not succeeded, he decided to try something different. He finally settled on a half-forgotten plan of Alderman Ulysses S. Schwartz.

First introduced in February 1922, Schwartz's measure was similar in many respects to a dozen other Municipal Ownership schemes. What set it apart was its method of purchase. In this plan, the city of Chicago would raise funds to buy out the transit companies by selling public utilities certificates. The bonds were to be backed by the assets and income of the transit properties being acquired. No tax dollars would be spent and the city's transit fund would remain intact. Operating profits would go into a special sinking fund. Once the certificates were retired, the city would have complete control of its mass transit system.[17]

Dever incorporated the Schwartz certificate plan into his transit message of June 1923. Purchase negotiations began shortly afterward. As previously noted, the city and the carrier companies could not agree on a price. The situation was complicated by the fact that a consortium of financiers managed

Political powwow at French Lick Springs: Edmund Jarecki, Thomas P. Keane, and Robert Sweitzer advising the mayor. *(Chicago Historical Society: DN 76, 874)*

the debt-ridden Chicago Surface Lines. The city had to deal directly with the bankers, and their price was $162 million, based on the formula of the 1907 Settlement: the mayor could take it or leave it.[18] As for the elevated lines, Chicago Rapid Transit had no set price tag, since it was not covered by the 1907 law. But in dealing with the "L" company, the mayor was dealing with Samuel Insull.

Insull was the most powerful utilities magnate in the country. His was the Horatio Alger story, the tale of a penniless English office boy who migrated to the New World, became personal secretary to a young inventor named Edison, and rose to the heights of fabulous wealth through brilliant ability and hard work. At sixty-four, the majestic Insull now controlled both of Chicago's main power companies (Commonwealth Edison Electric and Peoples Gas), as well as scores of other utilities throughout the Midwest.

His influence extended to banking, brokerage, manufacturing, and public transportation. He had also become a power in local politics, and he played it both ways: he gave large contributions to both the Thompson Republicans and the Sullivan-Brennan Democrats. He was a man to be reckoned with.[19]

For all practical purposes, Samuel Insull owned Chicago Rapid Transit. He was moving into the transportation field in earnest, having recently purchased stock in a number of interurban railroads. Insull had no particular desire to sell the elevated lines. He was going to upgrade the system, he had already announced $23 million worth of extensions and service improvements.[20] Would he sell out to the city? He did not need them to bail him out! Would he set a price for the "L" lines? Insull would not do that, though the 1918 CLTC plan had pledged $71 million to acquire the elevated. What would he set as a price tag? Insull still refused to name a figure. However, he did point out that Chicago Rapid Transit was capitalized at $90 million. If the city was really serious about purchasing the "L" system, that might be a reasonable number to discuss.[21]

So it remained into 1924. As the negotiations dragged on, the mayor considered other options. He might take the $40-odd million in the city transit fund and put together his own system. For that amount he could build a nice subway and a few surface routes to feed into it. Complete Municipal Ownership would be delayed for a time by introducing a third carrier; but in the long run, a municipal (muni) system might be just the tool needed for eventual "recapture" of the surface and elevated lines.[22] There were grounds for such hope. In Detroit, the city-owned Detroit Street Railways had recently completed the takeover of all privately held transit companies. In San Francisco, the city's muni system was attracting substantial patronage away from the mighty Market Street Railway. And while Dever was enduring the frustrations of protracted price haggling, New York City was in the process of creating a new authority to construct its first municipally owned subway line, the IND.[23]

The idea of a Chicago muni system had come from the Hearst press, the *Herald and Examiner* and the *American*. In New York, Hearst's papers had been allied with Mayor John F. Hylan in his long struggle for a city-owned subway. Hearst thought Chicago might take a lesson from how they did things in the Big Town. About a month after Dever assumed office, the *Herald and Examiner* was reporting that New York's Hylan had dropped in on the new Chicago mayor to advise him to construct his own subway, as Hylan was doing back home. After that, the two Hearst organs paid close and detailed attention to Dever's ongoing negotiations with the transit carriers. The *American* finally lost patience. On July 18, 1924, the paper published a long editorial titled "Wake Up, Mayor Dever," in which it told the mayor that he was wasting time trying to buy the run-down CSL and CRT. The city should begin work on a muni system instead. Worry about surface routes some other time, but start building a subway now, the *American* advised. The paper was careful to note that its chiding of the mayor did not mean it had deserted him in his efforts to reach a favorable transit settlement. It had merely "stepped out in advance and invited His Honor to follow." So concerned was the *American* that it get its message before Dever and the public, it even paid to have its editorial reprinted as advertising in the rival *Chicago Tribune.*[24]

By the end of the summer, however, Dever had decided against setting up a muni company. A third system on the scene would postpone final Municipal Ownership for too long. In Detroit, for example, it had taken thirty years to get all the transit lines. Dever did not want to prolong the issue; he wanted to settle it. Chicago had waited long enough. He must go ahead with a unification plan and work out a purchase price later.

However, a competing muni system was still a potent threat to hold over the heads of the reluctant private carriers, and administration officials continued to talk freely about the advantages of starting a third company. The city council, meanwhile, directed its transit engineer, Major R. F. Kelker, to draft a report on a municipal system of elevated and subway lines "to be operated independently of any negotiations with the existing transportation companies." The council also scheduled a series of public hearings on the transit problem, to begin in October. Just before the first hearing, Major Kelker announced his muni rapid transit plan. It called for a main line to run diagonally from Irving Park and Cicero on the Northwest Side, cross through the Loop in a subway under Clark Street, then head southwest to a terminal at Seventy-first and Ashland. There were also six extensions listed for future consideration. Kelker said that the planned route would be compatible with existing lines without duplicating their service. The line could stand on its own, or could easily be incorporated into a unified, comprehensive system.[25]

While Kelker's report was being debated on the front pages of the newspapers, the city council opened its transit hearings. Six transit plans were submitted. Samuel Insull proposed a set of seven CRT extensions, as well as the addition of express tracks to four existing lines. Henry Blair of the Surface Lines brought forward a program for combined municipal-private operation. There was also a proposal that the South Side car lines secede from CSL, another that the Chicago Motor Coach take over the street railway franchises, and still another from a group of private investors who wanted to build their own subway.[26] And there was Dever's plan.

The mayor's latest transit message proposed comprehensive Municipal Ownership, with the Schwartz certificate method used to finance the purchase. He said that the private carriers had shown themselves unwilling and unable to improve operations; furthermore, the public had lost confidence in them. It was time for government to take over. The city and the transit companies now agreed on all details of the acquisition, except the actual price to be paid. Once that item was settled, and unified transit a reality, work could begin on the long-awaited subway. The mayor said he would continue his efforts to these ends; he would resume purchase negotiations with the carriers. But he warned: "If . . . it becomes clear that a settlement cannot be brought on that basis because the persons holding the securities of the private companies cannot agree with the city on a fair price, then it seems to me the [solution] is the immediate building by the city of a rapid transit system." In the event such action became necessary, Dever felt that Major Kelker's muni proposal had "many commendable features."[27]

Response to the various transit plans was cautious. Chicagoans had talked about the subject for so long that it was difficult to believe improvement would ever come. The *Post* summed up the prevailing mood with an editorial titled "Everybody has a Right to Guess on Traction," in which the paper admitted that no one knew how the matter would finally be resolved. As the city council transit hearings began, most of the aldermen remained on the fence, watching for developments. A few became restless and formulated their own master transit plans, which merely added to the confusion. Even Bathhouse John Coughlin got into the act; his idea was to dig a fourteen-mile-long subway in open cut, then save money by not covering it over.[28]

Subway seemed to be the magic word in much of the debate. Instead of detailing a comprehensive traction package, many of the proposals simply assumed that a subway would cure all Chicago's transportation ills. Besides, subways were the public works fad of the 1920s, the confirmation that a city had arrived at big league status (in the 1980s, it would be 60,000 seat stadiums). A modern underground railway could ease congestion by accommodating longer trains at higher speeds, it was true. But the subway advocates often appeared more caught up in the booster spirit than with the desire to improve transportation. In Chicago, the drum-major of the prosubway parade was the *Tribune*. The paper devoted scant space to analyzing the many transit plans before the city council; instead, it used the hearings as an excuse to renew agitation for immediate construction of an underground line. Gathering up a good head of steam, the *Tribune* editorial writers finally went so far as to suggest the printing and distribution of 100,000 subway-boomer buttons with the arresting slogan "Dig it Now."[29]

But amid all the rhetorical hoopla, it was clear that only two transit plans would be seriously considered, the mayor's and Samuel Insull's—and Insull was a man accustomed to getting his own way. The magnate returned from a European vacation in November and began campaigning for his program. He appeared before the city council transit hearings, scoffing at charges his CRT company could not afford its proposed improvements. Insull observed that he represented almost $300 million in invested capital. The $23 million to be used for the elevated extensions was "a comparatively small amount"—he had raised one-third more cash for the Edison Company just that year. He told the aldermen he was prepared to give Chicago a modern rapid transit system but cautioned them that "if you do not want me to do it, you must accept the responsibility."[30]

Insull continued lobbying in other arenas after his council testimony. He shrewdly decided to hammer away at the subway issue. Mayor Dever had repeatedly said that the city could not have a subway until comprehensive Muncipal Ownership was a reality. Insull, however, declared that the subway should be built immediately—and that he was willing to run his trains through it. The mayor was standing in the way of progress, he said. When the two men's paths crossed at a real estate dealers' banquet, Insull put the question directly to Dever: "In the gas company, we constantly declare 'You can do it better with gas'; the florists tell us 'Say it with flowers.' Why don't you stop talking about traction . . . and 'Say it with shovels'?"[31] But the mayor would not be goaded. If the city went along with Insull's plans, he said, "the traction matter would still be where it is—and the city would have expended the millions in its traction fund." Dever repeated that he would settle for nothing less than a comprehensive solution to the transit problem. In this position, he received vigorous support from the *Chicago Post*, which called the cry of Dig It Now "childishly impatient" and reminded its readers that a subway would be only "a detail" of any city transit system. The mayor also reaffirmed his intention to buy out the private carriers at an equitable price, and then construct the subway. He would not let Samuel Insull or anyone else pressure him into squandering the city's traction treasury on a subway benefiting bankers and capitalists. He would not be swayed. "I am eternally right," he declared, "and the people will be with me."[32]

Was it commendable prudence or willful stubborness? After all, there was much to be said for flexibility. Perhaps the mayor was right in not wanting to dig a subway before the city had all the pieces of public transit, but some sort of accommodation had to be devised, or Chicago would lose another chance to solve its transit dilemma, perhaps the last chance. The *Daily News* spoke to this fear, saying: "In the Mayor's present mood, unless his program is adopted to the letter, stagnation and even retrogression will be the alternative. . . . Is this attitude consistent with the earnest and rational desire to give Chicago good transportation as soon as possible?"[33] The mayor had made his point; but, if he truly want to get a workable transit program, he would have to compromise.

And so he compromised. It was the only practical thing to do, and Dever was a practical man. The mayor modified his stand on the tranist purchase price. He agreed to an arrangement by which the city council and the traction interests would together appoint three engineers to appraise the value of the properties. When these appraisers announced that the $162 million sought by the surface carriers was a fair price, Dever accepted it. He also reached a settlement with Insull, approving a middle figure of $85 million for the elevated lines.[34] The mayor knew that the time had come for pragmatism. By bending a little, he was saving most of his program. He thought that he had contrived the best possible means of resolving Chicago's transit crisis. He thought that, at last, he had the answer to the riddle.

Others did not think so.

Armageddon

The first hint of opposition to the mayor's compromise came from the *Chicago Journal*. The afternoon daily had been the only newspaper to oppose the Chicago Local Transportation Company plan of 1918, and it remained suspicious of any transit buy-out. On December 6, shortly after Dever agreed to the appraisal procedure, the *Journal* warned its readers to expect a "whitewash" of the traction valuation. The paper revealed that three of the men being considered as appraisers had been part of "the notorious traction-grab ordinance of 1918." A few days later, the *American* joined the chorus: it claimed that the appraisal was a plot to give "a few expert cronies" a large fee while inflating the price of the transit properties. The Hearst organ also called on the mayor to stop dallying with the traction interests and get to work on that third, muni system.[35]

Dissension had also developed in the Democratic organization. The split in the party on Prohibition, so dramatically manifested at the Cermak banquet in October, had not been patched up by the New Year. Some of the ward bosses now thought that the mayor needed another message. They confided to reporters that they would be working against the Dever transit package. They cared nothing about the plan's merits; they merely wished to use the transit referendum as a protest against Prohibition enforcement. "Now watch our smoke," one anonymous statesman said. "If he puts his traction plan up to the people, we'll defeat it. . . . We've been waiting for the people to get a chance to show what they think of Dever's administration. And this is the chance."[36]

If a few closet insurgents looked forward to the referendum, many Dever loyalists dreaded it. The city council was in a dither. The mayor hoped to have his ordinance voted on at the regular aldermanic election, on February 24, 1925, and that caused concern. In order to appear on the ballot, the transit package had to be approved by the council at least thirty days in advance. The aldermen did not receive their printed copies of the bill until the second week in January, leaving them only two weeks to study it. Even friendly lawmakers thought that was being too hasty. Alderman Jacob Arvey, Dever's floor leader in the council, was heard to grumble that the administration was "trying to rush through in ten days something that took a number of lawyers many months to prepare." There were also doubts about scheduling the transit plebiscite on the same day as the city council elections. The aldermen knew that the mayor's plan was becoming controversial and that the mayor himself already *was* controversial. Perhaps it would be better to face the voters for reelection when they did not have such matters on their minds.[37]

So the city council remained cool to the mayor's ordinance. When Corporation Counsel Busch appeared before the aldermen to read the proposal, many of them got up and walked out of the chamber. Alderman Schwartz scheduled a series of meetings of his Transportation Committee to consider the ordinance; he had to cancel them because he could not get a quorum. One newspaper, observing these obstructionist tactics, characterized them with a term then starting to gain some notoriety: *passive resistance.*[38]

The mayor himself was not even in town. Confident that his traction package would sail smoothly through the council, he had gone off to New York to be honored for his law enforcement activities by John D. Rockefeller, Jr.'s, Committee of One Thousand. The *Tribune,* which was supporting the mayor's ordinance, took it upon itself to call Dever's attention to the deteriorating situation back in Chicago. The paper published an editorial headed "O Mister Mayor, Come Home!" It advised Dever to cease taking his ease among the lords of mammon and return to his own city to rally the troops; otherwise his ordinance was doomed. "This is no time for the amenities of life in Capua," the *Tribune* told the mayor. "Come by the night mail, or you won't find anything left when you get here."[39]

Dever wisely took heed of the warning. He returned home on the first train, he listened to the rumblings, and he quelled the revolt. He agreed to postpone the transit referendum until April 7, the date of the aldermanic run-offs. Meanwhile, George Brennan began to crack the whip. Grudgingly, the regulars fell into line.[40]

Some Democrats would not be convinced. One was Alderman Oscar Nelson of the North Side Forty-sixth Ward. Nelson had served a term as state factory inspector under Governor Dunne and was vice-president of the Chicago Federation of Labor. He also had been Margaret Haley's closest council ally in the war against School Superintendent McAndrew. Nelson was the Chicago labor leader most actively and directly involved in politics; and like many labor leaders, he had doubts about Dever's transit plan. The alderman felt that the city would not have sufficient oversight power. The ordinance vested transit authority in a nine-member Municipal Railway Board. Three members were to be appointed by the mayor of Chicago, three by the Schwartz certificate holders, and three by joint agreement. Since the mayor had independent choice of only three board members, the private investors could conceivably retain control of the other six seats. The administration was talking about selling over a *billion* dollars in certificates to finance the deal, which meant that the bondholders would keep their majority until every last one of those certificates was retired—in about seventy-five to a hundred years! That was four or five times longer than the maximum transit franchise allowed by state law. And all the while, the investors would be receiving a dividend of 5 percent per year. Such a plan was not even remotely Municipal Ownership, Alderman Nelson declared on the council floor. It was a give-away to the traction capitalists, and he would fight it to the death.[41]

For Dever's part, he tried to safeguard against any long-term private control of the new transit system. He recognized the merits of Nelson's complaints and ordered revisions in the ordinance; now the mayor of Chicago would get independent appointment power over a majority of the Municipal Railway Board once 51 percent of the certificates were retired. When the financiers objected to this change, Dever forced them to submit.[42] But outside criticism of the plan was increasing, and the critics becoming more numerous. A definite antiordinance coalition was developing, and it was gathering around the mayor's one-time transit mentor, Edward Dunne.

Dever had tried to enlist his old friend's support very early. In August 1924, the mayor had taken Dunne to lunch at the Congress Hotel and told him of his new plan for transit reform. He had also asked the former mayor to become one of his appointees on the Municipal Railway Board. Dunne had been interested but told Dever he wished to read the actual ordinance before making a final commitment. When the plan had finally been completed, the mayor had the first galley sheets sent to him. Dunne took them along to read on his annual Florida vacation. What he found was enough to make him doubt that the Dever ordinance fit his own definition of Municipal Ownership. Dunne had promised to postpone any announcement of his position on the plan until he had a chance to discuss it in person with Dever. When he was unable to reach the mayor for a meeting, he decided to go public with his opposition.[43]

Dunne accepted an invitation from the *Chicago Herald and Examiner* to analyze the Dever transit plan. In a lengthy, closely detailed essay—something of a sort not commonly found in the Hearst papers— the former mayor carefully dissected the ordinance. He observed that even the revised organization of the Municipal Railway Board gave the financiers too much power and that the entire plan was simply a "stock-jobbing" scheme. Since the city would not get immediate control of its transit system, the Dever plan could hardly be called a reform measure. "Giving it the name of Municipal Ownership does not, in fact, make it Municipal Ownership," Dunne declared.[44]

In contrast to Dunne's reasoned arguments, the rest of the Hearst press attacked the Dever ordinance with its customary bombast. The *Herald and Examiner* dubbed Dever's plan the *unloading ordinance* and refused to refer to it as anything else. Both Hearst papers ran daily editorials against the ordinance. In accepted yellow journalism fashion, they did not shrink from loading supposedly objective "news stories" with their diatribes. When Dever was being honored for his law enforcement work by the Rockefellers, the *American* darkly hinted that the mayor's crime fighting was merely a ploy to conceal the financiers' traction grab. Endorsement of the Dever ordinance by the moribund Municipal Voters' League brought *American* charges that the elitist "secret caucus" was trying to regain its "undemocratic" control of Chicago politics. The Hearst attacks finally become so oblique that some observers believed that they really did not concern transit at all but were merely a warm-up for Big Bill Thompson's comeback attempt.[45]

Still, the Dever ordinance had much support. The *Tribune*, the *Daily News*, and the *Post* had all approved the plan with varying degrees of enthusiasm. Insull was giving it tentative backing, while other business and banking leaders were strongly in favor of its adoption. Meanwhile, the administration rallied reluctant aldermen to the cause. On February 27, the city council passed the Dever traction ordinance by a vote of 40 to 5.[46]

Now the politicking began in earnest. Six weeks remained until the public referendum. The contest over ratification took on all the appearances of a major electoral campaign. One hundred thousand copies of the 63-page ordinance were printed and distributed. Another 100,000 pamphlets of the official summary were issued. Supporters of the Dever plan organized themselves into the Nonpartisan Citizens' Committee of One Thousand. This Committee of One Thousand established headquarters in the financial district and began activities with a speakers' bureau. Their plan was to blanket the city with pro-ratification orators. Alderman Schwartz, Corporation Counsel Busch, and the mayor himself took turns briefing the first 250 speaker-trainees on aspects of the ordinance. The committee missed no bets—it also set up a women's speakers' bureau under Mrs. Kellogg Fairbank.[47]

The ordinance backers had good cause for their thorough preparation. The opposition was girding for an all-out fight. The antiordinance forces opened their own offices just down the street from City Hall. They called themselves the Peoples' Traction League. Dunne was chosen as the organization's president, while the seven vice-presidents included ex-mayors Harrison and Thompson and Alderman Nelson. The league started training its own speakers and began to churn out propaganda pieces against the Dever ordinance. It also adopted a slogan: "It Shall Not Pass."[48]

Almost the entire Harrison-Dunne wing of the Democratic party deserted the mayor on the traction issue. George Sikes, the original Dever-for-Mayor man, wrote a series of articles for the *American* telling why he now opposed the mayor. Dunne continued his scholarly analyses of the ordinance's shortcomings in the Hearst papers and in the *Journal*. Harrison, as usual, was blunt and personal. He told the *Daily News* that he was against the Dever plan because George Brennan was for it, and "George is Samuel Insull's friend." He added that he was expecting large-scale vote fraud on the part of ordinance supporters, since "50,000 illegal voters" had robbed him of his delegate's seat at the Democratic National Convention the year before.[49]

WOULDN'T IT BE TOO BAD, AFTER ALL THESE YEARS OF FOOLING, TO PASS UP THE REAL THING?

The *Chicago Tribune's* viewpoint on the transit referendum: March 30, 1925. (© *Chicago Tribune Company, all rights reserved, used with permission*)

The Democratic leadership came out strongly in favor of the ordinance. Brennan pulled out all the stops, sending aldermen back into their wards to stir up public support, spending money lavishly, and warning backsliders about the consequences of unfavorable vote totals. The party leader put the whole prestige of his machine behind the transit package. But at the grass roots there were still those nagging doubts. Many aldermen and ward bosses were not thrilled with the plan. They supported it as an organization-backed measure, quietly rationalizing that the people would have the final say at the referendum. Others did not even bother to go through the motions. The most notable of the defecting regulars was Boetius Sullivan, son of the late boss, who broke with Brennan to accept a vice-presidency in the Peoples' Traction League.[50]

The Republicans, meanwhile, were notably silent. Thompson and his followers, of course were deeply involved in the antiordinance campaign, but little was heard from other sectors of the party. The Dever ordinance did enjoy almost unanimous endorsement from the business community, the backbone of the local Republican party. Certainly, many Republicans supported the plan on its merits. As for the rest, perhaps they just decided to sit back and watch the Democrats tear each other apart.[51]

The Progressives and Independents who had helped carry Dever to victory in 1923 split on the transit package. Harold Ickes jumped into the fray on the mayor's side and baited the opposition with his usual acerbic wit. Margaret Haley, who had become disillusioned with the mayor during the McAndrew affair, actively campaigned against the ordinance. Most of the others were more cautious. If they were skeptical of the Dever plan, they did not publicize it. They had no wish to turn the transit vote into a referendum on the mayor's performance in office; neither could they work for an imperfect plan and keep a clear conscience. So Raymond and Margaret Robins endorsed the ordinance but did not speak for it. Mary McDowell, still a member of the mayor's cabinet, simply announced that she favored the plan, then left town. Long-time advocate of Municipal Ownership Clarence Darrow remained silent. And Charles E. Merriam, though privately advising the mayor on ways to keep the transit debate off a personal level, refused to publicly support the Dever ordinance.[52]

Dever and his cohorts attempted to conduct a very rational campaign. They felt their plan was so clearly beneficial, they would only have to publicize it sufficiently to win voter approval. They emphasized four points: (1) Municipal Ownership was the only way to build necessary service extensions; (2) no tax money would be spent in purchasing existing carriers; (3) a unified, single fare would be established; (4) transit would be removed from politics. The ordinance supporters did not want the issue to become embroiled in personalities. Their task was to educate the electorate. "We are going to unusual lengths in advising the people of Chicago on this program," Dever told an audience of Logan Square Kiwanis, "[because] this is not a Democratic, Republican, or factional ordinance." It was a plan for all the people. It would give them modern transit service and end the bickering and the quibbling.[53]

However, the opposition did not take so reasoned an approach. The antiordinance newspapers continued to seize upon any scrap of controversy and exploit it. The *Journal* pointed out that the ordinance's Municipal Railway Board was to be made up of "men of high character," and claimed that the proposal was thus antiwomen. Next, the paper announced that loopholes in the Dever plan would put elevated structures onto the center parkways of the city's boulevards. The Hearst press also continued its attacks, accusing pro-ordinance unions of selling out in return for city jobs and predicting that the "traction trust" was about to seize total control of government. Edward Dunne and some of the more level-headed spokespersons of the Peoples' Traction League tried to keep to the issues. They talked of such matters as the lengthy terms of the traction certificates, the loss of city tax revenue from the private carriers, the lack of a stable fare structure—but who wanted to listen to all that? The voices of moderate dissent were drowned out by the cries of "Conspiracy!" "Fraud!" and "Sell-out!"[54]

And the frenzy increased as the day of referendum drew near. The ordinance foes reached new levels of creativity. Tomaz Deuther, a Northwest Side businessman opposed to the plan, announced that he would pay prizes of $100, $50, and $25 to the three precinct organizations in his district that delivered the largest vote against the Dever proposal. One local radio station sponsored a contest for the best antiordinance slogan, and received entries like these:

—Traction ordinance not so good
   Because it can't be understood

—On traction vote "No,"
   And save your dough.

—Our peace of mind will go forever
   If we adopt the plan outlined by Dever.

Significantly, nobody offered prizes for the best alternative to the Dever ordinance. But the opposition seemed to be have a good time with the issue, anyway.[55]

In contrast, the ordinance supporters were beginning to run scared. Rumors were again spreading that some committeemen were planning to knife the mayor over Prohibition, so the organization roused itself into a final flurry of activity. More fliers went out and new billboards were erected. Another round of neighborhood meetings were held, sometimes as many a thirty-three in a single night. Businessmen were called into ordinance headquarters and urged to electioneer for the plan with their employees. The mayor seemed to be everywhere, scurrying around from platform to platform, shouting himself hoarse in defense of his transit bill. It was also reported, though never confirmed, that the police were instructed to "ease off" on Prohibition enforcement while the mayor's ordinance was up for ratification.[56]

On the last weekend before the balloting, the Democratic organization held a gigantic rally at the Sherman House hotel. All the big chiefs and all the little ward lords were there, the reluctant rubbing shoulders with the eager. In the heady atmosphere of the packed ballroom, however, one might be tempted to forget they had any differences and remember that they were all Democrats. And when Anton Cermak took the lectern to tell the crowd why he supported the mayor's plan and how he was having his appeal printed in the Bohemian-language newspapers, could anyone doubt that the organization was primed to deliver again?[57]

The final *Tribune* poll on the traction plebiscite showed the contest to be dead even. What happened on April 7 was a surprise even for the bitterest foes of the Dever ordinance. The mayor's transit package was buried by a margin of nearly 20 percent. The final tally was: For, 227,033; Against, 333,789; for a majority opposed of 106,756. Only fourteen of the city's fifty wards voted in favor of the plan.[58] It was a crushing, humiliating defeat.

One can be comforted by the belief that the democratic process had been vindicated: that Dever had submitted a bad ordinance and the people had rejected it. The transit package was certainly not perfect. The purchase price was doubtlessly inflated. (When the city finally bought out CSL and CRT in 1947, the total paid for *both* companies was only $87 million.)[59] The Dever ordinance gave no guarantee that fares would stay down. The Schwartz certificate gimmick offered the real possibility of default, with resulting continuation of private control. There were also a great many little things wrong with the plan, and it was not really Municipal Ownership except in a long-range sense. However, it was probably the best package Dever could have put together. Cities must do more than see to everyday housekeeping chores; they must keep an eye to their future. The Dever traction ordinance was an honest attempt to provide for that future. It deserved kinder treatment from the voters.[60]

The geographic pattern of the balloting reveals little conclusive evidence. The ordinance carried in both a bloc of nine inner working-class wards surrounding downtown and in four white-collar independent wards strung out along the South Shore, plus in the Far North Side Forty-ninth Ward—the mayor's home. These areas had some of the best public transportation in the city. The strongest opposition came from the Far Northwest and Far Southwest sides, middle-class Republican areas with notoriously poor transit service.[61] Partisan considerations evidently outweighed the material benefits to be expected from transit reform. Yet there is more to the story than simple Democrat-Republican cleavage. What really happened to the Dever transit package is bound up with the power and personalities of Democratic party politics.

The party organization failed its mayor. The stronghold of the regular "machine" was the twenty-two wards on the Greater West Side. In his 1923 election, Dever had carried these wards by 66,000 votes, taking a majority in seventeen of them. Two years later, his transit ordinance lost the same wards by a margin of over 54,000 votes, carrying in only five districts. Despite their professions of loyalty, a number of ward leaders had not delivered and a number of others may have knifed Dever. Some of the returns are particularly striking. Cermak's Twenty-second Ward had given Dever over 75 percent of its votes in 1923, but now the powerful county board president could not manage even 40 percent for the mayor's transit ordinance. The shift was similar in the neighboring Twenty-first Ward, where Cermak exercised strong influence. The most dramatic change took place in the Twenty-sixth Ward, where alderman Joseph Mendel worked openly against the transit package. Dever had taken Mendel's ward with 89 percent in 1923, but the ordinance now scored only 21 percent. And the vote erosion was not limited to the West Side. In the South Side Eleventh Ward, to mention one example, Dever had won with 77 percent in 1923; in 1925 his traction ordinance could tally barely 23 percent.[62]

Wednesday-morning quarterbacks blamed the ordinance defeat on the mayor's Prohibition policy. One commentator estimated that up to two-thirds of the 100,000-vote margin against the bill was a result of the Beer War.[63] There is more than a little truth in this assessment. Certainly, a city that had voted 80 to 20 percent for Prohibition modification in November 1922 would not have dried up very much in two-and-a-half years. But voters are a strange breed. It is not overestimating their intelligence to suspect that they could have kept transit and Prohibition separate in their minds as they drew the curtain on the voting booth. If they chose to link the two, it is likely that they were encouraged to do so—or at least, not discouraged from it too energetically. The fact remains that in wards where the committeemen worked hard for the ordinance, it carried, even in the wetter wards. The North Side Forty-second Ward had gone 85 percent wet in the 1922 Prohibition referendum; on traction it voted 66 percent in favor of the mayor's bill, only slightly down from the 68 percent candidate Dever had polled in 1923. The figures are even more interesting in the Twenty-seventh Ward, 88 percent wet in 1922. There the mayor's ordinance took 67 percent of the vote, fully 3 percent *better* than Dever had done in 1923. Admittedly, these are isolated cases, but they indicate that with active support from all ward leaders the transit package could have had a fighting chance.

However, there was no way to determine whether Mayor Dever was more popular with the grass-roots voters than with the committeemen. His critics read the referendum results as they wished. Encouraged by the *Herald and Examiner*, some of the aldermen began to speak out against administration policies. They attributed the antiordinance vote to Dever's unpopularity and attributed the unpopularity to his dalliance with the reform crowd. The mayor had forsaken his working-class roots, they claimed. "It is all right for a Republican to go heavy on that reform stuff," one alderman conceded, "but in a big city like Chicago, with its meltingpot character, a Democrat doesn't fit into a fanatical reform picture." The politico continued: "Silk-hatting the LaSalle Street crowd is all right if you have been reared in that atmosphere and are one of them. But to give the impression that you've gone over to the silk-hatters after you've been raised under a fedora is fatal in politics in Chicago."[64]

And, of course, there was the matter of Prohibition. The anonymous alderman also suggested that continuing police raids were not winning the mayor many voters. Everyone knew that the cops had better things to do than "smelling around a basement flat to see if some partiarch from Warsaw or Leningrad had fermented cider on his table." This was just one more example of how Dever had lost touch. If the mayor wanted to get some work done in office and have any chance for reelection, it was time he returned to the fold.[65]

Dever had failed in the great aim of his administration: to bring about transit reform. His term was half over; his oldest political comrades had deserted him; and his party organization did not respect him. He who had been gloriously wet now found himself best known for the enforcement of a silly bluenose law. It was a bad situation for any politician.

But if two years were gone, two years were left. He must go on. There was still time to salvage his administration, still time to avoid relegation to the political ashcan. He could do it without sacrifice of his principles, he was sure. And he knew he would succeed: he was eternally right, and the people would be with him.

8

Hanging On

The Volstead Matter

■ Dever took the defeat of his transit ordinance gracefully. He issued a simple statement saying that "the people have spoken" and declared that he had no bitterness over the referendum's result. He promised to continue his fight for transit reform, while going forward with the work of his administration.[1] He knew that he must regain his lost initiative; he did not intend to become a lame duck for two years. However, the transit plebiscite was a watershed in Dever's mayoralty. He had put all his power and prestige behind and ordinance, and it had failed; now he was politically vulnerable. And more and more, outside forces were to challenge him, forces over which he could have no mastery. Despite his desire for a fresh start, old problems continued to plague him. The second half of Dever's term became a holding action. He could still react to events with his customary feistiness and vigor. But the agenda no longer seemed to be his.

Prohibition and its related crime problems came to surpass all other concerns. The issue had never really gone away, of course. Since Dever's inauguration, it had always been present, lurking in the shadows, sometime charging onto the scene to steal a headline or two, then retreating into darkness. In the final years of Dever's term, it came to center stage and stayed.

Not that this was all bad. Dever's war on bootlegging had made him a national celebrity. It was reported that the Mayor Who Cleaned Up Chicago was the second-most photographed person in the country, only after President Coolidge.[2] The public was interested in the man. Favorable articles continued to appear in the Sunday supplements and the drugstore monthlies, as journalists journeyed to Chicago to meet the remarkable statesman and discuss his work.

There was even a Dever biography of sorts. In April of 1924, *McClure's* magazine had printed Neil McCullough Clark's description of the Dever Beer War. Prohibition advocates found the article so inspiring that they arranged to have it published in booklet form. Distributed by the American Issue Publishing Company of Westerville, Ohio, the sixteen-page tract was titled *Mayor Dever and Prohibition: The Story of a Dramatic Fight to Enforce the Law.* It begins with a vivid account of corruption and wetness in Chicago at the time of Dever's inauguration. The tale then moves through the Torrio-O'Donnell bootlegging rivalry, the shooting of Jerry O'Connor, and the "drastic steps" taken by the mayor in response. At the end, the reader is taken on a tour of the new, dry, crime-free Chicago. Author Clark notes that an interested party can still purchase liquor in the city, but with so much difficulty that "the stealth of the transaction takes away . . . [one's] appetite." In short, "liquor has vanished from most of its accustomed haunts in Chicago because protection of the liquor traffic has disappeared. And protection has disappeared because William E. Dever is mayor." Clark's treatise went on to become something of a classic in dry circles. Even after Dever's death, copies of the booklet were still being circulated by prohibitionist organizations.[3]

Chicago's mayor was also attracting the attention of the rich and powerful. His tough handling of the liquor criminals won high praise from the newly formed National Committee of One Thousand for Law Enforcement. This was a Prohibition-lobbying coalition of wealthy financiers and industrialists who saw the Eighteenth Amendment as a bulwark of the social order and an effective tool in promoting worker productivity. Leaders of the "one thousand" included John D. Rockefeller, Jr., Elbert H. Gary of U.S. Steel, and Charles Schwab of Wall Street. Here was the country's economic royalty. President Coolidge invited them to the White House to discuss their plans for the nation over sausage and eggs. When the committee spoke, America listened.[4]

In January 1925, the Committee of One Thousand invited Dever to be guest of honor at its annual banquet in New York City. The mayor came and was an instant success. He seemed relaxed and at home among the money lords at the posh Waldorf-Astoria Hotel. He made his usual speech about not being a Prohibitionist but still having to enforce the law. He told his audience of the evils that had greeted him when he became mayor and reviewed the problems he had faced fighting them. Much of the trouble, Dever said, stemmed from the differing conceptions of Prohibition held by older-stock Americans and the more recent arrivals. In just the past decade, Chicago had been inundated with "five Negroes and twelve foreigners for every two white children born there." Because these people were not yet fully Americanized, they caused more than their share of difficulty. However, the mayor was confident that this was only a minor concern. "Law enforcement is not unpopular in this country," Dever assured his hosts. "Although it may cause annoyance, the great majority of the people of the country stand solidly for a vigorous enforcement of the laws."[5]

Dever's remarks were well received. The day after the formal banquet, a smaller reception was held at the Lawyers Club, and the mayor met with over fifty of the nation's corporate moguls. John D. Rockefeller, Jr., set the tone for the gathering, telling reporters that he had come because "I like to be near a man who has the courage of his convictions," and that "there are all too few of Mayor Dever's type today." Later, the Committee of One Thousand announced that it would give its full support to Dever's law-and-order campaign, working through its "local influences" in Chicago. Political pundits were impressed by the mayor of Chicago's easy rapport with the mighty capitalists. They noted that Dever had been honored as had "no Democrat in New York by a similar group since the days of Grover Cleveland." Such backing from men of high station "unquestionably makes Mayor Dever a prominent candidate for the Democratic nomination in 1928," declared one writer. The poor tanner had come a long way.[6]

Unfortunately, crime had not been banished from Chicago. Even as Dever was busy captivating the wealthy teetotalers of the East, a new storm was breaking out back home, a tempest of violence such as the city had never seen. The lavish praise of Rockefeller, Gary, and the rest was soon to seem hollow, or at best premature. And the sad irony of the situation, journalist Elmer Davis later observed in *Harper's Magazine*, was that "the greatest out-burst of robbery, homicide, and machine-gunning came after Thompson went out of office. It came under the best mayor Chicago ever had."[7]

The very success of Dever's Beer War was a good deal to blame. During Thompson's lax rule, Johnny Torrio had brought order to the bootlegging industry, stamping out independents and establishing a citywide syndicate. Individual subchiefs had definite territories. With occasional exceptions, everybody lived in simple peace and harmony—making money. But Dever's massive raids altered the situation. As the city began to dry up, bootlegging profits shrank. Local operators started quarreling among themselves over pieces of the rapidly disappearing pie. Ward politicians and police captains who disagreed with the mayor's policies aggravated matters, cutting new deals with the squabbling liquor traders. It seemed only a question of time until new gang violence would break out.[8]

The trouble began when Dion O'Banion became dissatisfied with his share under the Torrio syndicate. O'Banion and his mostly Irish gang controlled bootlegging in the Forty-second and Forty-third wards, just north of the Loop. The bantam-sized gunman operated out of a flower shop located directly across from Holy Name Cathedral, where he had sung in the choir during his innocent years. In the summer of 1924, the O'Banions began moving into the territory set aside for the Genna brothers' gang. The Gennas resisted their encroachments. Torrio, as head of the syndicate, attempted to maintain the peace between his subbosses, but O'Banion rebuffed him, making a few unkind remarks about Sicilians in the process. Then one day in November, three men sauntered into O'Banion's floral emporium to pick up a wreath. While the first man shook hands with the proprietor, his two companions produced pistols and pumped six bullets into the gangster-florist. They then left, without bothering to take their order. [9]

O'Banion's death caused a sensation throughout the city, and newspapers predicted a fresh wave of gangland mayhem. The mayor did what he could to downplay the event. He assured reporters that the O'Banion killing was merely the result of some "personal feud" and not the prelude to more violence. Meanwhile, Dever ordered Chief Collins to disarm all known hoodlums, to prevent any revenge by the slain mobster's friends. He also told the chief to begin yet another round of police transfers. [10]

The killing brought to light an incident quite embarrasing to the administration. Shortly before the recent election, North Side Democrats had sponsored a testimonial dinner for the politically influential O'Banion at the Webster Hotel. Among those present were Dever's public works commissioner, Colonel A. A. Sprague; and his chief of detectives, Michael ("Go Get 'Em") Hughes. Supposedly, the banquet had been planned to woo support from local labor leaders for Sprague's U.S. Senate campaign. When the mayor learned of the affair, he called both men on the carpet and told them to find some better dinner companions. Sprague was chastened—he had lost the election, and O'Banion's carefully cultivated wards had gone Republican. Hughes bridled at the mayor's rebuke, was demoted, then resigned. He gave the whole story to the press, claiming that he was the victim of political pressure exerted on the mayor. [11]

While this entertainment was going on, O'Banion's chums were busy burying their leader in a $10,000 casket, accompanied by twenty-six truckloads of flowers. They were also preparing their next move. Chief Collins's police evidently could not disarm the O'Banion clan fast enough, for on January 12, 1925, three men in a black touring car attempted to gun down Torrio-lieutenant Al Capone on the South Side. Less than a fortnight after that, two other triggermen seriously wounded Torrio himself while he was carrying a bag of groceries into his apartment building. The chronology of bloodshed then starts to become somewhat cluttered. It is enough to say that by the end of the summer of 1925, Chicago gangland was once again quiet. Along the way, the Genna brothers' gang had been wiped out, the remnants of the O'Banion mob had been pacified, and Capone had succeeded the gun-shy Torrio as chairman of the syndicate. [12]

Crime on the whole was increasing. This puzzled the professional criminologists, who had hoped Prohibition would usher in a more moral society. But the cold statistics verified what many people had begun to feel—general lawlessness was becoming more common. In the five years following the passage of the Volstead Act, for example, robberies in Chicago had gone up 35 percent; bombings had doubled; murders, rapes, arson, and felonies were on the rise. A peak of sorts was reached on July 30, 1925, when gunmen invaded the elegant Drake Hotel in a daring high-noon holdup. Even the Gold Coast was no longer safe. As police chief Collins admitted, Chicago's crime situation had become "the worst lawlessness since the Haymarket Riot."[13]

Many cures for the disease were brought forward. Chief Collins decided to initiate another series of police transfers. A group of businessmen paid to have posters hung in streetcars and elevated trains, listing the penalties to be meted out for various offenses. One visiting French cleric had a simple solution: he advised the city to set up a guillotine in the middle of Grant Park.[14]

No matter what the specific crime under discussion, many observers felt that it somehow related to Prohibition. A great deal of blame was laid on the Dever crusade. The police were being wasted, so the argument ran. As the *Chicago Tribune* saw it, "By throwing the emphasis on the closing of beer joints and pinochle games, police effort has been scattered and the security of persons and property has undoubtedly suffered. Activity has been focused on liquor, gambling joints, dives, card games—these are given the emphasis rather that the protection of life and property."[15]

Of course, many of the perpetrators of "life and property" crime were the same persons the police were chasing for liquor and gambling violations. But the perception of misdirected police energies was becoming popular. The *Tribune* continued its antienforcement editorials and was often joined by the Hearst press. The politicians began to take note as well. In November 1925, a city council subcommittee voted 9 to 2 to ask Chief Collins to withdraw his men from pursuit of dry-law offenders.[16]

Conditions in Chicago highlighted a nationwide trend. Prohibition was not performing as advertised. Temperance advocates had promised that the Eighteenth Amendment would bring about better health, wealthier citizens, safer streets, and an uplifted society. After six years of legislated sobriety the country had not yet reached Utopia. If anything, civilization had gone backward. Liquor was still available for those who wanted it, rival rum-drummers were turning urban avenues into approximations of early Dodge City, and public morality was in decline. Something was not working. Meanwhile, the wet leaders, who had known all along that the people would not lose their hankering for strong beverage, pointed to the breakdown of society and called for a total revision of the Prohibition laws.

In the spring of 1926, a U.S. Senate subcommittee began hearings on the dry statutes. The proceedings soon began to take on a distinct Chicago flavor. Representatives of the Better Government Association, the local political watchdog group with strong dry ties, testified that Chicago politicians were in league with organized crime to subvert the Volstead Act and commit other nefarious schemes. Stung by this criticism and anxious to revise wetward the nation's drinking laws, the Chicago City Council decided to dispatch its own delegation to the Senate hearings. In good organization style, they sent a balanced ethnic ticket: an Irishman (George Brennan), a Bohemian (Anton Cermak), a Pole (Stanley Kunz), and a Jew (Adolph Sabath). These four, and the others who joined them, repeated the theme familiar to all wets: Prohibition was not working; the people did not want it, it should be scrapped.[17]

The city's most renowned expert on Prohibition enforcement did not come to the hearings at first. That was before the testimony of Edwin A. Olson. Olson, the U.S. district attorney for northern Illinois, told the senators that the Volstead Act was being widely ignored in Chicago. He said that he received little cooperation from local authorities. State courts interfered with federal prosecutions, and political "good fellows" used their influence to preserve the liquor traffic. Outlaw cabarets openly flouted the law. Olson declared that Prohibition could be enforced in Chicago if given an honest chance—but it had not had that chance. To cite an example, he claimed that thousands of illegal stills were operating in the city. The police knew their locations, yet did nothing. If he had 5000 men under his command, Olson said, he could "pull out by the roots every still in Chicago in twenty-four hours."[18]

Dever was outraged by Olson's charges. When news of the U.S. attorney's allegations reached Chicago, the mayor jumped on a train and headed for Washington. He arrived at the Capitol with fire in his eyes and asked to appear as a witness before the subcommittee. The senators graciously agreed to schedule Dever for an afternoon session. He wound up testifying for two days.

The mayor began by responding to Olson's charges with some accusations of his own. Dever related that early in his term, he had called the U.S. attorney into his office and had told Olson he was not satisfied with federal Prohibition enforcement. Olson had still hedged, so Dever had threatened to take up the matter with the president. Then, according to the mayor, "[Olson] instantly responded; he became instantly an ultra public-welfare man." Since that time, the U.S. attorney had given the city administration valuable assistance in carrying out the law; but it had taken the mayor's pressure to get him cracking. As for the statement that the police could clear out all illegal stills in one day, that was plain nonsense. Dever said that he had "not the least doubt" that there were thousands of underground stills at work in his city. But nobody could get rid of them all unless they started conducting raids without search warrants, and that he would never do. "We claim that we are trying to bring about respect for law and order in Chicago," Dever explained. "If that means we must invade the homes of our people, we won't do it."[19]

Having thus disposed of Olson's allegations, the mayor turned to the Prohibition law itself. His observations must have been surprising to those who knew of him only as the great enforcer of dry ordinances. Dever declared that the entire liquor matter had been blown out of proportion. Prohibition had become the number one political issue in Chicago. Aldermen were elected or defeated mainly on their Volstead stand; judges were influenced in their court rulings because they had to run for reelection in wet districts. And for the chief executive of the city, there was the continuing obligation to carry out an unpopular law. Too much of his time as mayor was tied up in it. He wanted to be busy clearing land for parks or building bridges; instead, he was kept bogged down in the liquor mess. "It is almost impossible to give anything approaching good government along general lines [because] this one subject presses so strongly upon our attention," Dever told the senators. "Even I, who have tried to divest myself personally and as chief executive of the City of Chicago of the subject, find myself immersed in it . . . from morning to night."[20]

What to do about Prohibition was a complex question, Dever said. He allowed that there were many sincere and well-informed people on both sides of the issue, but so far their discussions had created more heat than light. Dever proposed that Congress establish a special commission to make a comprehensive, neutral, objective study of the Prohibition matter. He was convinced that such an unprejudiced body could uncover the truth beneath all the rhetoric and the nation would accept its findings, whatever they might be. He even offered to serve on such a commission, if that would help.[21]

Dever's testimony made the front pages of newspapers throughout the country. He appeared to have done much to dispel the image of Chicago as a wide-open frontier outpost. Two thousand people came out to Grand Central Station in the pouring rain to welcome the mayor home from Washington. Once again, there was talk of Dever as a future presidential candidate.[22] Then, William McSwiggin was killed.

Chicagoans had grown accustomed to gangsters liquidating each other. McSwiggin's death was something different: he was an assistant state's attorney in the office of Robert E. Crowe. On the evening of April 27, 1926—scarcely three days after the mayor's triumphant return from the senate hearings— young McSwiggin was gunned down as he emerged from a Cicero saloon with four other men. First reports indicated that a crusading prosecutor had been murdered in cold blood by fearful racketeers.[23] However, other facts soon began to materialize.

The slain lawyer's companions on the night of the shooting were members of the Klondyke O'Donnell gang, then engaged in a furious struggle against the Capone syndicate. Two of the men had recently been prosecuted for murder—unsuccessfully—by Mr. McSwiggin. What was an assistant state's attorney doing drinking beer in a speakeasy with known hoodlums? State's Attorney Crowe claimed that his young deputy had been gathering evidence for future indictments. Few people swallowed that one. The newspapers began to ask, in bold headlines: "Who killed McSwiggin, and Why?"[24]

The official investigation of the shooting was a farce. Grand juries were summoned, indictments issued, testimony taken; but nothing happened. The best guess was that the Capone mob had mistaken McSwiggin for the leader of the former O'Banion gang, Hymie Weiss. Al Capone himself was supposed to have led the attack, yet he went free. The McSwiggin case remained officially

Mayor Dever returns from the Senate Prohibition hearings in Washington. Among the greeters are Corporation Counsel Busch (front row, far left) and Police Chief Collins (on train steps behind Dever). *(Chicago Historical Society)*

unsolved.[25] But the stench of the affair was overpowering. Could anyone really believe that there were no ties between politics and organized crime in Chicago? Didn't the mayor know what was going on around him? Was he trying to cover up corruption, or was he simply naive?

All Dever's work restoring the city's image was shattered. And, as if on cue, the mobs resumed heavy warfare. Two pitched battles broke out on downtown Michigan Avenue within a five-day period. Then Hymie Weiss and his minions launched a full-scale, armed invasion of Capone's Cicero stronghold. A few weeks after that offensive failed, Weiss himself was murdered on the steps of Holy Name Cathedral. The belligerent forces finally agreed on a peace settlement after lengthy negotiations at the Sherman House hotel. Even with the end of hostilities, however, the perception that Chicago was a gang-ridden metropolis was more firmly established than ever. Where else did racketeers call a press conference to announce the terms of their territorial agreements?[26]

The mayor, meanwhile, had become more vocal in his criticism of Prohibition. He told the City Hall press corps that the liquor question was like a toothache—the pain of it made you neglect your more important business. In a Rockford speech, he even compared the problems caused by the dry law to those created by slavery before the Civil War; the Volstead Act was "a tremendous mistake," he said, and he would do "anything [I] can to correct it."[27] Dever also wrote an article called "Get at the Facts" for the *Atlantic Monthly* magazine. Partly a rehash of his senate testimony, it contained some new thoughts on the subject, as well.

Dever allowed that Prohibition had its good points. When it was accepted by the people, temperance helped bring about a better community. Of course, some groups did not view matters this way; for them, drinking was a treasured part of social intercourse and a requirement for good health. Their traditions inclined them toward wetness. Dever had always known this—he was an Irishman, after all—though he had not allowed his personal beliefs to deter his executive actions. The law was the law, as he had often said, but now he modified his views. On previous occasions the mayor had declared that even an unpopular law should be enforced. Now he sounded doubtful:

A large majority of the people here were and are opposed to Prohibition laws. They do not and they cannot by force be brought to respect them. Hence, such efforts as have been made to enforce the law in [certain] communities have been followed by social and political evils of the first rank. The wise legislator in a democracy will not attempt to impose law by any special programme, however desirable in the abstract, that will not receive the support of the people, if for no other reason than that such an attempt will in practice be found unworkable. It is not what the people should think, but rather what they actually believe, that determines whether they may be likely to respect and obey certain of our laws; and men . . . cannot be brought to support a policy that they believe to be oppressive and unjust.

Wholesale arrest of those who violated questionable laws was not productive. Rationality must overcome emotion. What this country really needs is an objective study of Prohibition, to "get at the facts."[28]

After three years of faithfully upholding the Eighteenth Amendment, Dever had concluded that enforcement did not work. Respect for the law had not been restored; the police department had not been revitalized; city streets had not been made safer. Once Dever had vowed to carry on alone if outside authorities did not aid his efforts. They had done little, and he had been unable to bear the burden alone. He had also discovered that you do not encourage the repeal of an unsound statute by compelling strict obedience to it. The mayor now realized that many folks—good citizens, to be sure—would simply not accept a bad law, would sooner disobey it than follow procedures and petition for a redress of grievance. Sometimes politics did not operate the way the textbooks said. He had let his idealism overcome his practicality. The delicate balancing act of being both reformer and ethnic politico, so important to Dever's electoral success, was out of kilter. And Dever had made a classic reformer's mistake, according to his mythical countryman Mr. Dooley. Many years before, Finley Peter Dunne's saloon keeper-philosopher had observed:

> [The reformer] managed to poke a few warrum laws conthrollin' the pleasure iv the poor into the stachoo book, . . . an' whin he's in office, he calls up the Cap'n iv the polis an' says he: If these laws ar-re bad, the way to end thim is to enfoorce thim." Somebody told him that, Hinnissy. It isn't thrue, d'ye mind. I don't care who said it, not if 'twas Willum Shakespere. It isn't thrue. Laws ar-re made to throuble people, an' the more throuble they make the longer they stay in the stachoo book.[29]

Dever could now agree with this assessment. Unfortunately, he had learned the lesson the hard way.

Dever did not respond to his revelation by throwing the city wide open. His personal integrity would not permit the flouting of any laws. Until the end of his term, he continued his dogged enforcement of Prohibition. It was a bitter experience; but nobody had ever promised that the life of a public official would be easy.

One hopes that Dever found consolation in following the path of duty. Perhaps he was comforted by the singular story, well-known at the time, of a certain New York City police commissioner of the 1890s. Confronted with a widely ignored Sunday saloon-closing law, the young official had decided on strict enforcement, hoping that the state legislature would thus be inclined to repeal the ordinance. The commissioner finally succeeded in shutting the taverns. But the blue law was not revoked and the commissioner's party suffered heavy losses at the next election. His own political career was supposed to be over. Yet he came back. The public, in spite of itself, was impressed by the young man's stubborn honesty and forthrightness. They recognized his special dedication. While he had lost in the short run, he gained over the long haul. The young commissioner's name was Theodore Roosevelt.[30]

The Other Side of Office

Dever did not spend all his time enforcing Prohibition. Although those matters took up an inordinate amount of his attention, the mayor was still able to pursue other, more rewarding activities. The Volstead-related violence spread a pall over the second half of Dever's administration, but government went on.

The "great public works projects" were a major source of pride for the mayor. Many long-range improvements reached completion during his term, and Dever got to slice a lot of ribbons. The widening of Ashland and Western avenues was finished, as was the northern extension of Ogden Avenue and the first section of South Lake Shore Drive. In 1925 the monumental Union Station opened after nine years of construction. Later that year the mayor presided at the dedication of the new Grant Park Stadium (now called Soldier Field).[31]

Then there were the projects initiated by the mayor himself. The most notable of these, of course, was Wacker Drive. He also built parks and viaducts and bridges, and his board of education erected a record number of schools. Dever's pet railroad consolidation project never progressed very far, but he had greater success with another type of transportation terminal. Late in 1924 the mayor announced plans to build an airport. Chicago was then the rail hub of America; if the country switched to air travel, His Honor wanted to be ready. He appointed a committee to study sites for the new facility. They finally selected a tract of vacant school-board land ten miles southwest of the Loop, near Sixty-third Street and Cicero Avenue. In May 1926, Municipal Airport opened. Although the first terminal was modest, the mayor's vision was eventually realized. By the start of the air age in the 1950s, Dever's airport had become the world's busiest.[32]

Dever also helped launch the biggest public works project any mayor could hope for, a world's fair. The Columbian Exposition of 1893 had been one of the great artistic triumphs of the late nineteenth century and had alerted the world of Chicago's arrival as a major metropolis. During the mid-1920s, local promoters began to discuss the possibility of staging a new fair. A fair would be good for business; it would also help restore the city's image, somewhat tarnished by the recent exploits of Big Bill and Big Al. Charles H. Wacker and Dr. Otto Schmidt of the Chicago Historical Society laid the idea before the mayor, and he took it up with great enthusiasm. Dever brought together a blue-ribbon citizens' commission to organize the project. He also agreed to serve as the group's chairman for a time, to aid in drumming up the necessary popular and financial support. The mayor was in a hurry—he wanted the fair to be held in 1933, the centennial of Chicago's first incorporation. After Dever left office, his successors carried on with the venture. In the summer of 1933, right on schedule, the Century of Progress Exposition opened its gates in Burnham Park. It was such a success that it ran for a second season.[33]

Transit reform was still bantered about during the second half of Dever's term, although the mayor seemed to have less heart for the subject after the defeat of his traction package. Still, the streetcar franchises would expire in 1927, and nobody knew what would happen then. One group of downstate legislators, led by Will County senator Richard J. Barr, concocted a plan for the state government to assume control of Chicago transit. Dever joined with

his recent referendum foes to beat back Barr's scheme; but the alliance was
only temporary. When the mayor attempted to secure a constitutional amendment giving Chicago complete "home rule" power over local transportation,
his plan was defeated in the state senate by the humiliating margin of 37 to
9. Dever continued to talk about transit. He spoke of building subways and
of modernizing the surface system rolling stock. He hinted about submitting
a new Municipal Ownership package. But in the end, he did nothing—and
neither did anyone else. Just before the streetcar franchises ran out, the city
council hastily passed a six-month extension of the existing grants. This
legislation was supposed to give the lawmakers some extra time to devise a
solution to the transit puzzle. All it did was drag out the agony. The Chicago
Surface Lines, and later the Chicago Rapid Transit, continued to operate
under such "temporary" franchises until the city finally bought out both
carriers in 1947. [34]

Fiscal matters were an ongoing concern. After the administration was forced
to abandon the Griffenhagen budget in 1924, the municipal deficit mounted
alarmingly. Dever tried again to cure the city's financial ills by ordering thirty-
day furloughs for all government employees during 1926, a projected saving
of $2.35 million. As can be expected, this bitter medicine was thoroughly
distasteful to the workers. They enlisted the city council in their cause, and
the aldermen passed a resolution instructing the mayor to secure council
approval before enacting such arbitrary cuts. Dever responded with the charge
that the council was attempting to usurp his constitutional privileges—the
same complaint the aldermen had made about the "executive budget" of
1924. When the mayor would not give way on the layoffs, the council simply
increased the 1926 departmental appropriations by an amount equal to the
wages lost by employees. So once more Dever was defeated on fiscal reform.
Although his department heads were able to improvise some economies, the
municipal budget for 1926 included a deficit of over $2 million. [35]

During this time, Dever took up the housing question in earnest. Mary
McDowell's Public Welfare Department had been involved in various ongoing
studies of the city's poor, culminating in a special conference on housing
problems in April 1926. As a result of the conference, the mayor and the
city council established the Chicago Housing Commission. This semiofficial
advisory body was charged with the task of improving the living conditions
of the city's low-income families. Reflecting the mayor's philosophy of pragmatic idealism, the housing commission was a mixture of social reformers
and business leaders: the former to provide "information and a sense of high
purpose," the latter to get things done. It lasted just over a year, as Dever's
successor chose to let it die a quiet death. The housing commission's major
accomplishment was securing the passage of a state law that eased the restrictions placed on developers of moderate-income housing, a law that had mixed
results. [36] Still, Dever was making a start. In his council days he had fought

for cleaner streets, better recreational facilities, sounder housing. Now, as mayor, he was helping to sustain that work.

Dever also continued to delight in the ceremonial duties of his office. He always seemed ready to greet any celebrity who passed through town and mug for the press photographers. He put on a ten-gallon hat when cowboy actor Tom Mix arrived at City Hall, he talked golf with his "old buddy" Jackie Coogan, he gave entertainer Al Jolson the key to the city. He was on hand to welcome Queen Marie of Rumania when that royal globetrotter, the forerunner of the media-hyped jetsetters, visited Chicago in 1926. When conventions opened, the mayor was there. He took part in inaugurating all manner of gatherings, from the American Bowling Congress tournament to the great Catholic Eucharistic Conference of 1926.[37] Perhaps Dever did not carry it all off with the same dash and aplomb as his New York City counterpart, "Beau James" Walker; but he did his best.

But when the speeches were over, when the bands had stopped playing and the flashpowder had ceased exploding, Dever would return quietly to the shelter of his Kenmore Avenue flat. He was still basically a homebody. Alderman Jacob Arvey, who knew Dever well, recalled that the mayor did not like to spend his evenings at weddings, wakes, and corned-beef and cabbage dinners. He enjoyed more private pleasures, such as reading a pulp detective thriller or going to a movie with Kate. The mayor was not one to stay late at the office; he brought his unfinished work home instead. After Kate had gone to bed, he would roll up his shirt sleeves, light a cigar, and retire to his study with his reports. He worked very late, preferring to rise late the following morning. Kate would be up before him, would have skimmed the morning papers, and would be ready to give him a digest of the day's news when he came to the breakfast table. As his term wore on, Dever tried to pace himself. His health was not always good. He took frequent vacations, usually for a week to ten days at a Southern spa: Excelsior Springs, Missouri, and Biloxi, Mississippi, were two favorites. He seems to have cut down on his hunting and fishing, spending more and more of his leisure hours on the golf course.[38]

Arvey remembered Dever as a not particularly hard-working mayor. That assessment must be qualified. Like most people, Dever did not enjoy spending a great deal of time on things that were uninteresting to him—which included everyday political matters. The mayor left patronage, deals, and general campaign planning to George Brennan and his lieutenants. Dever was still a good party man: he attended political functions when asked, and he remained an effective stump speaker. However, Dever preferred to deal with the "greater issues" of his office. He had moved up through the political ranks, had played the game as a pro. Now it frequently seemed to bore him. Something had changed Dever. Perhaps, it was the long years squirreled away in the courts; perhaps, it was the dignity of his present position; perhaps, it was his association with businessmen and with nonpartisan reformer types. Or maybe it was his own conception of creeping old age, that he had little time to waste on trifles. Dever was a fine city manager. With his love of ceremony, he would have made a splendid constitutional monarch. But, as Charles Merriam observed, the mayor of Chicago wears many hats. Like it or not, Dever was a ranking political leader. And politics, like government, went on.

Democratic Politics: 1925–1926

Shortly after the defeat of the Dever traction package, political reporter William H. Stuart wrote a brief article, "Separation Starts," for the *Chicago American*. The piece concerned the spring travel plans of the leading local Democrats. In 1923, Stuart noted, all organization bigwigs had vacationed together at French Lick Springs, Indiana. Now they were going their different ways. Only County Treasurer P. J. Carr had chosen to return to French Lick in 1925. Mayor Dever and Corporation Counsel Busch were in Excelsior Springs, Missouri; comptroller Martin J. O'Brien and city collector Thomas Keane were in West Baden, Indiana; parks' engineer Edward J. Kelly was in Springfield; Anton Cermak had gone off to California; and George Brennan had completely disappeared. Stuart attached great significance to the diversity of these vacation sites. For him, it was a visible indication that party unity was dissolving, that the Democratic machine was breaking down.[39]

Stuart was no friend of the Democratic regulars, but he did have a point. George Brennan had sought to continue old Roger Sullivan's work of putting together a comprehensive, multiethnic party organization. Brennan had improved on his mentor, winning allegiance from the Harrison-Dunne bloc, making inroads in Progressive Republican and Independent circles, and finally electing a mayor in 1923. Now, there were strains on the alliance and dissension within the regular ranks. Someone once called George Brennan the "centripetal force" within the Chicago Democratic party. During 1925 and 1926 he was taxed mightily to keep all the different elements of his party safely in orbit.

The Harrison-Dunne irregulars had long ago deserted camp and were raising their customary ruckus. Having helped beat down the mayor's transit ordinance, they grew heady with victory. They dreamed now of more power, of a return to those fine days when they were the dominant force in the local party. On August 31, 1925, the Harrison-Dunnites gathered to announce their latest combine—this time they styled themselves Democracy of Illinois. Once again they vowed to overthrow "boss domination" of the Democratic party. To begin with, they planned to run their own slate of candidates in the next spring's primaries. Leaders of the group included the usual anti-organization malcontents: Harrison, Dunne, O'Connell, Alderman Nelson, and the rococo former U.S. senator J. Hamilton Lewis.[40]

One of party leader Brennan's chief faults, the insurgents declared, was his bipartisanism. A dirty word in the 1920s, it meant selling one's own party to the enemy. According to the Harrison-Dunnites, Brennan had such an arrangement with the Crowe-Barrett Republicans. The conspirators would supposedly agree on which party was to win a certain election, and then the other side would slate a hopelessly weak opponent. On some occasions, the cooperation was even more sinister. If one party was stuck with a candidate who would not play ball but was too strong to oppose openly, the "bipartisan manipulators" of the candidate's own party would work quietly for the other side's nominee.[41]

For his part, George Brennan had no great fear for the "Ill Democrats." It was better to have them with you, he reasoned, but it was no great loss if they were against you. They were little more than an occasional nuisance. The charges of bipartisanism were really nothing new, mainly because undercover bipartisanism was nothing new. What was interesting was the insurgents' latching onto the Volstead issue. In their initial publicity releases, Democracy of Illinois called for lenient enforcement of the Prohibition laws, saying that the question should be left up to individual states. Most of the faction's leaders had been supporters of the dust-dry William G. McAdoo for president in 1924. Now they were talking wet.[42]

This was tactics, of course, but it demonstrated the continuing importance of the Prohibition issue, the issue that would not go away. Brennan knew that the mayor's liquor policy was a wedge splitting the party organization. And although the attacks of such outsiders as the Harrison-Dunnites did not ruffle Brennan, internal strife did. Many ward leaders were wondering whether Dever could be elected again; not a few questioned whether he *should* be. Certainly, the mayor's enforcement campaign had cost votes on his transit ordinance. As the *Tribune* observed, there was serious doubt whether the "moralistic load can be offset by the constructive achievements of the Mayor"; the next election might simply become a referendum on "Beer versus South Water Street." Administration loyalists like Alderman Stanley Adamkiewicz might boast of the "two hundred thousand Poles" eager to support the mayor's reelection because of his clean-up activities, but many party elders remained unconvinced. How long they would stay on board was anybody's guess.[43]

Ethnic rivalry also troubled Brennan. Democratic unity, it must be remembered, was an innovation. The party leader knew well that the future of his organization demanded the forging of alliances between the different nationality groups. To achieve this, he had helped promote the political careers of certain bright young people of non-Irish background who shared his pan-nationalist outlook. Among these "new breeders" were Anton Cermak, Joseph Kostner, and Jacob Arvey. The plan seemed to be succeeding, as the party had made notable gains in the city's varied ethnic communities. However, the old suspicions still remained. Many non-Irish politicos mistrusted the Brennanites, resenting the fact that the Gaelic brigade continued to fill thirty-five of the fifty seats on the party's central committee. On the other hand, many old-line Irish nationalists were contemptuous of the part the "foreigners" wanted to play in the Democratic establishment. Such close Brennan associates as Martin J. O'Brien and T. J. Crowe did not share the party leader's vision and appeared willing to repolarize the organization along nationality lines before they would share any more power with the non-Irish. The old ethnic wars threatened to break out anew at any moment.[44]

All thorough 1925, Brennan watched the cracks in the organization grow deeper. He managed to patch over some of them, calling upon both his remarkable talent of persuasion and his formidable powers as party boss. Then he played his masterstroke: he announced that he would run for the U.S. Senate.

Perhaps the old backroom boss thought that the time had arrived to become respectable. Perhaps he was trying to emulate his mentor, Roger Sullivan. Possibly, he was looking for a graceful way out of the everyday infighting of local politics. Whenever great decisions are made, there are numerous reasons. However, the crucial factor appears to have been Brennan's desire to keep the party together. Personal ambition must have had little to do with the senate idea, for the 1926 race was a definite long shot. Illinois was a Republican state. The Democratic votes coming out of Chicago were nearly always overwhelmed by the rural small-town returns from downstate. If that were not handicap enough, there was the added factor of G.O.P. dominance in national politics during the 1920s. The Republican senatorial nominee would enjoy so many advantages going into the contest that all the ambitious young men on the Democratic side stayed carefully away from candidacy. Nobody wanted to play sacrificial lamb—nobody but Brennan, that is.[45]

The senate campaign was Brennan's opportunity to preserve party unity. By heading the ticket, he hoped to act once more as the centripetal force. He had become party chief because of his ability to bring together diverse factions. His candidacy could serve as a visible rallying point for Chicago Democrats. It mattered little if Brennan lost his own election. Local and state offices were always more important to the organization, and to win those contests the regulars had to stay united. Thus Brennan decided to become a senatorial candidate in the spring of 1926.[46]

The details of Brennan's campaign do not concern our study, except in one connection. Early on, the candidate declared that he would run for the senate solely as an advocate of Prohibition repeal.[47] Quite a few eyebrows were raised, then, when the well-known Volstead-enforcing mayor of Chicago began to take an active role in the contest. Since at about this time Dever started to find serious fault with the Prohibition laws, cynics claimed that the mayor's conversion rather neatly coincided with Brennan's emergence as

a candidate. Whatever the motivation for his shift, Dever campaigned vigorously for his friend. In September, Brennan fell off a speaker's platform and
was hospitalized. Dever then assumed the full burden of the senate race. He
visited cities and villages throughout the state, carrying the injured candidate's
message to the voters. So, as the campaign drew to a close, its most prominent
feature had become the sight of Chicago's mayor scurrying around to such
far-removed places as Peoria and Rockford to denounce the Prohibition act. [48]

The elections went about as predicted. Brennan's slate had easily brushed
aside the "Ill Democrats" in the primaries, and the November balloting was
another organization triumph. The Democrats won all the important county
offices, including the patronage-rich post of sheriff. Although the Republicans
took a majority of the municipal judgeships, the Democratic party did well
enough in the other contests to register a net gain of 1400 patronage jobs.
As had been expected, Brennan was defeated for the U.S. Senate by Frank
L. Smith. But the party leader ran very well, carrying Chicago by 80,000
votes, and coming within 68,000 of winning statewide. Political analysts
noted that Brennan had scored considerable gains even in the city's Republican
strongholds. [49]

Brennan had held the party together. The organization had closed ranks
and performed admirably. Intraparty conflict had been submerged by party
unity. Brennan was playing for time, and he was doing it superbly. Every
election helped institutionalize the concept of a united party. While the Republicans were still involved in their family feuding, the Democratic party
of Cook County was evolving into an organized, efficient amalgamation of
diverse elements, a modern corporation engaged in the business of winning
elective offices.

The 1927 mayoral elections would come next. That would be the resiliency
test for the party organization. Victory would enable the Democrats to consolidate their control over local politics. The party machinery appeared to
be in fine running order as Brennan and the regular leaders began to prepare
for the new campaign. Meanwhile, the man who sat in the mayor's chair
pondered the political future and tried to decide what to do next.

9

The Unmaking of the Mayor
1927

The Reluctant Incumbent

■ It was not altogether certain that the mayor wanted a second term. Four years in the executive pressure-cooker had had their effect. Government had become a strain and politics an ordeal. Dever saw little need to go on, many reasons to retire. His health was not at its best. Kate was urging him to step down. There was a standing offer from a trust company for him to become a vice-president at $30,000 per year. He could travel: go to Europe again, or perhaps to the Holy Land. He would have time to play more golf. He could write his memoirs. Hadn't he done enough already? Hadn't he fulfilled his duty?[1]

Early in his administration, Dever had said that he would serve only one term. Nobody had taken him seriously—office seekers like to pose as reluctant suitors. But the mayor continued to drop hints to City Hall reporters that he intended to retire in 1927. Sometimes he spoke to them of the joys of private life. On other occasions, he mused about becoming a state supreme court justice or a U.S. senator. It was true that, most of the time, Dever talked as if he planned on remaining mayor indefinitely. As his term drew to a close, though, his retirement discourses become more frequent.[2] Even the cynics started wondering if perhaps there was some truth to it, that Dever really wanted out.

Not that there was universal support within the party for four more years of Dever. Some Democratic ward leaders were eager to be rid of him. The mayor's police policies had made him unpopular in certain sections of the city, and these politicians were convinced that he could not win again. One alderman, looking ahead to his own reelection campaign, observed that he would have to "forget Dever entirely" if he hoped to be successful. Another declared that the 9500-vote plurality Dever had won in his ward might become a 9500-vote deficit next time around. Alderman Toman and Congressman

Sabath both said flatly that the mayor could not carry their districts. As the party's slating conferences approached, anti-Dever pamphlets began to appear around City Hall cloakrooms. The anonymous tract-writers blasted the mayor's record on Personal Liberty and his "broken promises" on transit reform. They called on the party elders to dump Dever and find a more electable mayoral candidate.[3]

There was no shortage of potential mayors within the Chicago Democratic organization during those last weeks of 1926. Every time Dever made some enigmatic remark about his future plans new candidates came out of the woodwork. Anton Cermak still had his boosters: he had done a businesslike job running the county board and had had four years to make himself respectable. Ed Kelly was another possibility. The parks' engineer had shown real savvy while managing Brennan's recent senate campaign; he might be just the man to nominate as another "nonpolitical" candidate. Sheriff-elect P. J. Carr, another of Brennan's "new breeders" and the party's champion vote getter, was also frequently mentioned. Meanwhile, minor booms were under way for such men as Judge Joseph Sabath (the congressman's brother), South Side ward boss Pat Nash, and former Congressman James McAndrews. One veteran politico even suggested that George Brennan should run for the job himself.[4]

However, William E. Dever remained the first choice of the organization hierarchy. Brennan and his confidants simply felt that the mayor was their strongest candidate. Dever possessed the advantages of incumbency and a record of achievement. He promised the best chance of attracting large blocs of votes from independents, old Progressives, and straying regular Republicans. With ex-Mayor Thompson looming as the Republican nominee, only Dever was a sufficiently prominent public figure to face Big Bill on equal footing. Dever's candidacy would also help preserve party unity. Although a great many ward committeemen did not like the mayor, Brennan believed that they could be persuaded to close ranks around an incumbent; if Dever dropped out, there might be a wide-open primary fight that would tear the party apart. Of the other likely candidates, only P. J. Carr seemed to be a suitable alternative to Dever.[5] He had already served two terms as county treasurer, was young, handsome, and popular. But the sheriff-elect died suddenly on November 16, 1926. With Carr gone, it had to be Dever.

Yet the mayor still hesitated to commit himself. He knew that another campaign would resurrect the Prohibition contoversy; the poison-pen pamphlets had made that clear. Even Dever's supporters were bringing up the issue. One backer, writing the mayor to urge a second term, tactfully suggested that perhaps "police activity should be carried on in less spectacular fashion." Dever himself had publicly acknowledged that the Volstead matter had been blown into epic dimension. During his senate testimony, he had ruefully observed:

Suppose a man desires to be mayor of Chicago tomorrow. Suppose the great political parties should nominate separate candidates for that great office. . . . Who is going to win? The man who has had the longest public experience, and who has dealt most intimately with the great construction problems of Chicago? Is he going to win? Is that going to be the determining question? Not at all! Not at all! . . . He will go into office, whatever his character, however efficient or inefficient he may be—he will win dependent upon his attitude upon the Prohibition question.

Dever saw himself as a wet with the unhappy obligation of carrying out the dry law. He knew what many of the ward chiefs thought of his actions and was not about to be crucified on the Volstead issue. If he could not be guaranteed united organization support, he simply would not run.[6]

So Dever went on testing the political waters, inviting a variety of party elders to his fifth-floor office for consultation. The assessments he received were cautious and the enthusiasm of many was lukewarm. Most of his visitors saw a difficult campaign ahead. But George Brennan persisted in his conviction, and he was the one whose views mattered most. The party leader told Dever that he must be a candidate for another term. The city needed him, and so did the party. The carpers and critics within the organization would be silenced, Brennan pledged. The Democrats would stand steadfast with their mayor.[7]

Meanwhile, Julius Rosenwald was preparing to throw his considerable influence into the balance. Rosenwald assembled a select group of ten business heavyweights, including two railroad presidents and an assortment of banking executives, and called on the mayor at City Hall. They told him emphatically that he must run again. If he refused, Big Bill Thompson would likely be elected—and everyone knew what that would mean. "You have redeemed the city from the terrible ravages of the eight years preceding your election," Rosenwald said to Dever; "it is your duty to see that the good work is carried on." The businessmen promised Dever their full moral and financial support in the struggle ahead. Observers of the event made much of the fact that all but two of the delegation were registered Republicans.[8]

Rosenwald and his associates seem to have finally made up Dever's mind. After their visit, fresh reports began circulating that the mayor would definitely go for a second term. To give final confirmation to the rumors, George Brennan now orchestrated a series of "grass-roots" demonstrations of support. Delegations of party regulars were formed in each of the fifty wards, then trooped up to the mayor's office. One by one their spokesmen came forward to praise the chief executive and beg him to continue his wise leadership. Dever responded by telling the callers how touched he was by their loyalty. He had just about sorted matters out, he said, and would make an announcement shortly.[9]

The mayor addresses a Polish gathering at Riverview Park. Paying close attention is party leader George Brennan (just left of the microphone). *(Chicago Historical Society: ICHi 20810)*

Despite his aversion to a second term, Dever gave in to his sense of duty. Brennan, Rosenwald, and his own conscience convinced him that he was indispensable. The rugged election he faced could still be won: he was promised a solid party organization behind him and powerful support from the outside. Possibly most important in Dever's decision was his own sense that his work was unfinished. He was currently in the middle of numerous large-scale public works projects; the transit problem was still unresolved; government reorganization remained in limbo; the public schools had not been completely straightened out. He had been forced to spend too much time on police matters and had not accomplished all that he had set out to do. Perhaps the next four years would be better. And there was still the dream of national office.

On the last day of 1926, Dever made his decision public. He would seek a second term as mayor of Chicago. He would give it another chance.

The Return of Big Bill

When we last left William Hale Thompson, he was trying to stay out of prison. Early in 1923, state's attorney Robert E. Crowe had brought Fred Lundin and some other Thompson cronies to trial for raiding the public school treasury. Public furor over the scandal had forced Big Bill out of the mayor's race that year. He had gone off to Hawaii to soothe his disappointment, returning home only to be a character witness at Lundin's trial. Thompson's testimony had helped the "Poor Swede" win acquittal, but all was over between the two men. Thompson blamed his mentor for costing him a third term. He refused even to speak to Lundin. Where once there had been fraternal warmth, an icy feud developed.[10]

Over the next four years, Big Bill Thompson jumped all over the political gameboard, looking for a useful connection. Unlike the Democrats, who were building a unified organization, the Republicans of Chicago still dealt in factions and personality politics. Affiliations changed constantly; one contemporary political writer had to provide his treatise with an appendix of Republican factional chronology, to keep everything straight![11] Big Bill spent his exile trying to hitch onto whatever group could help him return to power. He also did his best to remain in the public eye. His movements during the Dever years are an important story. In many ways, the odyssey of William Hale Thompson illuminates the significant developments in the local Republican party.

After the Lundin trial, Thompson laid low for awhile. Nothing was heard from him until the last days of 1923, when he came out loudly for Governor Small's reelection. This had been expected and caused no sensation. What was more noteworthy was Thompson's decision to support ex-Governor Charles Deneen in the U.S. Senate primary against incumbent Medill McCormick. Big Bill was no great friend of Deneen, but he had ample reason to embrace him—most of it negative. Senator McCormick was one of the *Tribune*-owning McCormicks, and Thompson had a fine hatred for that newspaper. The defeat McCormick had handed Big Bill in the 1918 senatorial primary continued to smart, as well. Also a factor in Thompson's gambit was the presence of two prominent enemies in the McCormick camp: Robert E. Crowe and Edward Brundage. Crowe was personally despised, since his investigations had helped drive Thompson from office. Big Bill's animosity toward Brundage, the Illinois attorney general, was more a matter of courtesy toward Len Small; Brundage had once brought the governor into court on corruption charges. So Thompson and Small reached a convenient understanding with their long-time rival Charlie Deneen. The former mayor returned to the campaign trail in his grand old style, banging away at his foes, claiming that Brundage had "killed" Governor Small's wife (she had died of a heart attack the night of his acquittal). It almost seemed worth the effort. The Small-Thompson-Deneen candidates swept the Republican primaries. Of the enemy, only Crowe survived.[12]

During the summer lull between primary and general election, Big Bill concocted an outlandish scheme to stay in public view. He announced that he was organizing an expedition to sail for South America. His party would search for a legendary tree-climbing fish that Thompson said he had read of in "some scientific treatise." That July, thousands of curious citizens came down to the Michigan Avenue Bridge to watch the good ship *Big Bill* embark on its historic voyage of discovery. As the little cypress yawl moved slowly down the river toward South America, Thompson stood on the deck, waving his sombrero at the appreciative spectators. Once away from the crowds, Big Bill and his friends jumped ship and returned home by train. He was delighted by the publicity given his venture. Chicago voters had been reminded that William Hale Thompson was still around.[13]

Thompson resumed his energetic campaigning for Len Small and Charles Deneen, helping them defeat their lackluster Democratic opponents. But early in 1925, Big Bill suffered two severe blows to his comeback plans. After taking office for a second term, Governor Small began fraternizing with Fred Lundin and soon granted the "Poor Swede" control of state patronage jobs in Chicago. Since Small was well aware of the Thompson-Lundin feud (as was just about everyone in the state), he had obviously concluded that he needed Lundin more than he needed Thompson. Caught off balance by Small's action, Big Bill turned to Deneen for help. He offered to campaign for the senators's 1926 slate of candidates, in return for Deneen's support in the 1927 mayoral race. Senator Deneen had other plans, however; he was already grooming Edward Litsinger to be the next mayor of Chicago. Big Bill once more found himself out in the cold.[14]

This situation did not last long. Thompson had too large a personal following, was too effective a campaigner to be left at large. By 1926 he had hooked up with his one-time adversaries, Robert Crowe, Edward Brundage, and Charles Barrett. The newspapers labeled this latest Republican faction the *C-B-B-T.* As the price for Thompson's allegiance, the new alliance named Big Bill's friend George Harding as its candidate for sheriff.[15]

The C-B-B-T began a quiet campaign against the Small-Lundin and Deneen slates in the spring primaries of 1926. Thompson, though, had his own ideas about political tactics. He announced that the Republican primary that year would be contested on the issues of "America First" and "No World Court." Perhaps these slogans had some place in the U.S. Senate campaign; it was difficult to see what international relations had to do with the sheriff of Cook County or the assessor's office. Big Bill did not seem to mind; he continued to stump for his candidates as the only hope for preserving American freedom. And he also found time to tweak his personal rivals. In April, the one-time mayor of the country's second city appeared on stage at a Loop theatre carrying two caged rats. He addressed the rodents as Fred and Doc— for Fred Lundin and Dr. John Dill Robertson, Lundin's latest protege. While the overflow audience guffawed and cheered, Thompson carried on a spirited half-hour conversation with his two pets. The next day, "Big Bill's Rat Show" drew banner headlines in all the local papers. It was a vintage Thompson performance.[16]

Thompson and the C-B-B-T swept aside their competitors in the Republican primaries, then ran into some setbacks. The McSwiggin shooting and the aborted investigation proved highly embarrassing to State's Attorney Crowe, casting a shadow of suspicion over his administration. Meanwhile, the C-B-B-T-backed senatorial nominee, Frank L. Smith, had become the target of a federal probe into his imaginative methods of campaign financing. But Big Bill himself was riding high. He had found a secure political base for his return assault on the mayor's office.[17]

William Hale Thompson, like Carter Harrison, was a "personality" politician. He won elections and retained influence through the force of his own charisma. Even after eight years as mayor of Chicago, Big Bill had been unable to build a permanent political organization. Instead of fostering unity, he had kept the Republican party factionalized. He quarreled with McCormick, Deneen, Brundage, Crowe, Small, and a dozen others. Thompson could not work for a long-range goal, patiently assembling an enduring alliance of different forces. He operated on personal pique. When Small befriended Lundin, Thompson broke with the governor. Let Deneen say that he would not endorse Big Bill for mayor, and Thompson was off somewhere else, seeking immediate gratification. He was unable to swallow his personal pride and ambitions to build for greater future power, like Roger Sullivan and George Brennan. Thompson's vision extended no further than the next election. If he could improvise a makeshift coalition to pull him through an imminent contest, that was well and good. He would worry about the next election when it came. In this shortsighted philosophy, Thompson was not unique in his party; other Chicago Republicans operated on the same basis. Big Bill was merely the most visible.

With a new mayoral season coming upon him, Thompson moved into action. In October 1926, while his party was still busy trying to salvage the state elections, the Thompsonites held a kickoff campaign rally at the Medinah Temple. Five thousand of them gathered to be entertained by Sophie Tucker and harangued by Big Bill's corps of orators. They sang a marching song written for the occasion, "America First, Last, and Always." Finally, Thompson appeared. He passed out pledge cards and told his friends to go out and hustle signatures. He would run for mayor if the people demonstrated that they wanted him.[18]

What followed was inevitable. Even widespread Republican defeats in the November elections could not detract from the enthusiasm of the Thompson canvassers. On the evening of December 10, 1926, another meeting was called, this time at the Grand Ballroom of the Sherman House. One by one the ward leaders came forward with their neatly tied batches of pledge cards and dumped them on the stage. Thompson stood off to the side, sniffling with a head cold, as the pile grew. The master of ceremonies stepped up to announce that fully 430,000 voters had endorsed cards calling for Big Bill's restoration to power. The speaker then walked over to Thompson, plucked the cowboy hat from his head, and threw it onto the mound of paper. The ballroom rocked with screams and applause.[19] The 1927 mayoral race was on. It would be a campaign that Chicago would not soon forget.

Dever versus Thompson

As George Brennan had promised, the Democratic organization rallied around Dever. Cermak, Kelly, and the others were told they would have to swallow their personal ambitions for another four years; they went along quietly. Even the insurgents were peaceful. For a time it appeared Carter Harrison might enter the primary with the backing of Pat Nash, but the old warhorse finally declined the honor. Barrett O'Hara, Dunne's lieutenant governor, was in the race for awhile, then quit. Dever was left with only token opposition for the Democratic nomination.[20]

The Republican field was more crowded, with two challengers contesting Thompson. Edward Litsinger, who had run poorly against Lueder in 1923, was the candidate of Deneen and the senator's new ally, Brundage. Meanwhile, Dr. John Dill Robertson, one-time city health commissioner and more recently head of the West Parks Board, carried the tattered standard of Small and Lundin. It soon became obvious that Thompson had little to fear from either of these worthies. Robertson saw the handwriting on the wall early and dropped out of the primary, preferring to take a crack at the general election as an independent. Litsinger stayed in and proved to be as inept a candidate as the last time around. Big Bill soon forgot about him and set his sights on Dever.[21]

Thompson was swift to snatch the initiative of the campaign away from the Democrats. Dever felt he had accomplished much during his term and was prepared to contrast his administration with Thompson's erratic record in office. He hoped for a "polite debate" on issues of substance, but there was scant room for rational dialogue on Big Bill's agenda. Thompson did not talk of transit problems, or government reorganization, or even public works. He said that there was only one issue worth discussing in the current campaign: America First.[22]

Thompson had gotten a great deal of mileage out of the splendidly vague patriotism plank in past campaigns and reasoned it would be effective again. He also found a perfect target for his 100-percent Americanism in School Superintendent McAndrew. The grim-faced educator had performed creditably in office, but managed to antagonize a number of powerful ward leaders and most of the city's teachers. He was clearly a man heading for a fall. Now additional facts came out. It seemed that McAndrew had once made some disparaging remarks about the famous painting *The Spirit of '76*, saying that it was jingoistic and did not give an accurate representation of the horrors of war. He had also refused to let city schoolchildren collect money for the restoration of the storied warship "Old Ironsides." Meanwhile, McAndrew's allies on the school board had authorized a series of controversial history texts—books that said, for example, that the British considered George Washington a rebel and a traitor.[23]

When word of these transgressions reached Big Bill, he took up his sword. All these things constituted a pattern, he claimed. McAndrew was certainly not a good American; he must be a British agent. He was at the heart of King George's conspiracy to undermine American independence. The king would stop at nothing to get back his old colonies, Thompson bellowed, even if that meant corrupting the minds of impressionable schoolchildren. But never fear! William Hale Thompson had come to the rescue! All patriotic, right-thinking Americans should join his crusade to save their beloved land. They must get rid of that renegade McAndrew and get rid of the man who had helped put him in office: Dever.[24]

So Thompson roamed about from rally to rally, ranting against King George, McAndrew, and Dever, dedicating his energies to the task at hand. And while he moved among the voters, he began to sense another useful issue: Personal Liberty. Although he had a history of enforcing blue laws and was privately inclined toward the drys, Thompson's sensitive political nose was quick to sniff out public sentiment. He began to hammer away at Dever's Prohibition record, and hammer hard. He told one crowd: "The Dever administration has made one of the greatest records in Chicago's history for closing up business. When I'm elected, we'll not only reopen the places these people have closed, we'll open 10,000 new ones!" Thompson did not specify what sort of "businesses" he was discussing, but his message was unmistakable: Big Bill would let the city run wide open. He would not send his police out on the "trail of the lonesome pint." He was for Personal Liberty—first, last, and always. "I'm as wet as the Atlantic Ocean!" he roared.[25]

Many Dever supporters did not take Thompson seriously. The outrageous baiting of the British monarch convinced most of the independents and good-government reformers that Big Bill could be easily beaten; so they ignored Thompson as he built up strength. Harold Ickes saw what was developing and attempted to organize a coalition of independent Republicans but was met with monumental foot dragging. Many reasoned that there would be plenty of time to deal with Thompson after the Republican primary—if, indeed, he even survived it. Some thought it would be a simple task to finish off this moronic demagogue; the whole operation would cost only about $15,000, they laughed, "Who's afraid of the Big Bad Bill?" *Time* magazine called him a "vaudeville actor" and said he would be no match for "popular, able William E. Dever."[26]

The professionals knew their enemy better. George Brennan respected Thompson's skills as a campaigner and his large personal following. He recognized that Big Bill's two elections to the mayoralty had not come about through accident. And Brennan could also read the signs. By the middle of January the momentum was clearly swinging into Big Bill's direction. The Democratic leader decided he could wait no longer. Fully a month before the primaries he called in his committeemen to launch Dever's campaign.[27]

The mayor was sent out on the hustings to make a few speeches. Gone was the reluctance of earlier days. He told one audience that "I'm going in feeling as young, fresh, and strong as if I had never been in politics," and he seemed to mean it. Dever generally stuck to his own record, bringing up such things as Wacker Drive or the fifty-one schools he had built or the pure milk ordinance he had passed. He promised to continue his building program. He turned shovels to start the widening of LaSalle Street and the construction of the North Damen Avenue Bridge. He promised to build the long-awaited subway under State Street. As for the knotty problem of crime, Dever simply said that he had done his best. "No superman can be found to eliminate crime," he told a Norwegian fraternal group; "no such man exists because we are looking for [somebody] to save us from ourselves."[28]

The party primaries of 1927 were held on February 22—Washington's Birthday, the America Firsters happily noted. Dever was renominated by the Democrats with 149,453 votes against the 13,099 tallied by his minor league opponent. On the Republican side, Thompson buried Litsinger by a count of 342,337 to 161,947. Big Bill's total was the largest vote ever recorded in a Chicago primary.[29] Perhaps most ominous for the Democrats was the fact that Thompson's *victory margin* was larger than Dever's entire vote.

The Deverites had a ready answer for the huge Thompson totals. They claimed that many of the mayor's supporters had not bothered to vote in the uncontested Democratic primary, and that many more had crossed over to help nominate Thompson, the less formidable opponent. George Brennan pointedly called another meeting of his committeemen to bring the supposed bolters back in line. The mayor himself said that he was unconcerned with the primary results. He contended that Thompson had reached his peak and would decline in the weeks ahead. Dever predicted that the 160,000 Litsinger supporters would now move to his side. With the 150,000 voters he had already attracted and the 300,000 whom he said had stayed home, that would give him over 600,000 votes in the April 5 finale.[30]

With the battle lines now definitely drawn, the Chicago press became actively involved in the campaign. Dever received most of the newspaper endorsements. Four of the city's dailies backed him, as did leading Polish, Jewish, and Italian papers. Thompson's support came from his traditional allies, the two Hearst organs and the black *Daily Defender* (although he did manage to gain endorsement from the city's second Italian paper, the Republican leaning *L'Italia*).[31] As usual, the *Chicago Tribune* led the offensive against Big Bill; for the moment it forgot its running feud with Dever over Prohibition. With so much at stake, minor differences could be passed over. The day after the primaries, the city's leading newspaper laid out its scenario for the final campaign:

> No one is obligated to guess as to Thompson or as to Dever. The city has had experience with both and knows exactly what to expect. It is not exploring unknown territory. Both regions are mapped out and signposted. The issue is between common sense and plain bunk. It is between decency and disreputability, between sensible people and political defectives, between honesty in administration and the percentage system.[32]

Thompson's extraordinary victory was also sobering to the independents and the good government reformers, and they finally got around to girding for battle. Yet, they continued to run helter-skelter. Ickes got into a disagreement with Colonel Sprague over organizational matters and fired off a six-page letter to the mayor, asking him to arbitrate the dispute.[33] Dever was evidently unable to reach a decision, for he allowed the formation of two distinct campaign committees. Instead of the united front of 1923, Progressive-Independent-Republican-Reformer efforts were divided between the Independent Republicans for Dever Committee and the Peoples Dever for Mayor Committee. The two groups were not mutually exclusive, and there was some dual membership: Graham Taylor, for instance, was listed on both committees. But this arrangement led to a great deal of confusion and duplication. Although the regular Democratic leaders tried to bring the two factions together, they remained stubbornly separate throughout the campaign.

Of the two groups, the Independent Republicans for Dever Committee was more business oriented. Its membership included such people as merchants Julius Rosenwald, W. A. Wieboldt, and Sewell Avery; university presidents Max Mason and W. Dill Scott; and prominent socialites Potter Palmer, Edward Ryerson, Jr., and Louise deKoven Bowen. Attorney Orville James Taylor was chairman. The Independent Republicans for Dever initially hoped to raise $500,000 to conduct their campaign but soon had to lower their goal to $150,000. They concentrated on publishing full-page newspaper advertisements in the *Tribune* and other friendly journals and did not devote much effort to individual precinct work. Their dignified approach to the campaign was indicated by their choice of slogan: "Dever and Decency."[34]

The Peoples Dever for Mayor Committee, on the other hand, was led by Ickes and the more aggressive elements. Among these were Robins, Merriam, Jane Addams, Harriet Vittum, and Donald Richberg. As they had done in

1923, many of these prominent citizens went into the wards and actively stumped for Dever, with the regular Democratic organization helping coordinate assignments.[35] They fought hard, and they did not hesitate to adopt some of Thompson's tactics. When the Republican candidate returned to Chicago after a short vacation in the South, the Peoples Committee issued the following announcement:

> BIG BILL THE SHRINKING VIOLET—Citizens are advised that William Hale Thompson will arrive in Chicago shortly. With his usual modesty, he will attempt to slip into town unnoticed. Only one or two bands will be at the station to meet him. An appreciative citizenry ought to disregard William's shrinking habits and aversions to publicity. They ought to turn out in countless thousands to greet this heroic return from Georgia (named for King George). As they march down the street the citizenry will be able to tell William and the band apart if they look closely. William will be wearing a cowboy hat.[36]

The Peoples Committee continued their offensive throughout the campaign. They were a most effective part of the Dever effort. But one wonders how much more effective that effort might have been if they had been able to work together with the Independent Republicans for Dever.

The Democratic nominee, meanwhile, kept to his higher road. Dever had not wanted to campaign, and did so only because he was needed. He was determined to concentrate on real issues, addressing them coolly and rationally. He knew that the King George stuff was nonsense. "The job of being mayor of Chicago has to do with managing the business affairs of a big business city," Dever told reporters. "The mayor's duties have nothing to do with regulating international affairs [or] freedom for the downtrodden people of Mars." What he had in mind was a "decent, friendly discussion—without malice or sensationalism—of the needs and dangers of our city."[37]

The mayor balked at doing anything that would compromise the dignity of his office. For example, some Democratic publicists accidentally learned that Dever still carried membership in the tanners' union. Since no previous Chicago mayor had ever been a union man, they devised a plan to dress Dever in overalls and photograph him back at one of the old tanneries on Goose Island. It was as least as valid a tactic as all those pictures of President Coolidge allegedly farming in patent-leather shoes, and it might win some blue-collar votes. But Dever refused to go along with the scheme. He said he would not descend to the level of "that clown" Thompson: he would win the election on his own terms, and that was all there was to it.[38]

After awhile, though, Thompson's badgering got to the mayor. When Big Bill called him a "left-handed Irishman" for supporting King George's stooge McAndrew, Dever's Gaelic temper exploded. Nobody could call *him* a left-handed Irishman; Bill Dever was right-handed all the way! "My father's name was Emmett and that's my middle name," he told a St. Patrick's Day gathering, with more emotion than accuracy. "My grandfather was chased out of Ireland the day Robert Emmett was executed!" As for Thompson's repeated calls to patriotism, "nobody needs any blarney about 100 percent Americans." The Republican candidate was making an issue out of nothing. "We're all Americans First here," Dever said, "and nobody has a monopoly on that."[39]

While Dever was busy getting his Irish up, his supporters began their counterattack. Democratic speakers started asking questions about Thompson's close ties with Samuel Insull, and hinted that their opponent had been a tool of the transit and utilities trusts. They also dissected Big Bill's Prohibition record. They pointed out that Thompson had once signed a pledge to oppose Sunday closing laws, then reneged after taking office. Voters were also reminded of Big Bill's recent support for dry senatorial candidate Frank L. Smith. Nor did the Dever forces neglect the "America First" angle. They made dark references to Thompson's notorious pro-Germanism during the past war and delighted in contrasting his bellicose rhetoric with his nonexistent military record. "Where was Big Bill Thompson in the Spanish-American War and the World War?" Charles Merriam asked one rally; "I'll tell you—he was playing football in the Spanish-American War, and he hid under the bed in the World War!"[40]

The Deverites continued to hammer away at Thompson's dubious record as mayor. At one point, the Republican nominee announced that he would run on the slogan "Dever Didn't," since the incumbent had been a do-nothing mayor. The Democrats responded with a list of things that Dever "didn't do":

Dever didn't appoint school trustees who were sent to jail.
Dever didn't name a school-board attorney who was guilty of fraud.
Dever didn't make a fortune for real estate experts.
Dever didn't force his employees to contribute to his campaign fund.
Dever didn't have a whisper of scandal in the four years he has been mayor—
a record in Chicago.[41]

Some Democratic strategists felt that their campaign should be even more aggressive. They argued that dredging up old Thompson hypocrisy and scandals was not the answer. As the Republican primary had demonstrated, voters had a short memory. Dever's best chance lay in making a more emotional appeal to the citizenry. Candidates did not win elections by scoring debater's points. Chicagoans had to be made to feel what a grave calamity a Thompson victory would be.[42] As March wore on, the Dever campaign tilted more in this direction.

The race issue is instructive. The city's black population had been growing rapidly during the decade, and at first the Democrats sought to capture a share of their vote. The defection of some prominent black Thompsonites, coupled with Julius Rosenwald's endorsement of Dever, gave them high hopes. Big Bill's massive black vote in the primary ended this dream, so the Democrats decided to go the other way. A few days after the primary, squads of police descended on the Second and Third wards, padlocking businesses and arresting hundreds of black citizens. Chief Collins explained that he was simply enforcing public order by closing down illegal nightclubs and gambling houses; the Thompson forces screamed "voter intimidation" and "cossack raids."[43] Although it is impossible today to discover who was correct in this affair, what happened afterward is all too clear.

At one early campaign rally, Thompson had stopped to embrace a little black boy. Now the Democrats flooded the city with crude drawings of Big Bill kissing black babies. Shabbily-dressed black men began to appear in white neighborhoods, supposedly soliciting Republican votes but mainly panicking nervous property owners. A plot to lure thousands of black people to a fake Thompson rally in the "white only" Loop was uncovered. A black horseman in colonial garb was sent galloping through downtown streets, shouting "The British are coming! Tell Bill." Meanwhile, at Democratic gatherings, calliopes pumped out the song, "Bye, Bye, Blackbird."[44]

Dever himself took no part in this mudslinging; yet neither did he renounce it. He tried to stay above the battle. His supporters, however, actively played on white fears. Raymond Robins contended that Thompson "offers to open the city as a haven to all the lower type of colored man, the crap-shooters and the crooked Negroes from all parts of America." Former state's attorney Maclay Hoyne claimed that Big Bill had been responsible for the great 1919 race riot. Democratic leader George Brennan put matters more simply. "Mayor Dever will be re-elected," he said "[because] this is a white man's town."[45]

The Democrats' racist tactics should be viewed in their broader context. The party had long used the Prohibition issue to rally its ethnic alliance, since support for wet measures was one area where most of the nationality groups could agree. Dever's dry policies had made this approach impractical. Because there were still relatively few black voters and they seemed to be in Thompson's pocket, the race question was a ready-made substitute. It was one more way of keeping Brennan's coalition together. Nor need the reformers be abandoned. If they were not as virulently racist as some of the ethnic groups, many of these people viewed blacks with condescension and suspicion: witness Robins's crap-shooter tirade. Racial bias was such an ingrained feature of the times that even the enlightened were afflicted with it.[46] Using the spectre of black power to build inter-ethnic unity came hand-in-hand with the emergence of a substantial black presence in the city during the 1920s. It has remained an unfortunate practice in Chicago politics down to the present.

As in 1923, religious bigotry made its appearance in the mayoral campaign.

Before the battle got hot. Mayoral candidates Thompson and Dever with their wives (1927). *(Chicago Historical Society)*

Thompson's "King George" rantings served as the vehicle. Whispers began to be heard that Big Bill was not really gunning for the British monarch, as everyone thought; his actual target was George Cardinal Mundelein, the powerful Roman Catholic archbishop. Both ultra-Catholics and Ku Klux-types peddled this wacky interpretation to their respective constituencies. Many other sectarian charges were thrown around as well, and both sides seem to have been equally guilty. It was just another bizarre factor in a bizarre campaign, which had become so ludicrous that visiting philosopher Will Durant left Chicago wondering whether democracy was dead.[47]

There was a third candidate involved in the donnybrook. Doctor Robertson was listed on the ballot as the nominee of something called the People's Ownership—Smash the Crime Rings Party. Fred Lundin's candidate went his lonely way, spewing forth venom against both major candidates and receiving less and less attention as the campaign heated up. Dever ignored him completely. Big Bill made a few nasty remarks about the doctor's eating habits, then turned to more important matters. No one thought Robertson had the least chance of winning. Discussion of his candidacy centered mainly on whether he would draw away more votes from Dever or Thompson.[48]

Perhaps that would be important. For the first time in memory, both parties were united. The Republicans had surprised themselves by coming together after Big Bill's primary victory. Senator Deneen and his protege Litsinger made their peace with Thompson and Crowe. Even the wandering Brundage came back. Only Small and Lundin remained aloof, backing Robertson—and maybe that did not hurt so much, after all. In any event, the newly friendly Republicans were so pleased with their alliance they held a banquet in celebration. They gathered at a North Side hotel a week before the election, to trade flowery toasts and saccharine tributes while damning the perfidy of the Democrats. Forgotten were the recriminations and the insults of the past. The *Tribune* watched these strange political fellows bedding down together and could not help recalling their past enmity. The paper wryly commented that there was no need for the Democratic nominee to plan an elaborate final campaign assault against his opponent. "Mr. Dever's case [against Thompson] could be made complete merely by presenting Republican evidence against the Republican candidate."[49]

Sour grapes, the Thompsonites retorted; and they had good reason to be smug. Thompson's personal magnetism and the party's united front seemed to be having their effect. The *Tribune's* own straw poll continued to show Big Bill with a lead over Dever of about 52 to 44 percent (with 4 percent for Robertson). The paper was forced to search for any good news it could read into those figures. On some days Dever's vote might move up a bit, and the *Tribune* would confidently announce that a major shift was underway. But the percentages always returned to about the same split, and the newspaper began to run out of explanations. At the rival *Herald and Examiner,* the pollsters found Big Bill was out in front by 100,000 votes. Since that paper was backing Thompson, it could merely report the totals without any convoluted analysis. [50]

One factor in Thompson's campaign should not be ignored. The Democrats charged that organized crime was supporting Big Bill, and they were undoubtedly correct. All segments of the Chicago underworld mustered together under the Republican standard. Dever's war on bootlegging had seriously inconvenienced these businessmen; Thompson's pledge to open "ten thousand new places" was appealing. So the mob pitched in. Such noted gangland figures as Big Tim Murphy, Jack Zuta, and Vincent ("Schemer") Drucci were often seen attending Thompson functions or hanging around campaign headquarters. A few of them even held membership cards in the William Hale Thompson Republican Club. Al Capone himself contributed up to a half-million dollars to the Republican war chest, and was known to display a framed picture of Thompson on his office wall, between the portraits of Washington and Lincoln. But to the Democratic cry that "every hoodlum in town" was backing him, Big Bill only smiled. He even began an address to an audience of Republican society matrons with the burlesque salutation "My Fellow Hoodlums."[51]

The last days of the campaign brought new explosions. The Thompsonites warned that the Democratic race-baiting was about to touch off a riot. On the other side, the Dever forces charged that Big Bill's chum, State's Attorney Crowe, was preparing to ignore vote fraud. They got a friendly judge to appoint a special election supervisor, and now it was the Republicans' turn to scream that the election was being rigged.[52] Police Chief Collins armed his men with submachine guns and began rounding up underworld characters. On the day before the election, Thompson stalwart "Schemer" Drucci was mysteriously killed while in police custody. The shooting galvanized the Thompsonites into playing their final card. To confront Chief Collins's police "cossacks," they mobilized their own private legion. "The time for statements was over; only sterner stuff counted now," Thompson apologist William H. Stuart later recalled. He went on to boast:

> Capone men, an army of them, spread through the "bad lands" of the West Side that night and in the early hours of election morning. There were none more ferocious in political or bootlegging warfare; none better trained. They were enlisted against the "Dever and Decency" gunmen. Their orders were to meet and beat the enemy at the enemy's own game. They did. Steal the election from Thompson? Not where the Capone mob was marshaled![53]

On that note, Chicagoans prepared to choose their mayor.

Denouement

April 5 dawned cloudly and cool. For a Chicago election, the balloting was relatively quiet. Only a handful of voters were openly harassed at the polls and no more that two election judges were kidnapped. No one was reported killed. In fact, despite the threats of weather and mayhem, nearly a million people cast ballots, a city record. Most of the voters appeared cheerful enough, though a few folks were seen to jump whenever an automobile backfired.[54]

Early returns were inconclusive. For a time it appeared that election night would be a long one. But then Thompson began to move in front. Dever was left further and further behind as the hours passed and Big Bill's lead mounted. Before midnight, it was evident that the Republicans had won by a landslide.

Dever polled 432,678 votes to Thompson's total of 515,716. Robertson trailed far back with 51,209. The percentages closely followed the *Tribune* straw polls: Dever, 43.3 percent; Thompson, 51.6 percent; Robertson, 5.1 percent. The mayor was able to win only twenty-two of the city's fifty wards, as Big Bill rolled up a plurality of 83,038 votes. Added to Dever's humiliation was the fact that he actually received 3,000 fewer votes than his new running-mate for city treasurer, Matthew Szymczak.[55]

The mayor lost big in a number of traditional Democratic strongholds. The twenty-two Greater West Side wards had gone for Dever by a plurality of over 66,000 in 1923. Now they deserted him, as they had in the traction referendum. Thompson carried the Greater West Side by a margin of nearly 27,000, a swing in plurality of over 93,000 votes. Some of the shifts were remarkable. In the Twenty-sixth Ward, Dever's 1923 plurality of nearly 8000 votes became a Thompson margin of 1895: a Democratic percentage drop from 89 to 41. Next door in the Twentieth Ward, the Dever plurality of 5275 now became a Thompson victory of 3622 (a drop for the Democrats from 81 percent to 35 percent). The Thirty-first Ward shifted from Democratic by 5548 votes to Republican by 1205 (the percentage drop for the Democrats was from 84 to 43). And these represented only the extreme cases. Even where the mayor held on, it was usually by greatly reduced margins. In Congressman Sabath's Twenty-first Ward, Dever's previous 5000-vote plurality was cut to 72. Martin J. O'Brien's Twenty-ninth Ward went Democratic by fewer than 1000 votes; the mayor had carried it by over 5000 votes the last time around. In the Thirty-third Ward, Dever's 1923 plurality of 6020 votes was shaved to 95.[56]

Dever made gains in a few places. He carried the Progressive-Independent Fifth and Sixth wards near the University of Chicago, a neighborhood that had gone for Lueder four years earlier. The mayor also won big in his home Forty-ninth Ward on the far North Side, moving from a 2000-vote deficit to a plurality of over 4500. He improved his showing somewhat in the South Side Eighth Ward and in other scattered places.[57] But that was the extent of his progress; everywhere else, he lost ground.

Looking at the totals from an ethnic perspective is instructive. John W. Allswang's general survey of nationality voting in Chicago covers ten groups. His figures show sharp Democratic declines among nine of the ten. The only one of Allswang's groups to register Democratic gains was the native born whites. In the first election, Dever had taken 43 percent of their votes; this time, he won 55 percent.[58]

Dever's improved showing with this group is an interesting development, since it runs counter to a nationwide trend. Although there had been various alliances between old-stock reformers and urban ethnic politicians during the high days of progressivism, the situation changed after World War I. One reason was that the "cultural questions" separating the two groups (such as Prohibition and restriction on immigration) proved so divisive that cooperation on other issues became difficult.[59] Tribalism ran rampant. Dever himself had felt the scourge of the era's nativism with the anti-Catholic propaganda of the 1923 campaign. He had also been supported by many of the city's better-known WASP reformers that time and had won. During his four years in office, he did little to alienate the suspicious bulk of the "native Americans," while impressing them with his law-and-order policies, his support for civil service, and his honest administration. Chicago's old-stock voters were won over by Dever, despite the nativism hinted at in Thompson's America First slogan. With this group at least, Brennan's slating of his Irish marginal man had paid dividends.

The most dramatic shift in Dever's vote is among the blacks. In 1923, Dever had beaten Lueder in the city's three predominantly black wards by about 6300 votes. Four years later, the same Second, Third, and Fourth wards combined to give Thompson a margin of about 60,000; Allswang's figures report Dever's share of the Negro vote falling from 53 percent in 1923 to just 7 percent in 1927.[60] Blacks had been apathetic in the first election. Now they turned out in record numbers to show support for Thompson, the man many of them called the *Second Lincoln*—and they turned out to answer the Democrats' racist campaign as well. Yet Dever did not lose the 1927 election because of Thompson's strength in the black community. The black electorate still numbered less than 10 percent of the city's voters, and it is possible that the Democrats' tactics stirred up enough backlash votes to offset whatever black votes they had to write off. Of course, this cannot be proven or disproven. The raw numbers suggest, however, that Dever lost the mayoralty in the white ethnic wards.

Three scholars have gone beyond Allswang's general study to analyze the voting behavior of the city's Italians, Poles, and Jews. Using precinct voter registration lists, Humbert S. Nelli calculated the decline in Dever's Italian vote: from 79 percent in 1923 to 45 percent in 1927. Nelli credits the shift to the "key issue [of] enforcement or non-enforcement of the liquor law." The strong influence of underworld elements in Italian area wards seems to have been at least partly responsible for the Thompson triumph in this community. Only in the First Ward, where the Capone syndicate refrained from using its political muscle, did Italian precincts remain with Dever. Lacking a strong commitment to either party, Italian voters were especially receptive to issues that affected them as a distinct nationality group. Thompson's courting of Italians, coupled with ethnic anger against the Dever war on "Sicilian gunmen," helped complete the process of moving the Italians into the Republican column.[61]

Edward R. Kantowicz computes Dever's 1927 Polish vote to be 54 percent, down from 83 percent four years earlier. Like Nelli in the Italian study, Kantowicz puts the blame squarely on the Volstead matter. Dever had won the Poles' support in 1923 as an "inoffensive" Democrat—he had done nothing to antagonize them, so they voted for their party as usual. By 1927, however, the Poles had had enough of Dever's police policies. They were also critical of the mayor for what they felt was their under-representation in city government.

When the astute Thompson pledged to turn City Hall into "the capital of Poland," many disgruntled Poles were inclined to give Big Bill a chance. Thousands of them crossed party lines to vote Republican.[62]

Edward Mazur's study of the Jewish vote discloses some interesting statistics. The writer divided his sample into Eastern European Jews and German Jews. The Eastern Europeans, working class and relatively new to America, lived on the city's West Side. These voters broke with the Democrats on the Personal Liberty issue. Mazur notes the relatively low totals recorded by Dever in the Twenty-first, Twenty-third, and Twenty-fourth wards, and concludes that the Jewish ward leaders did not expend much effort for the mayor. He calculates that Thompson carried the ninety-two Eastern European Jewish precincts by a margin of 55–41 percent. However, among German Jews, the voting pattern was strikingly different. These people were settled mostly in middle-class areas of the South Side. More fully "Americanized" and politically sophisticated than their ghetto bretheren, they were less likely to be swayed by campaign sloganeering or the attitude of local precinct captains. German Jews supported Dever; they liked his curbs on lawlessness, and they did not trust Thompson. In this point of view, they were in the company of the city's "native American" bourgeoisie, whom they more closely resembled in socioeconomic status. Mazur's figures for the ten German Jewish precincts show Dever at 62 percent, Thompson at 35 percent.[63]

The impact of Dever's labor policies on the 1927 election is difficult to assess. Four years earlier, Dever had come into office heralded as the friend of the working man. As mayor he had treated unions fairly, and had skillfully arbitrated a number of their disputes with management. His attempts at cutting the municipal payroll, although not popular with those involved, do not seem to have damaged his standing with labor groups as a whole. Only his handling of the McAndrew affair had created any great hostility by labor toward Dever. During the campaign, the mayor's opponents naturally played this up. Taking the lead was Alderman Oscar Nelson—still nominally a Democrat, though that would change once the election was over. Nelson renewed his bitter offensive against the school superintendent, while also raising questions about the labor views of Dever's school board appointee Helen Heffernan. This had the effect of shifting attention away from Thompson's labor record, which was spotty at best and antiunion at worst. For their part, president John Fitzpatrick and other leaders of the Chicago Federation of Labor supported Dever, and the roster of the Dever for Mayor Trade Union Committee reads like a who's who of the city's labor chieftains. And yet, the forces of organized labor do not seem to have shown much enthusiasm for Dever or worked very hard for his cause. Various explanations of this psychology of indifference spring to mind. Perhaps the labor leaders could not fully trust anyone like Dever who got along so well with business. Maybe it was a case of the unions expecting too much of the mayor: they had believed Dever to be their man, and when he let them down on the matter of McAndrew, it seemed like a betrayal of everything. David Dolnick, who studied Chicago's labor politics during the 1920s, concluded that the support of organized labor divided evenly in the mayoral election. Considering the final result, that is not bad for Dever. But it is not as good a showing as his record might have predicted.[64]

News of Dever's loss to Thompson stunned the nation. Outsiders were baffled by the victory of a disgraced buffoon over the country's best mayor. *The Forum* magazine was convinced that Big Bill had somehow "hypnotized " the mass of Chicago voters. Nels Anderson of *Century Magazine* called the election "the triumph of the gang." The *St. Louis Star* blamed the results on the Windy City's psyche, saying "Chicago is still a good deal of a wild west town, where a soapbox showman extracting rabbits from a gentleman's plug hat gets a better hearing than a man in a sober suit talking business." Will Rogers, though speaking tongue in cheek, accurately summed up America's disappointment with Chicago: "They was trying to beat Bill [Thompson] with the better-element vote. The trouble with Chicago is that there ain't much better-element."[65]

Why had Dever lost? In the years since the election, some observers have asserted that the Democratic leaders secretly knifed their candidate. Cermak's biographer claims that the Bohemian chieftain cut down the mayor because of the Personal Liberty issue; he cites the low Dever vote in Cermak's Lawndale wards as evidence. Donald Richberg placed the blame higher up. He declared that party leader Brennan had dumped his mayor under pressure from Samuel Insull, who had threatened to "destroy" the Democratic organization if Dever was allowed to win. Fletcher Dobyns and (according to Gottfried) Charles E. Merriam also thought that Brennan and the Democrats had abandoned their nominee.[66]

The conspiracy theory has a certain attractiveness. There is comfort in thinking that the superior man lost because of some underhanded dealing, rather than through an honest verdict of the people. It somehow vindicates one's faith in the wisdom of democracy. But the simplest explanation is usually the best: Dever was defeated because he was less popular than Thompson. The Democratic organization might not have worked very hard for the mayor in 1927; but it is more logical to assume that the lethargy was a result of voter hostility and not its cause.

The party bosses had little to gain and much to lose by engineering Dever's defeat. Cermak might be angry about the liquor issue or about being passed over again, but he knew that he would be a frontrunner for 1931. So why sabotage Dever? Well, it is claimed, Cermak wanted to rid the Democratic party of its Irish domination and did not mind wrecking the organization to do so. He knew Thompson was a clown. Cermak had less to fear by putting him in the mayor's chair than by letting Brennan and the Irish retain power. The voters would turn on Big Bill; Cermak, with his new organization, would be ready.

This is a nice explanation—particularly because it is the way things actually happened during the next four years. But Cermak had no crystal ball in 1927. Nothing is certain in politics, except uncertainty. Given time and power, the Republicans might very well have built up their own machine, one that could have thwarted Cermak's ambitions for the mayoralty. And, as we have seen, Brennan was already working actively to bring the non-Irish into positions of prominence within the party; he was certainly not Cermak's enemy. Besides, it was well known that Dever was eager to leave City Hall, opening the way for a new mayor at the end of his second term. So it would seem that Cermak's best bet for future power lay with loyally reelecting the mayor, helping nurture the Democratic organization, and from that position preparing for 1931. That was the practical approach.

It is also unlikely that Brennan sabotaged Dever. The mayor was a close personal friend; and while that does not preclude subversion, it does make it improbable when joined with political advantage. Brennan was simply better off with Dever than with Thompson. The mayor's office gave Brennan patronage and power. He had no reason to surrender that to the Republicans. Any "bipartisan deal" he might have made surely would have netted him less that he had with Dever in office. As for the reported threats from Samuel Insull, one should remember that Donald Richberg was a long-time antiutilities lawyer and a bitter enemy of the tycoon. And if Brennan truly did fear Insull, would it not be more useful to reelect Dever and face Insull from a position of strength rather than from one of weakness?[67]

So the voters abandoned Dever for their own reasons. Prohibition appeared to be the main cause. Democratic ward leaders said as much in postelection interviews. Charles E. Merriam agreed that it was "by all odds the most important factor," and the mayor himself seemed to feel the same way.[68] The greatly reduced Dever vote in the wetter wards certainly supports this thought. Here Prohibition, as a symbol, is just as important as the actual fact that intoxicating beverages were banned. Chicagoans were probably not any more lawless in their attitudes than the residents of other large cities, despite the contemptuous remarks of some outsiders. Dever's local enforcement of the dry law had gotten tied up with all the bitter cultural conflicts that were plaguing the country as a whole. By 1927, the Prohibition question had taken on mythic dimensions that overrode rational thought or reasonable discussion. Thus Dever had found his entire administration virtually held hostage to a single issue.

A number of contemporary writers explored these deeper meanings in their commentaries on the Dever-Thompson election. They saw elements of a class struggle. Picking up on Will Rogers's remarks about the "better element," Elmer Davis of *Harper's Magazine* blamed the reformers for Dever's loss. Their support had been a deathblow. The reformers' trouble was that they concentrated on what the voters *should* or *ought to* do, instead of on what those electors really wanted: they had tried to "jam virtue, or what is called virtue, down the public throat." Thompson had won because he understood what the people wanted. He was an artist in politics, a person who might not know much, but still knew those things he had to do. His victory was no mystery; the real mystery was how Dever had managed to get 430,000 people to vote for him.[69]

The *New Republic* also read the results along these lines. The magazine believed that the growing power consciousness of foreign-stock voters had given the election to Thompson. These newer Americans had found their place in the country's society. They had helped create a new, urban culture and were now beginning to transform the old order. Politicians had long treated the ethinc Americans as an unthinking bloc of voters to be callously manipulated; that was no longer the situation. The foreign-stock citizens would now assert themselves as full-fledged Americans and do as they pleased. They were not gullible enough to be taken in by the politician's rhetoric: Thompson had not fooled them with his King George prattle or his pose as the Great Wet Father. But Big Bill had at least taken the trouble to cultivate them; Dever had not.[70]

The Democrats had not abandoned the ethnics, of course. They could not afford to and they knew it. Yet many of the foreign-stock citizens seemed to have felt that the party was taking them for granted while it played up to the reform crowd; and they despised the WASPs for their snobbish disdain. Thompson catered to these feelings. Nels Anderson vividly recalled one of Big Bill's speeches to a West Side audience:

> The crowd had come to his bosom. "They call you low-brows and hoodlums—they call me that too," [Thompson said]. "We low-brows got to stick together." He named the enemies of the plain people: the newspapers, except Hearst's; the two universities, the social workers, the political purity folks. . . . When he hurled defiance, gave the lie or mocked, he plunged his hearers into rhapsodies of laughter, howling for Big Bill, the *regular* guy.[71]

Thompson might be a rich man's son and Dever the child of workers, but the masses of everyday voters swung over to the man who spoke their language. The Deverites could respond only with limp pleas to vote for "Dever and Decency." And as one veteran politico sneered, "Who the hell is attracted by decency?"[72]

In 1923, Chicago Democrats had captured the mayoralty by building a solid coalition of various ethnic blocs, then joining it with the Progressive-Independent forces. Party boss Brennan had slated Dever to hold the ethnic alliance together while attracting support from the "respectables." But as mayor, when Dever started to reach out for these new elements, he pulled the party away from its traditional center of strength. Coalition politics is difficult enough in peaceful times; the tribal atmosphere of 1920s Chicago made it virtually impossible—particularly with the totem of Prohibition looming over the landscape. The multiethnic alliance began to come apart.

Dever the little-known judge had been a dream candidate. Once he had to govern, reality overtook fantasy. Good intentions, and even good performance, were not enough. As it turned out, the same factors that attracted the WASPs to Dever alienated the ethnics. His dignity, his cold intelligence, his law-and-order policies—these might have been an asset on Lake Shore Drive, but they were a definite handicap on Milwaukee Avenue, Halsted Street, or Roosevelt Road. Brennan had thought Dever would be the man to play it both ways, the "marginal man" who could be a bridge between the foreign stock and the old stock. The boss had miscalculated, and he had paid the price. The Democratic party would have to regroup, rethink, and reinvigorate itself. And it would have to do so without Dever. His time was now past.

10

The Least-Known Chicago Mayor

Emeritus

■ With the election over, Dever moved quickly to be rid of his burden and have Thompson take charge. "Let him come, the sooner the better," he said. "I want to get out as soon as I can legally turn over the office." And he meant it. He arranged to have Thompson sworn in at the earliest possible date, then left for Excelsior Springs with Kate before his own term was officially completed. It was the first time in the city's history that an outgoing mayor had not attended his successor's inauguration.[1]

He was glad to step down. "I have always felt that being mayor was a four year job," Dever told reporters. "Any man faithfully performing the duties of the office must be prepared to serve only a single term." He had not enjoyed being mayor, and preferred to have associates address him as "Judge" once again. He said that he would have refused to run for a second term if the Republicans had selected anyone else but Thompson. The job of mayor was something of a zoo. "I am happy to be out of the City Hall," Dever confided to a friend; "the work there was not only arduous, but I never felt quite safe."[2]

He still retained faith in the ultimate triumph of his ideals. He wrote to Graham Taylor that he was a "little disturbed" about the direction events had taken, though he was confident the city would survive four more years of Thompsonism. The people would get wise to Big Bill. "Temporarily, Chicago is in for a little difficulty," Dever conceded; "but there is, after all, a fine spirit here which can be invoked under the right auspices whenever the city is really in danger."[3]

A few weeks after Dever left office, the self-appointed guardians of that spirit decided to honor their hero with a testimonial dinner. Unfortunately, it was a flop. Two thousand people were expected at the Congress Hotel; fewer than 800 came. In retrospect, the banquet seems a fitting epilogue to the mayoral campaign. It was hazily conceived, hastily planned, and poorly executed. As Harold Ickes complained, the Dever testimonial was "distinctly a gold coast affair," run by Sprague, Farwell, Busch, and others of "that type." The banquet committee made no attempt to attract a wide cross-section of the community. Incredibly, the regular Democratic organization was completely ignored. George Brennan found out about the dinner only when he received a general "dear sir" invitation; when he arrived at the hotel, the ushers did not recognize him, and seated him in the gallery. Speakers were scheduled, cancelled, then rescheduled. The high point of the evening was the unveiling of a specially commissioned bust of "the Judge," which was to be placed in the Chicago Historical Society's museum. On the whole, the newspapers passed over the event—nobody had really publicized the banquet, and anyway, Dever was old news.[4] The ex-mayor was touched by it, however, and it did make his defeat easier to swallow.

Dever had many offers of employment to choose from when he left City Hall. For a time he seriously considered going into legal practice with his son Dan. He finally accepted a position with the Bank of America, a local trust company owned by one of his school board appointees. Dever's title was vice-president and trust officer, though basically, he was window dressing. He went about his duties conscientiously, but was dispensable enough to be allowed nine weeks of vacation during his first six months on the job. The bank directors knew what role they wanted him to play. Large display ads calling attention to Dever's association with the company were placed on streetcars and in the newspapers. A typical announcement, appearing in the *Tribune* under a fatherly portrait of the former mayor, read:

COME, TALK WITH WILLIAM E. DEVER ON TRUST MATTERS.
Former Mayor Dever is head of this bank's trust department. All Chicago knows him as a wise counselor, a safe guardian, and an able administrator. He is here to advise you about the handling of investments, the creation of living trusts, and concerning the best means of protecting those who may need protection after you have passed away.
He is here to direct the carrying out of your instructions in any form of trust agreement or in wills.
Come talk with him at any time.
He will be glad to meet you.[5]

As the Bank of America's chief public relations asset, Dever had to put up with any number of gawkers or schemers who wandered in off the street. (One persistent client, for example, kept bothering him for a $500 loan for a trip to Washington to "expose" the ex-mayor's enemies before Congress.) Still, it was a pleasant life. The vice-president's salary and Dever's sagacious real estate investments gave him an ample income. He began to travel extensively. During the first two summers after his retirement from office, William

Dever in retirement. *(Chicago Historical Society: ICHi 20813)*

and Kate sailed to Europe for month-long holidays. They also made side trips to their favorite spas in Missouri and Mississippi. They only turned down an offer to visit the Robinses in Florida when "the Judge" belatedly decided he was taking too much time off from his job.[6]

Dever remained a popular after-dinner orator. He was addressing more business groups now, speaking to chambers of commerce, railroad executives, and corporate lawyers. His talks generally stuck to a central theme: the businessman should take a greater interest in public affairs. Dever was certain that bringing sound managers into municipal government could put an end to inefficiency and corruption. The problem was attracting these gifted people to take up the task. "If businessmen would move in closer to city affairs, forgetting political, racial, religious, or local prejudices, we would see how easy it is to get things done," he told a Milwaukee audience. "When [the business leader's] interest is aroused, he is most capable."[7]

The public continued to be interested in the former mayor's observations and opinions. Reporters still sought his comments on political events; they even tracked him down in Paris for his views on President Coolidge's decision to retire from office. A high-school journalist named Edward Levi wrote him, asking Dever to compose an article on municipal politics. Northwestern University engaged him to lecture to a course in political thought and arranged to have his speech broadcast. Antiprohibition groups continued to solicit him for his counsel and for the use of his name.[8]

By now, however, Dever's political activity was confined to the spectator's role. He watched with disgust Thompson's "trial" and removal of School Superintendent McAndrew and the other excesses of the new regime. Privately, Dever considered Big Bill a Catholic-baiter who had beaten him with gutter tactics. He refrained from public comment on his successor, though his bitterness occasionally surfaced. He happened to run into Thompson at a funeral, and the affable mayor offered him his hand. Dever refused to take it, turning his back on the man. When the voters ousted Thompson's ally Robert Crowe from the state's attorney's office, Dever felt himself vindicated.[9]

Within his own party, he played only a minor part. He attended few political gatherings and delivered no stump speeches. He made his customary journey to the Democratic National Convention in 1928, helping to nominate Al Smith for president. But when George Brennan died shortly after the convention, Dever was left even more isolated. He did not become involved in the struggle for power that followed, Byzantine maneuverings that eventually put Anton Cermak in the chairman's seat. The party was moving forward without him. New York's governor-elect Franklin D. Roosevelt did write him after the presidential election debacle, to ask his advice on the party's future; but that seems to have been merely a courtesy request.[10]

His health, never the best, was starting to deteriorate. Shortly after returning from Europe in the summer of 1928, Dever began to get stomach pains.

He thought he had an ulcer. He spent a few weeks in the hospital, but that did not seem to help. Early in 1929, he resigned from the bank and went to Florida for a rest. He soon found the climate "too warm" and came back to Chicago.[11]

The pains grew worse. "The Judge" decided to seek help at the Mayo Clinic. The doctors put him on a special diet, which he ignored, and told him to stop smoking cigars, which he refused to do. He started losing weight, dropping over fifty pounds in a matter of months. Old friends who called on him at his apartment were horrified by his gaunt appearance—Raymond Robins offered to summon his personal physician from New York to treat his "Uncle Bill." By August 1929, yellow jaundice had set in. Dever returned to the Mayo to demand an operation. The staff took X-rays, informed him that the trouble was in his pancreas, and said that surgery would not help. They did not tell him he had cancer.[12]

He returned once more to Kenmore Avenue. On September 3, as was his custom during convalescence, he spent the morning propped up in the front sun parlor of his flat, looking at the street. Two of his nieces came over to visit. About noon he began to feel weak, so he stretched out on the living room couch. Somebody put the Cubs game on the radio. He listened for awhile and remarked at how well his favorite team was doing this summer. Shortly before two o'clock, he put out his cigar, turned his head toward Kate, and smiled. Then he closed his eyes and died.[13]

Dever's death took the city by surprise. His illness had been common knowledge, but only his family had realized its seriousness. Now that he was gone, the tributes began to roll in. Mayor Thompson said that he was "very sorry" to hear of his predecessor's death and reminded reporters that he had thoughtfully established a Quiet Zone on the streets around his old foe's residence. Edward Dunne declared that he was "shocked," and that Dever and he had been "close friends, and intimately associated in politics." Anton Cermak said that Dever's passing removed "one of my oldest and dearest friends." Party wheelhorse Martin J. O'Brien predicted that the dead man's career, "from humble boy to mayor of a great city, should be inspiration to the boys of this generation." In the city council, where the aldermen gathered to discuss a suitable memorial to the late mayor, Jacob Arvey observed that although any "monument of stone [might be] obliterated by the ravages of the elements," Dever's record of achievement "can never be erased from the memory of man."[14]

The press was a bit more restrained than the politicians, though the sentiment was similar. In the main, the journalistic eulogies dwelt on Dever's simple integrity. The *Chicago Times* called the man "a conscientious, loyal executive [who] performed his duties honestly and courageously, with no blaring of trumpets." The *Post* remembered him as "a citizen who gave the best he had in the service of Chicago," adding that "the enemies he made were to his credit." *The Chicagoan* magazine said of Dever that "he spent his life in politics without becoming a politician"—and meant it as a compliment. Half a continent away, Dever's passing also made news. The *New York Times* said the former mayor was a "symbol . . . of public honesty," whose life was "one of solid, moral dignity." The Catholic diocesan paper of Brooklyn, the *Tablet*, declared that "such men [as Dever] commend the Catholic faith more than a library of apologetics." But perhaps the most elegant tribute was John B. McCutcheon's cartoon in the *Chicago Tribune*. It pictured the maiden Chicago laying a wreath inscribed "in grateful memory" on the bier of the late mayor. The cartoon was titled "The Kind She Can't Afford to Lose."[15]

The funeral was held three days later. Tom Keane, Joe O'Donnell, and other old friends carried Dever's casket from the apartment to the hearse, then joined the parade of political princes that marched behind it the half-mile to St. Ida's Church. The city and county offices were closed in mourning, and they were all there (all except Thompson—there was an "illness" in his family). Five thousand people had gathered on the sidewalks and in the streets outside the church when the cortege arrived. Those who could not get inside stood out on Broadway, listening to the requiem mass over loudspeakers. At the conclusion of the service, Cardinal Mundelein stepped forward and personally blessed the casket. Then the procession was moving again, taking Dever to Calvary Cemetery in Evanston, where he would rest in a borrowed vault.[16]

The crowds began to disperse. Some of the politicians followed the cortege to the cemetery. But many of them lingered outside the church, knotted together in small groups, talking. There was a judicial election coming up. . . .[17]

The Footnote

In the sixty years since his death, Dever has been largely forgotten. Paul M. Green, a student of the Chicago Democratic organization, called him "the least-known Chicago mayor elected this century."[18] The description is accurate. For those who have any familiarity with his career, he is merely a curiosity. Not so long ago, a writer for the popular *Chicago* magazine summarized Dever's administration this way:

> In 1923, Thompson slipped a bit and reform candidate William E. Dever got to be mayor for a while (in Chicago, reform mayors are called interim mayors).
> Dever didn't feel the sense of tolerance and comradeship for Chicago gangsters that Big Bill had. Dever meant to strike the fear of God in those gangsters and make them stop attending one another's funerals.
> The new mayor issued some chilling statements. He gave chief of police Morgan A. Collins this order: "Collins, there's a dry law on the nation's books.

This town will immediately become dry."

Nothing happened.

Dever went to the public: "The gangsters are to be disarmed and jailed or driven out of town. Every one of the 6000 policemen is to be thrown into the fight, and public opinion is counted on to spur municipal and state court judges into cooperation."

Still nothing happened.

Then Dever got really tough and ordered the police to close the speakeasies.

This gave Big Bill Thompson his campaign issue: "The Dever administration has made one of the greatest records in Chicago's history for closing up business. When I'm elected we will not only reopen the places these people have closed, but we'll open 10,000 new ones."

Al Capone took heart and threw his considerable support behind Thompson in the next election.[19]

This is the picture of Dever that has come down to us: a quixotic figure among the hardheaded realists of Chicago politics, whose electoral demise proved the foolishness of trying to bring clean government to the city. How legitimate is this assessment?

For one thing, Dever was no ivory-tower idealist; he was a professional politician and party regular. As a young man, he had gravitated toward the reformers. He entered politics through the auspices of the Municipal Voters' League and the social settlement movement. Once in office, he learned to play the game of politics well. Dever got along with everyone, and his congeniality was perhaps his greatest asset as a politician. He was not ruled by doctrine. Aside from some general Progressive aspirations toward municipal efficiency and power to the people, he developed no comprehensive philosophy of government.

Nor was Dever a mere party hack. Politics meant more to him than just a battle to win elections and divide the spoils. He had visions of a finer city in a greater society. His support for social welfare programs as alderman and mayor, his continued advocacy of Municipal Ownership, his determination to keep partisan hands off the school system—all speak of Dever's wish to use government's power to promote a better life for all. His reform credentials were valid. But first of all, he was a politician.

His election as mayor in 1923 was not a reform uprising against an entrenched machine. Other cities had developed long traditions of that exercise: New York City comes readily to mind, with its "fusion" crusades against Tammany Hall every dozen or so years.[20] Chicago was different. The local Democratic organization was still struggling to overcome internal factional division, and Dever's victory was actually a consolidation of that process. During the 1920s in Chicago, "reform" had largely come to mean opposition to Big Bill Thompson. Merriam, Ickes, and the other clean-government activists were inclined to accept anyone who might rid the city of Thompson.

George Brennan shrewdly capitalized on this fact by slating Dever. Here was a candidate who far exceeded the reformers' minimum requirements. In Dever they had a man who shared their probity, who sought their counsel, who spoke their language—someone with whom they were personally comfortable. After twenty years' association with him, they felt as if Dever was one of them. The reformers embraced him wholeheartedly, casting their lot with the new Democratic organization. Brennan had his coalition, and the "goo-goos" had aided him. By the time they grew disillusioned in the late 1930s, the machine they had helped build was firmly in power. Reformers were not able to mount a serious challenge for the mayoralty until 1955, and did not finally capture the office until 1983.[21]

Dever was a symbol. He was the unification of the new Democratic order, all wrapped up in one blue serge suit. He brought together the regular organization of Sullivan and Brennan and the old, mildly-reformist Harrison-Dunne faction, and charmed the Progressive-Independent bloc. Dever was one of George Brennan's "new breed," a step up from the saloon keepers and the provincial Gaelic brigade of the early Hopkins-Sullivan days.[22] True, he was a straight Irish Catholic. Yet, he had grown up in an environment different from most of his co-nationalists, had not become that one-dimensional cardboard-cut-out figure of Paddy the Mick. Dever could cross cultural lines and be at home in many circles. An Irishman who acted like a WASP, he was the marginal man of politics who could unite all these different elements.

Such versatility was important, for having an ethnic Catholic as mayor was unusual in Chicago. Before Dever, only Edward Dunne had served a full term in office—and that for only two years.[23] Like Dever, Dunne did not fit the "Paddy" stereotype; he was eminently bourgeois, had spent his childhood in Peoria, and had been educated abroad. The Municipal Ownership rhetoric of his campaign, coming as it did during the high days of the Progressive Era, had further diverted attention from Dunne's roots and religion. Dunne had been respectable. He was not a creature of the machine but was associated with the "clean" wing of the Democratic party. He attracted substantial support from Republicans. And yet, Dunne was never able to build an effective political organization. He lost his bid for reelection as mayor in 1907 and could not even win nomination in 1911. His election as governor in 1912 was achieved only because of the Bull Moose split in the Republican Party. By 1916 Dunne was out of power for good, his political star in descent.[24]

In the meantime, the regular Sullivan organization was developing talented young men of varied background who might reach for the mayoralty and beyond. There were Catholics of many national pedigrees: Robert Sweitzer, P. J. Carr, Joseph Kostner, Michael Igoe, Edmund Jarecki, and others. There were Jews like Henry Horner and Jacob Arvey, and even a Bohemian Protestant (Anton Cermak). The ethnic peoples were gaining citizenship, were voting, and were becoming a key factor in the city's political equation. The representatives thrown upward from these groups were also growing more sophisticated, more cosmopolitan in their appeal. They were poised on the brink. Sweitzer, the German-Irish county clerk, tried twice for the mayoralty and failed. Then Dever broke through.

Once elected, Dever recognized his task as a "respectable ethnic." He often told Knights of Columbus suppers or other such gatherings that he would show the critics an Irish-Catholic could govern wisely; he had not forgotten the whispering campaign that had been waged against him. He was particularly careful in his relations with the city school system. The bigots had warned that Dever's election would lead to Catholic domination of public education. He responded by appointing a strictly nonsectarian school board, mostly Protestants. He was so scrupulous in avoiding favoritism that some Catholics complained the mayor was not being fair to his own people.[25]

His Prohibition policy is also revealing. Dever was a committed wet. He thought the Volstead Act was ludicrous and felt from the start that defending it in Chicago would be politically dangerous. Yet, he embarked on the most ambitious Prohibition enforcement campaign in the country. By 1926, he knew that he had failed. He publicly admitted as much, then went right on enforcing the law until the day he was turned out of office. Part of the reason, he said, was to destroy the corrupting influence that bootlegging had on government in general and the police department in particular. More frequently, however, he spoke of his desire to preserve the law. It was very abstract, very philosophical—the language of the seminar room, not the political club. Once again, Dever seemed to be making a point of demonstrating his integrity. Whatever his motivations, he underscored the fact that an Irish Catholic could have political standards as high as a WASP Brahmin.

Still, Dever could play the pragmatist, could compromise when it was politically advantageous and his ideals were not offended. Consider his attempts to reach a transit settlement. As much as anything, Dever was elected mayor as an advocate of transit reform. He still carried his youthful enthusiasm for the Municipal Ownership cure-all. When it became evident he could not get all he wanted in a transportation plan, he made concessions; he took the best package available. Dunne and his true believers could not forgive Dever's defection from the glorious lost cause of 1907. Rather than work for three-quarters of a loaf, they joined with those who opposed the Dever plan for other reasons and together brought it down. If they could not have the perfect settlement, they would have none at all. Dever, meanwhile, had served transit reform better than any of them, developing a comprehensive, workable plan that brought a unified transportation system closer to reality than ever before.

Dever's relations with the city council reflect the role he saw himself playing and the limits on him. He treated the council cordially and cautiously; he did not push it too hard. If a "moral issue" like law enforcement or keeping politics out of the schools were not involved, the mayor could find it advisable to give in. His actions on the fiscal problems are an example. The aldermen jealously guarded their budget-making privileges. When they resisted the mayor's attempts to curb their spending, Dever backed off, and the council kept possession of the municipal purse. In later years, other mayors would exercise great influence over the city council—during the Daley era, the body became a virtual rubber stamp. Dever never enjoyed such power. Granted, he was the mayor of Chicago; but he did not control the Democratic party machinery. Without that weapon, any confrontation with the council might be long, loud, and bloody. (Recall the three-year-long battle of the Washington administration against the "Vrdolyak 29.") Dever had been slated in the interests of party unity. Now that some harmony had been achieved, he would not rock the boat. If Dever did not become master of the city in the manner of a Cermak or a Daley, it was because he did not have the tools and was not prepared to fight for them.

As a leader, Dever was a good administrator. He selected able people to work under him, and his administration was free of scandal. Yet he lacked a personal touch. Somewhere between his days as a fighting, workers' alderman and his accession to the mayoralty, he had lost it. Perhaps it was a casualty of his isolated years on the bench. Whatever the reason, Dever had changed. The barrier was there.

Charles E. Merriam inadvertently alludes to this in a tale about Dever's handling of a minor labor dispute. According to the professor, a group of firemen had come to City Hall to see the mayor, crowding into his outer office. When their leader became agitated, Dever snapped at him "Who do you think you are talking to?" and ordered the firemen to get out and go back to work. Merriam relates that the visitors left meekly, only to return later and apologize for their conduct. He concludes that Dever acted wisely: the men respected him.[26] That much is evident. But they probably did not love Dever or even like him very much. It is said that when Cicero spoke, men commented upon his eloquence; when Demosthenes spoke, they said "Let us march." Dever could attract admiration for his talents, deference for his integrity. But he could not make the public march.

The paradox of Dever's career is that his identification with reform, which made him electable as mayor and even something of a national figure, also drove him from office. Reform politicians seem to wear out quickly in Chicago. Dunne, as we have seen, declined in political fortune after his single term as mayor. The other reform-oriented contender of the era, Charles E. Merriam, was nearly elected mayor in 1911 but never made a credible race after that. Dever, who was much more of a practical political professional than either of these men, gave promise of overcoming this failing, of being something more than another reform "morning glory." Yet he, too, went down.

As Dever in victory was a symbol of machine consolidation, in defeat he is representative of Chicago reform and its demise. During this transition era, the united party organization supplanted the personality politics of the past. And strangely enough, as politics became based less on personality and more on organization, the need for a special type of candidate charisma grew. Past political cults had frequently developed around figures of such remote, Olympian bearing as a Daniel Webster, a James G. Blaine, or (closer to home) a Carter Harrison II. The modern politician had to have a more down-to-earth appeal. It was as if they had to offer reassurance that the mystical individual bond between voter and candidate still endured. Here, both Dever and Progressive reform were found wanting. Honest, idealistic, and committed, there was no doubt that Dever meant well. In fact he seemed to good to be real; and that was a problem. The people became uneasy with perfection, tired of orderliness. Chicago progressivism, for all its skills and accomplishments, did not endure because the public did not accept it as natural. It always appeared to be something imposed by the Better Classes, always a bit aloof and therefore a bit alien. Reform did not spring from the public heart—it might be "for the people," but it did not often seem to be "by the people" and hardly ever "of the people." There was no bond of unconscious, reciprocal trust. Thus voters could reject what an outsider might objectively consider their best interests. Like the people it serves, the politics of democracy is not always rational. If George Brennan could have program-med a computer to produce the perfect Democratic mayoral candidate for 1923, he would have gotten Dever. On paper he was the ideal nominee. Logic argued for him that year. Logic also argued for him when he lost in 1927. Just as logic argued for the reforms of Progressivism. And just, perhaps, as logic argued that intoxicating beverages be made illegal.

Prohibition was a two-edged sword that made Dever a household name, lifted him to within dreaming distance of the White House, and finished him off in the end. After four years in office, Dever had convinced the American population that an Irish Catholic Democrat could be trusted with the keys to City Hall. The ethnic groups were another matter. They were the traditional power base of the Democratic party. They voted not only with their heads but with their hearts and their guts. And these "hyphenated Americans" had no use for Dever's Prohibition policies. The old catch-phrase Personal Liberty is most appropriate here, for more was involved than whether a person could buy a glass of beer. Personal Liberty was a sacred concept for the ethnics even if they did not often articulate it as such. Many of them had come to the new land to escape government oppression. To have the police searching someone's home for a bit of beverage seemed a betrayal of what America was supposed to be. It made little difference to them whether the mayor was enforcing the statute to speed its repeal, to purify the police department, or to advertise his official scruples. Dever's actions challenged them at a basic point—their idea of what it meant to be free.[27] No matter how many parks, schools, or public baths the mayor dedicated; no matter how persistently he courted the ethnic voters; there would remain the seeds of mistrust. This would be powerfully demonstrated in 1927.

Was Dever a failure? He certainly struck out in a primary test of political leadership; he could not retain his office. Though he left behind sizeable material accomplishments and a record of uncommon honesty, the impression one comes away with from studying Dever is of great expectations unfulfilled. He did some grand things; one suspects he should have been able to do more. And yet, this reaction must be tempered. It is only when Dever is weighed against these high hopes that he is found wanting; by any objective measurement his administration was a success, temporary though it might have been. We should not be too hard on Dever because he was not a LaGuardia or one of the Roosevelts. Few of our politicians have possessed the rare qualities of vision, leadership, and practical virtue that characterize such people; that is why they have become legendary. The shortfalls of even the gifted public men like Dever bring the extraordinary merits of these masters into clearer focus. The circus audience can never fully appreciate the tightrope walker until one of the performers loses his balance and plunges into the net. Then, when he returns to the top to leap and prance upon the wire again, the public is chastened. They can now see how really difficult it is to perform some singular activity, like walking on the high wire—or being a political leader.

In the grand scheme of Chicago politics, Dever's final place is nebulous. Anton Cermak is commonly recognized as the first "machine" mayor of Chicago. It can be argued that the title should be Dever's. Organization consolidation was a process begun under Roger Sullivan and continued with George Brennan. When Cermak finally knocked Thompson into political oblivion in 1931, he ushered in a solid half-century of regular Democratic rule. Yet the pieces were all in place as early as 1923.[28] Dever's election that year was the climax of the long struggle for party unification.

From a purely evolutionary point of view, Thompson's victory in 1927 was a fluke. Dever should have won—not necessarily because he was the better man, but because he had the better political organization behind him. When he lost, it was a rejection of him personally and his policies; it was not a repudiation of this party or the organization concept.

So when all was through, Dever lost more than power or office; he lost even his rightful place in the history books. He has become little more than a footnote in other men's careers. If he is thought of today, it is in terms similar to that *Chicago* magazine article.[29] He is the legendary epitome of political naiveté in the city that has elevated politics from an art to a religion. He is the mayor who "cleaned up" Chicago.

Epilogue

■ After her husband's death, Katherine Conway Dever continued to live at the Kenmore Avenue flat. She took an active interest in local politics and also closely followed the career of William's kinsman, Paul Dever of Massachusetts. She died in 1939.

Daniel Dever ran for alderman of the Forty-ninth Ward the year after his foster-father's death. Although he led in the preliminary election, he lost in the run-off. He returned to his career as an attorney and sought no other elective offices. Dan Dever died in 1958.

George Dever worked as a real estate investment broker. He did not enter politics. He died in 1961.

Arthur Lueder, the man Dever had defeated for mayor in 1923, remained federal postmaster for Chicago until the Democrats won the White House in 1933. After serving as president of a brewery, he was elected to two terms as state auditor.

Big Bill Thompson was defeated for reelection by Anton Cermak in 1931. He became a pathetic figure, wandering around at political gatherings, trying to hatch new plots for another return to power. He never made it. When he died in 1944, almost $1.5 million in cash was found in his safe deposit boxes.

After becoming mayor, Anton Cermak resigned as chairman of the Cook County Democratic party; however, he remained undisputed boss of the organization. He also became a force in national politics. In February 1933, he was shot while chatting with President-elect Roosevelt at a Miami rally and died some weeks later. To this day there is still controversy over whether the gunman was aiming at Roosevelt or Cermak.

Carter Harrison and Edward Dunne made peace with the regular organization and easily slipped into the roles of elder statesmen. Both men used their retirement for literary ventures. Dunne composed a five-volume history of Illinois. Harrison wrote a two-volume autobiography.

Charles E. Merriam continued as professor of political science at the University of Chicago. He also worked for the Roosevelt administration. His son Robert followed in his political footsteps, serving as an alderman and unsuccessfully running for mayor of Chicago.

Harold Ickes became Secretary of the Interior under Franklin D. Roosevelt. He served nearly thirteen years, a record in the office.

Raymond and Margaret Robins kept on with their work for political and social reform, particularly in the women's trade union movement. They lived in Florida and New York.

Graham Taylor remained associated with the Chicago Commons settlement house until his death in 1938. Some years later, the buildings became a boys' home.

Jacob Arvey, Dever's floor leader in the city council, eventually became chairman of the Cook County Democratic party. He is most renowned for bringing both Adlai Stevenson II and Paul Douglas into political prominence.

After his service as police commissioner under Dever, Morgan A. Collins resigned from the force and retired to private life. Colonel Sprague and Francis X. Busch remained politically active; when Cermak became mayor, they returned to their old cabinet positions.

Both of Chicago's leading business entrepreneurs fell on hard times in the 1930s. Samuel Insull's utilities empire collapsed; acquitted in a sensational fraud trial, he died penniless. On the other side of polite society, Al Capone was convicted of income tax evasion and sent to Alcatraz.

The City of Chicago has erected two monuments in memory of Mayor Dever. The William E. Dever Intake Crib, dedicated in 1935, helps provide the city with fresh drinking water. Since it is located nearly three miles out in the lake, it gets little tourist traffic.

The other memorial is the William E. Dever Elementary School. It also opened in 1935, on the far Northwest Side, at 3436 North Osceola Avenue. There is a painting of the one-time mayor of Chicago in the school office, the only commemoration of the man for whom the building is named. And like the general adult population, the children of the Dever School seem to know little of the local statesman who was once the second most famous political leader in the country. A ten-year-old boy summarized it best: "Mr. Dever? I think he was a mayor or something. But mainly, I think he's dead."

Appendix

Table 1

Vote for Mayor by Wards, 1923
(two-party vote)

Ward	Dever	Lueder	Ward	Dever	Lueder
1	10,862	1,599	26	9,125	1,155
2	8,276	3,717	27	8,965	4,885
3	9,077	7,044	28	8,293	5,784
4	7,912	8,163	29	12,782	5,753
5	7,537	9,025	30	14,257	6,529
6	8,062	8,877	31	6,805	1,257
7	7,723	6,029	32	6,820	2,736
8	7,376	8,327	33	8,257	1,637
9	4,779	5,962	34	6,338	2,649
10	4,853	4,714	35	4,786	6,248
11	8,387	2,471	36	5,310	7,271
12	8,727	5,324	37	8,634	11,522
13	7,039	894	38	7,021	5,597
14	10,940	3,166	39	9,184	6,679
15	10,270	6,057	40	6,221	10,470
16	9,538	6,745	41	5,540	8,176
17	7,307	8,793	42	7,920	3,586
18	9,127	7,437	43	5,827	5,209
19	7,707	10,654	44	5,778	6,923
20	7,312	2,037	45	7,060	5,626
21	7,663	2,326	46	5,266	7,719
22	7,922	2,587	47	6,864	10,423
23	8,081	4,397	48	5,983	7,837
24	9,157	6,140	49	8,869	10,884
25	6,946	2,802	50	5,928	7,752
			Total	390,413	285,094
			Plurality	105,319	

Source: Official Canvass, Board of Election Commissioners
(Mayoralty: April 3, 1923)

Table 2

Vote for Transit Proposition by Wards, 1925

Ward	Yes	No	Ward	Yes	No
1	6,623	2,055	26	1,222	4,545
2	3,273	3,505	27	6,298	3,041
3	3,125	5,272	28	2,906	6,195
4	4,693	4,531	29	7,604	6,758
5	7,341	4,553	30	6,158	9,358
6	6,442	5,814	31	1,252	5,239
7	6,556	6,398	32	2,454	6,527
8	7,357	12,152	33	1,824	4,147
9	3,274	4,759	34	2,761	3,916
10	1,979	4,427	35	1,880	6,251
11	2,588	8,646	36	2,073	7,213
12	3,694	9,406	37	8,930	13,580
13	3,445	1,721	38	1,983	6,396
14	6,310	4,417	39	4,900	14,747
15	5,051	9,654	40	5,666	12,867
16	3,418	6,435	41	4,519	9,623
17	5,666	8,854	42	5,930	3,059
18	4,425	7,493	43	2,455	5,535
19	8,903	11,700	44	5,405	7,851
20	4,141	2,169	45	2,191	7,043
21	2,639	3,816	46	3,786	7,188
22	3,257	4,907	47	5,558	14,023
23	4,667	6,414	48	6,222	6,915
24	5,747	1,840	49	8,595	7,452
25	4,094	2,498	50	5,754	11,354
			Total	227,033	333,789
			Majority "No"		106,756

Source: Official Canvass, Board of Election Commissioners
(Transit Proposition One: April 7, 1925).

Table 3

Vote for Mayor by Wards, 1927
(two-party vote)

Ward	Dever	Thompson	Ward	Dever	Thompson
1	11,076	3,931	26	4,853	6,948
2	1,791	24,169	27	7,164	8,565
3	3,484	27,715	28	6,035	10,377
4	6,848	20,107	29	12,059	11,095
5	13,148	10,236	30	16,998	13,479
6	12,220	10,843	31	3,864	5,069
7	15,416	12,967	32	5,392	5,204
8	13,226	13,256	33	5,603	5,562
9	6,766	7,654	34	6,416	5,812
10	4,547	7,913	35	4,254	9,150
11	6,882	5,253	36	5,027	10,293
12	8,433	10,031	37	14,647	16,366
13	6,379	3,214	38	6,431	8,529
14	10,160	7,685	39	13,621	15,709
15	15,268	13,437	40	9,877	18,139
16	9,049	9,288	41	10,961	15,709
17	8,389	8,977	42	6,879	6,255
18	11,727	10,803	43	5,601	8,431
19	15,822	14,240	44	6,887	8,386
20	4,200	7,822	45	5,897	9,378
21	6,239	6,161	46	6,668	9,515
22	7,721	4,688	47	7,893	12,754
23	10,282	7,338	48	8,037	9,619
24	8,174	5,361	49	16,797	12,223
25	6,740	4,608	50	10,827	13,935
			Total	432,678	515,716
			Plurality		83,038

Source: Official Canvass, Board of Election Commissioners
(Mayoralty: April 5, 1927).

Table 4

Democratic Percentages by Wards, Mayoral Elections, 1923 and 1927
(two-party vote)

Ward	Characteristics	1923	1927
1	The Levee; Coughlin-Kenna ward; Democratic stronghold	87	74
2	Near South Side; black	69	7
3	Mostly black	56	11
4	Kenwood; some black	49	25
5	Hyde Park; University of Chicago; usually heavily Republican	46	56
6	Woodlawn; usually Republican	48	53
7	South Shore; usually Republican	56	54
8	Grand Crossing-Calumet	47	49
9	Pullman-Roseland	44	47
10	South Chicago; steel mill area with significant Polish vote	45	36
11	Bridgeport; Old Irish area with many Germans and Poles	77	57
12	Southwest Side; Poles moving in	62	46
13	Back-of-the-Yards; P. J. Carr's old ward; Irish and Polish elements	92	66
14	Canaryville; Irish area	78	57
15	Far Southwest Side	63	53
16	Englewood; part of Senator Deneen's stronghold	59	49
17	Deneen's own ward; some "lace curtain" Irish	45	48
18	Another Deneen ward; less affluent	55	52
19	Morgan Park-Beverly; middle- and upper-class WASP	42	53
20	Lower West Side; one-third black	81	35
21	Sabath's ward; Polish and Bohemian	77	50
22	South Lawndale; Cermak's ward; heavily Bohemian	75	62

Ward	Characteristics	1923	1927
23	Similar to 22nd (Bohemian and wet)	65	58
24	North Lawndale; Rosenberg-Arvey ward; heavily Jewish	85	50
25	Johnny Powers's ward; working class; strongly Democratic	71	59
26	River ward; many Italians	89	41
27	River ward; lodging-house district	65	46
28	Sullivan's old ward, now led by Pat Nash; Irish, Polish, and blacks	59	37
29	Garfield Park; home of Crowe, Sweitzer, and Martin J. O'Brien	69	52
30	Austin and far West Side; strongly Democratic	69	56
31	Chicago Commons area; Dever's former ward (old 17th); Poles, Italians	84	43
32	Working class, Polish and Italian district	71	51
33	Kunz's ward; "Polish Downtown"	84	50
34	Keane's ward; more affluent Poles	71	52
35	Humboldt Park	43	32
36	West Humboldt Park, Republican stronghold	42	33
37	North Austin; middle class; large Swedish vote	43	47
38	Logan Square; Adamowski's ward	66	43
39	Avondale; rapidly growing with large influx of Poles	58	46
40	Irving park; middle class, Republican area	37	35
41	Far Northwest Side; fast growing, middle class	40	41
42	Near North Side; polyglot area, "Gold Coast and the Slum"	69	52
43	Lincoln Park; parties closely matched	53	40
44	Brundage's ward; many Germans	45	45
45	Heart of German community	56	39
46	Oscar Nelson's ward; many Swedes	41	41
47	Ravenswood	40	38

Ward	Characteristics	1923	1927
48	Uptown; middle class, heavily Republican	43	46
49	Rogers Park-Edgewater; Dever's home ward; usually "rock bound" Republican	45	58
50	Rosehill; new growth area	43	44
	Citywide	57.8	45.6

Notes

Chapter 1. Beginnings

1. *Chicago American* (April 17, 1923). The mayor's family name is pronounced in various ways; he always pronounced it to "to rhyme with 'sever.'" See *Chicago Tribune* (January 21, 1923).

2. *Chicago Tribune* (April 16, 17, 1923); *Chicago Daily News* (April 17, 1923).

3. The *Chicago Post* (April 17, 1923) declared that "there has never been such an inauguration." The *Chicago Herald and Examiner* of the same date echoed the sentiment, calling the event "the greatest inaugural ceremony" in the city's history; the paper also remarked that "the most astounding feature [was] the number of persons who sought to be present at the moment when Chicago installed a new mayor." The *Chicago Tribune* marveled at the spontaneous gathering, suggesting that the Chicago Colosseum might have been an appropriate site for the inauguration.

4. *Chicago Daily News, Chicago Herald and Examiner, Chicago Tribune* (all April 17, 1923).

5. *Chicago Herald and Examiner* (April 17, 1923).

6. Numerous pictures of Dever are on file in the William E. Dever Scrapbooks, Chicago Historical Society, Chicago. The *Chicago Tribune* comments are from April 17, 1923.

7. *Chicago American* (April 17, 1923).

8. Photographs of the dignitaries on the inauguration dais are in the *Chicago Daily News* and *Chicago Tribune* (both April 17, 1923).

9. *Chicago Herald and Examiner, Chicago Tribune* (both April 17, 1923).

10. *Chicago Tribune* (January 21, 1923).

11. William E. Dever (hereafter referred to as *WED*) to Clarence W. Diver (February 19, 1915), William E. Dever Papers, Chicago Historical Society, Chicago.

12. *United States Census of Population, 1900: Massachusetts*, vol. 81, E.D. 1525, sheet 14. The conditions faced by the arriving Irish immigrants are described vividly in Oscar Handlin, *Boston's Immigrants*, rev. ed. (Cambridge, MA: Belknap Press of Harvard University Press, 1959).

13. *Chicago Tribune* (January 21, 1923); *Boston Globe* (April 3, 1904, February 11, 1923).

14. *Boston Globe* (April 3, 1904), *Boston Directory . . . 1858* (Boston: Adams, Sampson, and Co., 1858), p. 406.

15. *United States Census of Population, 1880: Massachusetts*, vol 18, E.D. 425, sheet 31. The exact date of the Devers' move to Woburn is uncertain. It was probably 1859; in 1860, Patrick Dever appears on the tax rolls as a landowner. See *Tax List of the Town of Woburn* (Woburn, MA: Middlesex Journal Office, 1861), p. 13.

16. For Worburn's early history, see Samuel Sewall, *The History of Woburn, Middlesex County, Massachusetts* (Boston: Wiggins and Lunt, 1868); *Woburn* (Boston: Edison Electric Illuminating Co. 1909); and *Woburn Daily Times*, 75th Anniversary Edition (October 21, 1976).

17. *Woburn Daily Times* (February 1, 1923, August 15, 1923).

18. *Chicago Daily News* (May 16, 1925).

19. Ibid.; James H. Doherty to Katherine Conway Dever (May 19, 1923), Dever Papers.

20. *Chicago Daily News* (May 16, 1925).

21. Ibid.

22. The figures for Irish employment as laborers and domestics are from the 1850 *U.S. Census of Boston;* they are found in Handlin, p. 253. Patrick Dever's land-ownership was a distinct rarity. Although many Irish immigrants acquired real estate in the late 1860s and 1870s, few held it as early as Patrick. See Stephan Thernstrom, *Poverty and Progress: Social Mobility in a Nineteeth Century City* (Cambridge, MA: Harvard University Press, 1964), pp. 29, 172–80.

23. *Boston Post* (November 15, 1925).

24. Edward M. Levine, *The Irish and Irish Politicians* (Notre Dame, IN; University of Notre Dame Press, 1966), Chapter 4.

25. See *Chicago Tribune* (March 30, 1923). Another example of the prominence given Dever's public schooling can be found in Frederick Rex, "The Mayors of the City of Chicago from March 4, 1837, to April 13, 1933" (typescript, Municipal Reference Library, Chicago, 1933), p. 109.

26. LaGuardia's role as the ultimate marginal man in politics is described in Arthur Mann, *LaGuardia: A Fighter against His Times, 1882–1933* (Philadelphia: J. B. Lippincott Co., 1959).

27. The 1880 census gives Patrick Dever's address as "Chestnut Street, Woburn." The Dever children and their birthdates are Mary (1857), Charlotte (1858), William (1862), Harriett (1865), Joseph (1867), Catherine (1869), Daniel (1872), and Lillian (1874).

28. *Chicago Daily News* (March 13, 1923); *Woburn Daily Times* (February 1, 1923).

29. *Chicago Journal* (October 15, 1924); *Woburn Daily Times* (February 1, 1923).

30. *Olean Evening Times* (January 24, 1923); certificate of marriage between William E. Dever and Katherine Conway, Dever Papers.

31. *Boston Globe* (April 19, 1923); *Chicago Post* (January 20, 1923).

32. The precise sequence and dates of Dever's early career are unclear. Various sources provide contradictory information. We do know that Kate Dever paid the voter's registration fee in Woburn at the end of 1886 (see Poll Tax Receipt [November 1, 1886], Dever Papers). Dever stated in a number of interviews that he and his wife had lived in Boston for a time before moving to Chicago. In this case and others, I have tried to reconstruct the most probable order of events.

33. *Brooklyn Eagle* (September 8, 1929).

34. *Boston Post* (August 15, 1923); *Chicago Tribune* (January 20, 1923).

35. Quoted in Lloyd Lewis and Henry Justin Smith, *Chicago: The History of its Reputation* (New York: Harcourt, Brace, 1929), p. 113.

36. See Sir John Leng's 1876 impressions in Bessie Louise Pierce, ed., *As Others See Chicago: Impressions of Visitors, 1673–1933* (Chicago: University of Chicago Press, 1933), pp. 219–21

37. Bessie Louise Pierce, *A History of Chicago*, 3 vols. (New York: Alfred A. Knopf, 1937–1957), 3:501, 519

38. Ibid., Chapters 3–6; Perry Duis, *Chicago: Creating New Traditions* (Chicago: Chicago Historical Society, 1976), pp. 101–11.

39. The DuSable witticism is quoted by Albert E. Dickens in *Forty-four Cities in the City of Chicago* (Chicago: Chicago Plan Commission, 1942), p. 20. The population figures are from Pierce, *History* 3: 515–16.

40. Pierce, ibid., 2:13–19, 3:26–37. For a detailed treatment of the process, see Paul F. Cressey, "The Succession of Cultural Groups in the City of Chicago" (Ph.D. dissertation, University of Chicago, 1930).

41. Harold M. Mayer and Richard C. Wade, *Chicago: Growth of a Metropolis* (Chicago and London: University of Chicago Press, 1969), p. 152.

42. Mike Royko, *Boss: Richard J. Daley of Chicago* (New York: E. P. Dutton & Co., 1971), p. 24.

43. Mayer and Wade, pp. 152–54; Pierce, *History*, 3:22–28, *Historic City: The Settlement of Chicago* (Chicago: City of Chicago, 1976), supplemental community maps.

44. Mayer and Wade, p. 154; Pierce, *Others See*, pp. 275–80; Thomas Lee Philpott, *The Slum and the Ghetto: Neighborhood Deterioration and Middle-Class Reform in Chicago, 1880–1930* (New York: Oxford University Press, 1978, Chapter 1). See also Oscar Handlin, *The Uprooted*, 2d ed. (Boston: Little, Brown & Co., 1973), Chapter 6.

45. Pierce, *History*, vol. 3, Chapters 7–8.

46. The early history of West Town is described in Homer Hoyt, "Inventory Gives Low-down on Near Northwest," *Real Estate* 16 (April 26, 1941): 11–14; *Local Community Fact Book: Chicago Metropolitan Area* (Chicago: Chicago Fact Book Consortium, University of Illinois at Chicago, 1984), pp. 62–66; and Dominic A. Pacyga and Ellen Skerrett, *Chicago: City of Neighborhoods* (Chicago: Loyola University Press, 1986), pp. 166–74.

47. *Lakeside Annual Directory of the City of Chicago: 1889* (Chicago: Chicago Directory Co., 1889), p.493. During 1909–1911, Chicago's street numbering system was changed. The present address of the Devers' first Chicago home would be 666 North May Street.

48. *Chicago Daily News, Chicago Post* (both March 13, 1923).

49. *Chicago Post* (March 13, 1923).

50. *Chicago American* (September 5, 1929); Ovid Demaris, *Captive City* (New York: Lyle Stuart, 1969), pp. 179–80. Thomas E. Keane, the son of Dever's friend, succeeded his father as Democratic committeeman of the Thirty-first Ward. During the Daley administration, as city council floor leader, the younger Keane was regarded as Chicago's second most powerful political leader.

51. *Boston Globe* (February 11, 1923); *Boston Post* (August 15, 1923, November 15, 1925); *Chicago Daily News* (May 16, 1925).

52. *Boston Post* (August 15, 1923).

53. Interview with Ray Berry, Chicago (July 30, 1980). Mr. Berry was assistant dean of Chicago-Kent College of Law, the successor institution to Dever's school.

54. *Chicago Daily News* (March 13, 1923).

55. *Chicago Journal* (March 14, 1923); *Chicago Post* (March 13, 1923).

56. Dever's account books give some indication of the scope of his practice, though only the books for 1905–1908 have survived; see Account Books, Dever Papers. Dever describes his murder trial in *Chicago Daily News* (March 13, 1923).

57. *Lakeside Annual Directory of the City of Chicago: 1893* (Chicago: Chicago Directory Co., 1893), p. 458; *Lakeside Annual Directory of the City of Chicago: 1897* (Chicago: Chicago Directory Co., 1897), p.565. The current numbers of the addresses would be 663 North May Street and 1113 West Chicago Avenue.

58. *United States Census of Population, 1900: Illinois*, vol. 43, E.D. 541, sheet 2; *Woburn Daily Times* (February 1, 1923).

59. *Book of Chicagoans: 1905* (Chicago: A. N. Marquis, 1905), p. 162; *Chicago Daily News* (March 13, 1923).

60. Graham Taylor, *Chicago Commons through Forty Years* (Chicago: Chicago Commons Association, 1936), pp. 139–40.

61. *Chicago Daily News* (March 17, 1923); *Chicago Journal* (March 14, 1923).

Chapter 2. Political Apprenticeship: 1900–1910

1. The information on Chicago and Cook County governments is drawn from three sources: Charles E. Merriam, *Chicago: A More Intimate View of Urban Politics* (New York: Macmillan Co., 1929); Charles E. Merriam, Spencer D. Parratt, and Albert Lepawsky, *The Government of the Metropolitan Region of Chicago* (Chicago: University of Chicago Press, 1933); and Harold F. Gosnell, *Machine Politics, Chicago Model* (Chicago: University of Chicago Press, 1937).

2. There have been numerous studies of urban machine politics and the ward-boss system, including the works of Merriam, Gosnell, and others cited in these notes. Two major accounts were written during the era under study (1890–1910), offering today's reader all the advantages and disadvantages of a contemporary view: see James Bryce, *The American Commonwealth*, 3d ed. (New York and London: Macmillan Co., 1895), vol. 2, Chapters 59–68; and M. Ostrogorski, *Democracy and the Organization of Political Parties* (New York and London: Macmillian Co., 1902), vol. 2, Chapters 6–7. For a different perspective, see the era's most noted apologia for boss rule, William L. Riordan, ed., *Plunkitt of Tammany Hall*, paperback ed. (New York: E. P. Dutton, 1963).

3. Merriam, *Chicago*, pp. 95–97; Carroll Hill Wooddy, *The Chicago Primary of 1926* (Chicago: University of Chicago Press, 1926), p.33.

4. See Carter H. Harrison, *Stormy Years: The Autobiography of Carter H. Harrison* (Indianapolis: Bobbs-Merrill Co., 1935); and Lloyd Wendt and Herman Kogan, *Lords of the Levee: The Story of Bathhouse John and Hinky Dink* (Indianapolis: Bobbs-Merrill Co., 1943).

5. Bessie Lousie Pierce, *A History of Chicago*, 3 vols. (New York: Alfred A. Knopf, 1937–1957), 3:375–77; Paul M. Green, "The Chicago Democratic Party, 1840–1920: From Factionalism to Political Organization" (Ph.D. dissertation, University of Chicago, 1975), pp.45–84.

6. Merriam, *Chicago;* pp. 94–95; Wooddy, pp. 14–15; Joel Arthur Tarr, *A Study of Boss Politics: William Lorimer of Chicago* (Urbana: University of Illinois Press, 1971), Chapters 5–6.

7. Pierce, vol. 3, Chapter 10; Claudius O. Johnson, *Carter Henry Harrison I, Political Leader* (Chicago: University of Chicago Press, 1928), Chapters 10–11.

8. Louise C. Wade, *Graham Taylor, Pioneer for Social Justice, 1851–1938* (Chicago: University of Chicago Press, 1964), pp. 72–73.

9. Graham Taylor, *Pioneering on Social Frontiers* (Chicago: University Chicago Press, 1930), p. 29.

10. Ibid., pp.32–33; Louise Wade, p. 74.

11. William T. Stead, *If Christ Came to Chicago!* (Chicago: Laird and Lee, 1894), pp. 159–69.

12. Quoted in Louise Wade, p. 74.

13. Allen F. Davis, *Spearheads of Reform: The Social Settlements and the Progressive Movement, 1890–1914* (New York: Oxford University Press, 1971), pp. 188–89.

14. Stead, *passim;* Emmett Dedmon, *Fabulous Chicago,* 2d ed. (New York: Atheneum, 1981), pp. 257–59.

15. Wendt and Kogan, pp. 144–49; Taylor, pp. 58–60; Hoyt King, *Citizen Cole of Chicago* (Chicago: Horder's, Inc., 1931). For a firsthand account of the origins of the Municipal Voters' League by one of its leaders, Alderman William Kent, see Joel A. Tarr, "William Kent to Lincoln Steffens: Origins of Progressive Reform in Chicago," *Mid-America* 47 (January 1965): 48–57.

16. Wendt and Kogan, Chapter 15; Taylor, pp. 60–61; "Introduction to the Preliminary Report of the Municipal Voters' League" (Pamphlet, 1900), p. 1.

17. The literature on Progressivism is one of the most extensive in the field of American history. A particularly thorough bibliographical essay is contained in Arthur S. Link and Richard L. McCormick, *Progressivism* (Arlington Heights, IL: Harlan Davidson, Inc., 1983), pp. 119–40; the rest of the book is a good general overview of the subject. Three useful interpretary anthologies are Arthur Mann, ed., *The Progressive Era: Liberal Renaissance or Liberal Failure* (New York: Holt, Rinehart and Winston, 1963); Arthur Mann, ed., *The Progressive Era: Major Issues of Interpretation,* 2d ed. (Hinsdale, IL: The Dryden Press, 1975); and Louis L. Gould, ed., *The Progressive Era* (Syracuse, NY: Syracuse University Press, 1974). Among the more influential general studies, embracing a variety of perspectives, are Benjamin Parke DeWitt, *The Progressive Movement* (New York: Macmillan Co., 1915); Richard Hofstadter, *The Age of Reform: From Bryan to F.D.R.* (New York: Alfred A. Knopf, 1955); Samuel P. Hays, *The Response to Industrialism, 1885–1914* (Chicago: University of Chicago Press, 1957); Robert H. Wiebe, *The Search for Order, 1877–1920* (New York: Hill and Wang, 1967); John D. Buenker, *Urban Liberalism and Progressive Reform* (New York: Charles Scribner's Sons, 1973).

18. Melvin G. Holli, *Reform in Detroit: Hazen S. Pingree and Urban Politics* (New York: Oxford University Press, 1969), Chapter 8. For Medill's career as mayor, see David L. Protess, "Joseph Medill: Chicago's First Modern Mayor," in Paul M. Green and Melvin G. Holli, eds., *The Mayors: The Chicago Political Tradition* (Carbondale: Southern Illinois University Press, 1987), pp. 1–15.

19. Lincoln Steffens, *The Autobiography of Lincoln Steffens* (New York: Harcourt, Brace and Co., 1936), p. 423.

20. Louise Wade, Chapters 1–3.

21. Ibid., pp. 129–30.

22. Taylor, pp. 56–58; "Municipal Voters' League: Why it Should Receive Public Support" (pamphlet, n.d.), p. 4.

23. Taylor, *Chicago Commons through Forty Years* (Chicago: Chicago Commons Association, 1936), pp. 70–71.

24. Graham Taylor, "By Graham Taylor," *Chicago Daily News* (March 17, 1923).

25. Ibid.; Taylor, *Chicago Commons,* pp. 70–71.

26. *Chicago Chronicle* (February 25, 1900).

27. Ibid.

28. Undated newspaper clippings, Dever Scrapbooks.

29. Ibid.

30. Ibid.

31. Ibid.; *Chicago Daily News Almanac: 1901* (Chicago: Chicago Daily News, 1901), p. 292. This annual publication is the most convenient source of Chicago elections returns during Dever's career; it is hereafter cited as *CDNA*.

32. Davis, p. 166; Graham Taylor, "New Hope in Our Ward Politics," *The Commons* 6 (April 1901): 15.

33. Edward Van Der Rhoer, *Master Spy* (New York: Charles Scribner's Sons, 1981), p. 19; Allen F. Davis, "Raymond Robins: The Settlement Worker as Municipal Reformer," *Social Services Review* 33 (June 1959): 131–41; Hugh D. Camitta, "Raymond Robins: Study of a Progressive, 1901–1917" (Honors thesis, Williams College, 1965).

34. Taylor, *Chicago Commons*, pp. 259–60; Graham Taylor to Raymond Robins (September 1, 1902); John Smulski to Raymond Robins (May 31, 1901); both in Raymond Robins Papers, State Historical Society of Wisconsin, Madison.

35. For Dever's 1901 refusal to run, see *The Commons* 6 (May 1901): 15. Regarding Dever's growing prominence in the ward Reform movement, it should be noted that the other four speakers at the foundation dinner were all well-known local figures: Taylor, Robins, Alderman Smulski, and club president Joseph O'Donnell.

36. *The Commons* 7 (April 1902): 20.

37. Ibid.; Davis, "Raymond Robins," p. 134.

38. Polish language pamphlet (undated), Graham Taylor Papers, Newberry Library, Chicago.

39. *Chicago Daily News* (March 28, 1902).

40. *Chicago Daily News, Chicago Record-Herald* (both March 28, 1902).

41. *Chicago Daily News* (February 24, 1902).

42. Undated newspaper clipping, Dever Scrapbooks.

43. Ralph R. Tingley, "From Carter Harrison II to Fred Busse: A Study of Political Parties and Personages from 1896 to 1907" (Ph.D. dissertation, University of Chicago, 1950), p. 118; untitled Municipal Voters' League pamphlet (n.d.), Dever Scrapbooks.

44. *Boston Globe* (February 11, 1923); *Chicago Journal* (March 14, 1923).

45. *Chicago Daily News* (June 15, 1902); *CDNA: 1903*, pp. 381–82.

46. *Chicago American* (June 7, 1902).

47. *Chicago Post* (March 14, 1923).

48. Ibid.

49. Undated newspaper clippings, Dever Scrapbooks.

50. *Chicago Examiner* (December 28, 1903). The Ogden Avenue extension did not generate the traffic envisioned, and by the 1980s had been closed and built over again north of North Avenue.

51. Thomas Lee Philpott, *The Slum and the Ghetto: Neighborhood Deterioration and Middle-Class Reform in Chicago, 1880–1930* (New York: Oxford University Press, 1978), pp. 85–88. For Jane Addams's thoughts on the resilience of such leaders as Powers, see her article "Why the Ward Boss Rules," *The Outlook* 58 (April 2, 1898): 879–82.

52. Samuel P. Hays, "The Politics of Reform in Municipal Government in the Progressive Era," *Pacific Northwest Quarterly* 55 (October 1964): 159–69; Gabriel Kolko, *The Triumph of Conservatism* (New York: Macmillan Publishing Co., 1963).

53. Philpott, pp. 86–88, 285.

54. Malcolm W. Bingay, *Of Me I Sing* (Indianapolis: Bobbs-Merrill Co., 1949), p. 149.

55. For more on the Progressive split over Municipal Ownership in Chicago, consult Richard E. Becker, "Edward Dunne: Reform Mayor of Chicago, 1905–07" (Ph.D. dissertation, University of Chicago, 1971).

56. *Chicago Record-Herald* (March 27, 1902).

57. Harrison, Chapter 12; Wendt and Kogan, Chapter 15.

58. Alan R. Lind, *Chicago Surface Lines: An Illustrated History*, 3d ed. (Park Forest IL: Transport History Press, 1979), p. 449.

59. Harrison, pp. 244–45.

60. *Chicago Journal* (October 1, 1904); *Chicago Record-Herald* (October 4, 1904).

61. Harrison, p. 252; *Chicago Tribune* (January 18, 1905).

62. *Chicago Post* (January 27, 1905); *Chicago Record-Herald* (January 11, 1905); *Chicago Tribune* (January 18, 1905).

63. Becker, pp. 54–58; Harrison, p. 255; *Chicago Post* (January 30, 1905).

64. *Chicago Post* (April 7, 1905); *Chicago Tribune* (March 19, 1906).

65. Becker, pp. 99–100. Dunne's own account of the battle for Municipal Ownership is in Edward F. Dunne, *Illinois, The Heart of a Nation* (Chicago and New York: Lewis Publishing Co., 1933), vol. 2, Chapter 66. See also Ray Ginger, *Altgeld's America*, reprint (New York: New Viewpoints, 1973), Chapter 12.

66. *Chicago Chronicle* (October 10, 1905).

67. Becker, p. 100; *Chicago Inter-Ocean* (January 19, 1906). It was also suggested that the council shifted to favoring Dunne's plan when the transit companies opposing the plan would not pay sufficient bribes (Ginger, p. 300).

68. Becker, pp. 131–32; Lind, p. 450.

69. Becker, p. 144; *Chicago Tribune* (Feburary 12, 1907).

70. Edward F. Dunne to Walter L. Fisher (February 6, 1907); Charles Werno to Walter L. Fisher (February 7, 1907); both Walter L. Fisher Papers, Library of Congress, Washington, D.C. Fisher later became Secretary of the Interior during the Taft administration.

71. "Settling Chicago's Traction Question," *The Outlook* 85 (March 1907): 537.

72. The articles, published under the title "A Traction Debate," ran in the *Chicago Daily News* from March 5 through March 19, 1907. Dever declined payment for his writings; see C. H. Dennis to WED (March 14, 1907), Dever Papers.

73. *Chicago Daily News* (March 5, 1907).

74. Election figures are from *CDNA: 1908*, p. 259. Busse was one of the city's more controversial politicians. He was anathema to most of the reformers; Harold Ickes, for one, considered him a "near hoodlum" (see "Fred Busse," biographical sketch, Harold L. Ickes Papers, Library of Congress, Washington, D.C.). To his supporters, however, Busse was a caring man who associated with disreputable people in order to straighten them out; this view is advanced in Charles H. Hermann, *Recollections of Life and Doings in Chicago* (Chicago: Normandie House, 1945), Chapter 21. The most recent study of this mayor's career is Maureen A. Flanagan, "Fred A. Busse: Silent Mayor in Turbulent Times," in Green and Holli, pp. 50–60.

75. Lind, pp. 450–51.

76. *Chicago Post* (March 8, 1906).

77. Tingley, pp. 207–12.

78. Harold F. Gosnell, *Negro Politicians* (Chicago: University of Chicago Press, 1935), p. 85.

79. Ibid.; *Chicago Record-Herald* (November 9, 1906). The official canvass certified the election of Thomas B. Lantry, the top Democratic vote getter in the two-year-term category (Lantry, 90,754; Barnett, 90,450). There was some suggestion that Barnett had been counted out, but this was never proven.

80. *Chicago Record-Herald* (February 27, 1907).
81. *Chicago Daily News* (March 5, 1907).
82. For superior court judge: McSurely, 164,518; Dever, 151,677. For mayor of Chicago: Busse, 164,702; Dunne, 151,779. *CDNA: 1908*, pp. 259, 321.
83. *Chicago Daily News* (August 10, 1908).
84. *Chicago Daily News* (August 8, 1908).
85. *Chicago Daily News* (August 10, 1908). See also E. J. Batten to WED (August 10, 15, 19, 1908); Ernie G. Grey to WED (August 11, 1908); all in Dever Papers.
86. Edward Dunne to WED (August 24, 1908), Dever Papers.

Chapter 3. Judicial Years: 1910–1922

1. *Chicago Record-Herald* (April 3, 1906); *CDNA: 1907*, p. 361.
2. *Chicago Record-Herald* (January 6, 1910).
3. Kunz's career is described in Edward R. Kantowicz, *Polish American Politics in Chicago: 1888–1940* (Chicago and London: University of Chicago, 1975), pp. 64–69.
4. *Chicago Record-Herald* (January 6, 1910).
5. *Chicago Tribune* (March 17, 1910); *Chicago Daily News* (February 9, 17, 1910).
6. *Chicago Daily News* (April 2, 1910); undated newspaper clippings, Dever Scrapbooks.
7. *Chicago Tribune*, undated, Dever Scrapbooks.
8. *Chicago Record-Herald* (March 25, 1910).
9. *Democratic Bulletin* (March 23, 1910); F. Rogalski, quoted in *Chicago Tribune* (March 21, 1910); *Chicago Journal* (March 10, 1910).
10. Campaign letter (March 31, 1910), Dever Papers.
11. *Chicago Daily News* (April 5, 1910); undated newspaper clippings, Dever Scrapbooks.
12. *CDNA: 1911*, p. 403. The vote totals by precinct are in *Chicago Tribune* (April 6, 1910).
13. Raymond Robins to Margaret Dreier Robins (May 14, 1910), Robins Papers.
14. *Chicago Tribune* (July 12, 1910).
15. *Chicago Tribune* (July 13, 1910).
16. *Chicago Tribune* (July 14, 1910).
17. WED to Mayor Fred Busse and the Chicago City Council (November 28, 1910), Dever Papers. For the superior court vote, see *CDNA: 1911*, p. 399. After his resignation, Dever's aldermanic seat was filled by special election. His successor was none other than Stanley Walkowiak.
18. Edward M. Martin, *The Role of the Bar in Electing the Bench in Chicago* (Chicago: University of Chicago Press, 1936), pp. 11–13; Harvey M. Karlen, *The Governments of Chicago* (Chicago: Courier Publishing Co., 1958), pp. 141–43.
19. Martin, p. 13; Albert Lepawsky, *The Judicial System of Metropolitan Chicago* (Chicago: University of Chicago Press, 1932), pp. 169–71.
20. Dever's salary as an alderman was $3,000. During 1905–1908, his legal practice brought in about $3,500 per year. This gave him an annual income of approximately $6,500. His investment income is not known. See Account Books, Dever Papers.
21. Thomas Lee Philpott, *The Slum and the Ghetto: Neighborhood Deterioration and Middle-Class Reform, 1880–1930* (New York: Oxford University Press, 1978), pp. 86–87, 288–92.
22. *Lakeside Annual Directory of the City of Chicago: 1912* (Chicago: Chicago Direc-

tory Co., 1912), p. 379; *Lakeside Annual Directory of the City of Chicago: 1916* (Chicago: Chicago Directory Co., 1916), p. 472.

23. Dever's involvement in Irish-American affairs and the Irish independence movement is noted in *Chicago Herald and Examiner* (November 23, 1919) and *Chicago Tribune* (January 4, 1922); see also Thomas H. Prendergast to WED (September 25, 1920), Dever Papers. His dinners for orphans are described in *Chicago Herald and Examiner* (November 27, 1914), and *Chicago Journal* (May 16, 1916). For Dever's identification as a friend of labor, see David Dolnick, "The Role of Labor in Chicago Politics since 1919," (M.A. thesis, University of Chicago, 1939), p. 14.

24. Some of Dever's speaking activities are detailed in *Chicago Tribune* (October 6, 1912); *Chicago Record-Herald* (November 21, 1913); C. Kelly to WED (January 29, 1916), Dever Papers. The building dedication is noted in Graham Taylor to WED (November 15, 1916), Dever Papers.

25. *Chicago Daily News* (November 20, 1914); *Chicago Tribune* (October 10, 1916).

26. *Chicago American* (April 3, 1913).

27. The Lorimer trial is recounted in Joel Arthur Tarr, *A Study of Boss Politics: William Lorimer of Chicago* (Urbana: University of Illinois Press, 1971), pp. 309–13; see also Dever Scrapbooks, vols. 6–8, "Lorimer Trial."

28. See campaign letters (May 25, 31, 1916); Edward R. Bryant to WED (May 29, 1916); all in Dever Papers. Election returns are in *CDNA 1917*, p. 595.

29. Karlen, p.143; Lepawsky, pp. 169–70; Martin, p. 12.

30. The selected cases are listed in Francis X. Busch, "William E. Dever" (memorial pamphlet, Chicago Bar Association, 1929). The cases cited are *Consumers Co. v. City of Chicago*, 208 Ill. App. 203; *Reynolds et al. v. North American Union*, 204 Ill. App. 316; *Postal Telegraph Cable Company v. B & O–Chicago Terminal Railroad Company*, 29 Ill. App. 304.

31. *Read et al. v. Central Union Telephone et al.*, Defense Brief, pp.1–2; *Read v. CUT*, Final Decree (July 10, 1917), pp. i–iii; J. Warren Stehman, *The Financial History of the American Telephone and Telegraph Company* (Boston and New York: Houghton Mifflin Co., 1925), p. 209.

32. *Read v. CUT*, Final Decree, pp. 19, 24–25.

33. Ibid., pp. 97–98.

34. For a description of the Progressives' ambivalence toward big business, see Richard L. McCormick, "The Discovery that 'Business Corrupts Politics': A Reappraisal of the Origins of Progressivism," *American Historical Review* 86 (April 1981): 247–74. Dever's reputation as a prolabor judge is noted in Dolnick, p. 14. See also Royal E. Montgomery, *Industrial Relations in the Chicago Building Trades* (Chicago: University of Chicago Press, 1927), p. 74.

35. *Chicago Tribune* (July 12, 1917); Stehman, p. 209; *Moody's Analysis of Investments (1919)*, II; *Public Utilities and Industrials*, p. 1948; *Bell Telephone News* 10 (January, 1921), p. 27.

36. For details of the Black Sox case, see Eliot Asinof, *Eight Men Out* (New York: Holt, Rinehart, and Winston, 1963).

37. Graham Taylor to WED (November 24, 1913), Dever Papers; *Chicago Daily News* (March 20, 1923).

38. *CDNA: 1923*, p. 743.

39. Paul M. Green, "The Chicago Democratic Party, 1840–1920: From Factionalism to Political Organization" (Ph.D. dissertation, University of Chicago, 1975), pp. 123–31. Green's study is generally favorable to the Sullivan consolidation; for a hostile account, see Fletcher Dobyns, *The Underworld of American Politics* (New York: Fletcher Dobyns, 1932), Chapter 3.

40. Charles E. Merriam, *Chicago: A More Intimate View of Urban Politics* (New York: Macmillan Co., 1929), pp.281–87; Carter H. Harrison, *Stormy Years: The Autobiography of Carter H. Harrison* (Indianapolis: Bobbs-Merrill Co., 1935), Chapters 25–27; Barry D. Karl, *Charles E. Merriam and the Study of Politics* (Chicago and London: University of Chicago Press, 1974), pp. 66–72.

41. Carroll L. Wooddy, *The Chicago Primary of 1926* (Chicago: University of Chicago Press, 1926), 14–16; Lloyd Wendt and Herman Kogan, *Big Bill of Chicago* (Indianapolis: Bobbs-Merrill Co., 1953), Chapter 8; Harold Zink, *City Bosses in the United States* (Durham, NC: Duke University Press, 1930), Chapter 15.

42. Green, pp. 148–62; Harrison, Chapter 30; Charles H. Hermann, *Recollections of Life and Doings in Chicago* (Chicago: Normandie House, 1945), pp. 196–98; *Chicago Tribune* (June 18, 1911).

43. Harrison, pp. 339–40; Lloyd Wendt and Herman Kogan, *Lords of the Levee: The Story of Bathhouse John and Hinky Dink* (Indianapolis: Bobbs-Merrill Co., 1943), pp. 303–304; Alex Gottfried, *Boss Cermak of Chicago: A Study of Political Leadership* (Seattle: University of Washington Press, 1962), p. 81.

44. *Chicago Tribune* (February 24, 1915); Harrison, pp. 345–48. For Sullivan's senatorial campaign, see Walter A. Townsend, *Illinois Democracy*, 5 vols. (Springfield, IL: Democratic Historical Association, 1935), 1:317–19.

45. Thompson has been the subject of several biographies. For his early career, see Wendt and Kogan, *Big Bill*, Chapters 1–7; and John Bright, *Hizzoner Big Bill Thompson: An Idyll of Chicago* (New York: Jonathan Cape and Harrison Smith, 1930), Chapters 1–6. The latest scholarly study of Thompson is Douglas Bukowski, "Big Bill Thompson: The 'Model' Politician," in Paul M. Green and Melvin G. Holli, eds. *The Mayors: The Chicago Political Tradition* (Carbondale: Southern Illinois University Press, 1987), pp. 61–81.

46. Wendt and Kogan, *Big Bill*, pp. 100–115; Zink, p. 296.

47. Almost from the start of his term, Thompson diddled with the civil service system. In this connection, his reputation was particularly damaged by the suicide of Dr. Theodore Sachs, the respected former head of the Municipal Tuberculosis Sanatorium: Sachs's suicide note blamed "unscrupulous politicians" for his death, and it was well known that the mayor and Sachs had feuded over personnel matters. Thompson also lost popularity when he began to enforce the Sunday saloon-closing laws. See Wendt and Kogan, *Big Bill*, Chapters 11–13. In the April 1916 elections, the Democrats captured twenty-one of the thirty-five contested adlermanic seats: see *Chicago Tribune* (April 5, 1916).

48. *Chicago Tribune* (May 12, 1916). The Chicago Democratic organization was to be modeled on New York City's Tammany Hall. In later years, antimachine author Fletcher Dobyns would even refer to the Chicago Democrats as "Tammany"; see Dobyns, Chapter 4.

49. *Chicago Tribune* (June 19, 1918, September 12, 1918).

50. Wendt and Kogan, *Big Bill*, pp. 161–71; Eugene Perlstein, "The Progressive Movement in Chicago: 1919–1924" (M.A. thesis, University of Chicago, 1948), pp. 5–11.

51. Green, pp. 364–69. Between 1919 and 1975, only two Democratic mayoral primaries were contested. In both cases, the organization candidate easily triumphed: Edward Kelly over Thomas Courtney in 1939, and Richard J. Daley over Martin Kennelly and Benjamin Adamowski in 1955. For details on these campaigns, see Roger Biles, *Big City Boss in Depression and War: Mayor Edward J. Kelly of Chicago* (DeKalb: Northern Illinois University Press, 1984), pp.67–70; and Eugene Kennedy, *Himself! The Life and Times of Mayor Richard J. Daley* (New York: The Viking

Press, 1978), Chapter 9.

52. Quoted in Tarr, p. 199.

53. Harrison, p. 274. As evidence of the masses' low mentality, Harrison cited "the shrieks of adult delight that welcome the Pop-Eye, Mickey Mouse and kindred absurdities on the silver screen."

54. The Irish versus non-Irish interpretation can be found in a number of works. See Gottfried; Kennedy; Mike Royko, *Boss: Richard J. Daley of Chicago* (New York: E. P. Dutton and Co., 1971); John M. Allswang, *A House for All Peoples: Ethnic Politics in Chicago* (Lexington: University of Kentucky Press, 1971).

55. Sullivan's courting of the non-Irish is detailed in Green, passim; see also the same author's article "Irish Chicago: The Multi-Ethnic Road to Machine Success," in *Ethnic Chicago*, ed. Peter d'A. Jones and Melvin G. Holli (Grand Rapids: William B. Eerdmans Publishing Co., 1981), pp. 212–59. For the ethnic division of the 1910 harmony ticket, see *Chicago Tribune* (July 12–14, 1910). Harrison describes Dunne's strength among Irish voters in *Stormy Years*, pp. 266, 274.

56. Sullivan died of a heart attack on April 14, 1920. The Roger C. Sullivan High School was opened during Mayor Dever's administration, in 1926. It is located at 6631 North Bosworth Avenue.

Chapter 4. The Making of the Mayor: 1923

1. William H. Tuttle, Jr., *Race Riot: Chicago in the Red Summer of 1919* (New York: Atheneum, 1970), pp. 203–207.

2. For details on the school system's woes during the Thompson years, see George S. Counts, *Schools and Society in Chicago* (New York: Harcourt, Brace and Co., 1928), pp. 251–63; Mary Herrick, *The Chicago Schools: A Social and Political History* (Beverly Hills, CA: Sage Publications, 1971), pp. 137–42; and Lloyd Wendt and Herman Kogan, *Big Bill of Chicago* (Indianapolis: Bobbs-Merrill Co., 1953), pp.174–76.

3. The Thompson-*Tribune* feud was of long standing, exacerbated by the bitter 1918 Republican U.S. Senate primary, in which Big Bill was defeated by Medill McCormick, brother of the paper's publisher, Colonel Robert R. McCormick. Also Thompson had instituted a number of libel suits against the *Tribune* over the years; see John Bright, *Hizzoner Big Bill Thompson: An Idyll of Chicago* (New York: Jonathan Cape and Harrison Smith, 1930), pp. 125–26, 204, and Lloyd Wendt, *Chicago Tribune: The Rise of a Great American Newspaper* (Chicago: Rand McNally and Co., 1979), Chapter 20. For details on the experts' fees cases, consult Charles E. Merriam, *Chicago: A More Intimate View of Urban Politics* (New York: Macmillan Co., 1929), pp. 24–30.

4. Bright, pp. 178–79; Wendt and Kogan, *Big Bill*, pp. 194–96.

5. The pageants have been most recently described in Perry Duis and Glen E. Holt, "Chicago as It Was: Big Bill's Pageant of Progress," *Chicago* 29 (September, 1980): 112–14, 116. See also Bright, Chapter 14.

6. Bright, pp. 196–97; *Chicago Daily News* (November 8, 21, 1922).

7. The decline of the MVL is detailed in Joan S. Miller, "The Politics of Municipal Reform in Chicago during the Progressive Era: The Municipal Voters' League as a Test Case, 1896–1920" (M.A. thesis, Roosevelt University, 1966).

8. *The City Club Bulletin* 15 (1922): 145, 151. Darrow is quoted in the *Chicago Daily News* (December 19, 1922).

9. *Chicago Tribune* (January 3, 1923).

10. *Chicago Daily News* (December 26–29, 1922; January 2, 1923).

11. *Chicago Daily News* (January 4, 1923); *Chicago Tribune* (January 7, 1923).

12. *Chicago Daily News* (January 4, 1923). The organization's charter read: "Resolved: It is the utmost importance that Chicago secure a competent, progressive, and honest mayor, who will stop the wanton waste of public funds, protect the public schools, and guard the lives and property of our citizens. To this end, we organize the Citizens' Mayoralty committee, that, regardless of party, race, or religion, shall unite to accomplish the following: (1) The nomination at the Republican primary by Republicans alone, and at the Democratic primary by Democrats alone, two outstanding men of proved ability and integrity as candidates for mayor, (2) And, in order to secure such nominations, to urge upon the local Republican and Democratic leaders, respectively, the presentation of such men to the voters at the primaries." Shortly after this charter was promulgated, the group changed its name to the Nonpartisan Citizens' Mayoralty Committee. See also *The City Club Bulletin* 16 (1923): 4.

13. *Chicago Tribune* (January 11, 1923).

14. Quoted in "Senatorial Campaigns," *Time* 8 (August 9, 1926): 9.

15. Biographical information on Brennan is from Walter A. Townsend, *Illinois Democracy*, 5 vols. (Springfield, IL: Democratic Historical Assn., 1935), 2:34–37; Merriam, pp. 182–84; Parke Brown, "Brennan of Illinois," *Century Magazine* 112 (September 1926): 593-601; "Brennan and the Vanishing American Boss," *Literary Digest* 98 (September 1, 1928): 34–36.

16. Arthur W. Thurner, "The Impact of Ethnic Groups on the Democratic Party in Chicago" (Ph.D. dissertation, University of Chicago, 1966), pp. 68–70, 77–82; William H. Stuart, *The Twenty Incredible Years* (Chicago and New York: M. A. Donohue and Co., 1935), p. 182. Recall that John Hopkins, elected mayor through Sullivan's efforts in 1893, served only a partial term.

17. For examples, see *Chicago Daily News* (November 8, 11, 27, 1922; December 15, 1922). In later years, Harrison claimed that he could have had the Democratic nomination for the asking, and that even running as an Independent he would have "won in a walk." Carter H. Harrison, *Stormy Years: The Autobiography of Carter H. Harrison* (Indianapolis: Bobbs-Merrill Co., 1935), p. 479.

18. *Chicago Daily News* (December 21, 22, 1922). A total of eighteen names were finally submitted to the Democratic Party Managing Committee for consideration. Of these, the *Daily News* reported that ten were under serious scrutiny. Dever's name was on the list of eighteen but not among the "top ten," as of December 21.

19. Cermak biographical information is from Alex Gottfried, *Boss Cermak of Chicago: A Study of Political Leadership* (Seattle: University of Washington Press, 1962), Chapters 1–8.

20. Ibid., pp. 133–34. Cermak owned a real estate company and various small businesses in Pilsen and South Lawndale.

21. Harold L. Ickes, *The Autobiography of a Curmudgeon* (New York: Reynal and Hitchcock, 1943), pp. 247–48.

22. Alderman Schwartz's story quoting O'Connell is in Edward Herbert Mazur, "Minyans for a Prairie City: The Politics of Chicago Jewry, 1850–1940" (Ph.D. dissertation, University of Chicago, 1974), pp. 269–70. A somewhat different version of the same story is in Stuart, pp. 183–85.

23. Quotations are from George C. Sikes to Martin J. O'Brien (November 11, 1922), Dever Papers.

24. Dever had been touted as a mayoral possibility for many years, of course. The first serious mention of the judge as a contender for 1923 appeared in the *Chicago Herald and Examiner* (December 15, 1922). Political reporter Charles N. Wheeler noted that Dever had "stood true blue from the beginning of the traction fight of

1907," and that he had a "sterling record on the bench, and has kept in close touch with political and social affairs." As previously mentioned, the *Chicago Daily News* considered Dever a dark horse on December 21.

25. Two descriptions of the Brennan-Dever meeting are in Brown, pp. 596–97; and Stuart, pp.183–85.

26. Quoted in Brown, p. 597.

27. *Chicago Tribune* (January 18, 1923).

28. *Chicago American, Chicago Daily News, Chicago Herald and Examiner* (all January 17, 1923); *Chicago Journal* (January 18, 19, 1923).

29. *Chicago Tribune* (January 19, 1923). Cermak's biographer suggests that Brennan's fear of another Democrat building up his own following was one of the main reasons Dever was chosen over Cermak. See Gottfried, pp. 132–34.

30. The most famous Chicago example of "save-the-machine" slating of a blue-ribbon candidate is the 1947 nomination of Martin Kennelly for mayor. Incumbent mayor Edward J. Kelly had grown unpopular, and party chairman Jacob Arvey decided that the Democrats needed a businessman-nonpolitician to retain power. Kennelly served two terms, then was unceremoniously dumped when the party elders determined that the crisis had passed. See Arnold R. Hirsch, "Martin H. Kennelly: The Mugwump and the Machine," in Paul M. Green and Melvin G. Holli, eds., *The Mayors: The Chicago Political Tradition* (Carbondale: Southern Illinois University Press, 1987), pp. 126–43. For Murphy's role in promoting Progressive programs and upright candidates, consult Nancy Joan Weiss, *Charles Francis Murphy, 1858–1924: Respectability and Responsibility in Tammany Politics* (Northampton, MA: Smith College, 1968), Chapter 5. The alliance of old-stock reformers with urban ethnic politicians is described in John D. Buenker, "The Progressive Era: A Search for a Synthesis," *Mid-America* 51 (July 1969): 185–89; see also his book *Urban Liberalism and Progressive Reform* (New York: Charles Scribner's Sons, 1973).

31. For 1923, the Chicago City Council was restructured. There were to be fifty wards instead of thirty-five, with only one alderman for each ward. Aldermanic elections were also declared to be nonpartisan, an action that merely removed official party labeling and not political competition.

32. *Chicago Journal* (January 19, 1923). Geographic factors evidently played a part in setting up the Democratic ticket. Dever was then living on the North Side (Forty-ninth Ward), Gorman was a South Sider (Fourteenth Ward), and Cervenka was a West Sider (Twenty-second Ward).

33. Wendt and Kogan, *Big Bill*, pp. 206–207. Lueder had originally been proposed for mayor by Senator McCormick (Wendt, *Tribune*, p. 479). The Committee of One Hundred, which was dominated by the Brundage-McCormick Republicans, named the postmaster their candidate on January 16 (see *Chicago Daily News*, January 16, 1923).

34. Gottfried, p. 134. Thompson considered running as an Independent, but finally withdrew on January 25 (*Chicago Post* [January 23, 1923]; *Chicago Tribune* [January 26, 1923]).

35. Valentino's endorsement of Judge Barasa was reported in *Chicago American* (February 21, 1923). The results of the February 27 Republican mayoral primary: Lueder, 130,350; Litsinger, 75,117; Millard, 51,448; Barasa, 47,685 (*CDNA: 1924*, p. 729).

36. Biographical information on Arthur Lueder is from *Who's Who in Chicago and Illinois: 1931* (Chicago: A. N. Marquis Co., 1931), p. 607; and John Clayton, ed., *The Illinois Fact Book and Historical Almanac, 1673–1968* (Carbondale and Edwardsville: Southern Illinois University Press, 1970), p. 148.

37. *Chicago Tribune* (February 6, 1923). The Democratic open houses were held until the February 27 primaries. After that, Dever went out into the wards for more active campaigning.

38. *Chicago American* (March 27, 1923).

39. *Chicago Daily News* (January 23, 1923). Dever's first campaign speech was delivered at the Iroquois Club, a Democratic bastion, on January 22; in it, he introduced most of the themes he would make familiar in the weeks ahead.

40. *Chicago Tribune* (January 23, 1923).

41. *Chicago Herald and Examiner* (February 2, 1923).

42. Dever's program is outlined in "Campaign Pledges" (undated political broadside), Dever Scrapbooks.

43. *Chicago Herald and Examiner* (February 9, 1923, March 11, 1923); *Chicago Daily News* (February 13, 1923); *Chicago American* (March 13, 1923).

44. *Chicago Herald and Examiner* (March 14, 18, 1923); *Chicago Post* (March 9, 1923).

45. *Chicago Post* (March 20, 1923); *Chicago Tribune* (March 21, 23, 1923).

46. *Chicago Herald and Examiner* (March 16, 1923).

47. Harrison introduced Dever at the candidate's maiden speech as the Iroquois Club (*Chicago Tribune* [January 23, 1923]). Years later, in his second autobiography, Harrison claimed to have quit the Dever campaign after only fourteen days, fed up with Dever's supposed capitulation to George Brennan (Carter H. Harrison, *Growing up with Chicago* [Chicago: Ralph Fletcher Seymour, 1944], p. 319). As so often happened, "Our Carter" recalled events the way he wished; actually, he was still campaigning for Dever two months after the keynote speech. See Harrison's pro-Dever article in *Chicago Journal* (March 24, 1923), and one of his speeches reported in *Chicago Herald and Examiner* (March 20, 1923).

48. *Chicago Journal* (March 21, 1923).

49. *Chicago Herald and Examiner* (March 20, 1923). In his book *The Twenty Incredible Years* (Chicago and New York: M. A. Donohue and Co., 1935), Hearst reporter William H. Stuart takes the Brennan-Reformers alliance to task. He implies that Brennan dreamed up the whole Dever candidacy on his own and only later called in the "intelligent and public-spirited citizens" to rubber-stamp his selection. He also claims that Mrs. Fairbank was given the post of Democratic National Committeewoman in return for going along with Brennan's scheme (ibid., pp. 185–86). In assessing these and other Stuart interpretations of events, one should note that the reporter was a long-time foe of the regular Democratic organization and a close-enough friend of Big Bill Thompson to be offered the job of public works commissioner after Thompson's return to power (*Chicago Daily News* [April 6, 1927]).

50. *Chicago American* (March 1, 1923). Ickes is quoted in *Chicago Journal* (March 2, 1923).

51. Some endorsement examples: Sprague in *Chicago American* (February 16, 1923); Merriam in *Chicago American* (March 1, 1923); Robins in *Chicago Herald and Examiner* (March 5, 1923); Lathrop in *Chicago Herald and Examiner* (March 7, 1923).

52. Harold L. Ickes to Margaret Dreier Robins (April 5, 1923), Robins Papers. The Independent Dever Club opened its offices at the Morrison Hotel on March 20 (see *Chicago Herald and Examiner* [March 20, 1923]).

53. *Chicago American* (March 2, 1923); *Chicago Herald and Examiner* (March 23, 1923).

54. *Chicago American* (February 15, 1923); *Chicago Herald and Examiner* (March 2, 3, 1923).

55. Final poll, *Chicago Tribune* (March 30, 1923): Dever, 33,054; Lueder, 28,256. Final poll, *Chicago Journal* (March 31, 1923): Dever, 20,861; Lueder, 16,640. Although

the *Tribune* did not formally endorse a candidate, Senator McCormick wrote a scathing article against Dever in his family newspaper (see *Chicago Tribune* [April 1, 1923]). The shift in newspaper backing is reported in *Chicago Herald and Examiner* (April 2, 1923).

56. *Chicago Tribune* (March 18, 1923); *Chicago American, Chicago Daily News, Chicago Tribune* (all March 27, 1923).

57. Broadside (undated), Agnes Nestor Papers, Chicago Historical Society.

58. *Chicago Tribune, (March 30, 1923); Chicago American* (March 29, 1923); Harold L. Ickes to Margaret Dreier Robins (April 5, 1923), Robins Papers.

59. *Chicago Journal* (March 28, 1923, April 2, 1923).

60. *Chicago Journal* (April 2, 1923); *CDNA: 1924*, pp.727–37.

61. *CDNA: 1924*, pp. 727–37.

62. Although the change from thirty-five to fifty wards precludes detailed comparison of the two mayoral elections, the arrangement of wards into North Side, (greater) West Side, and South Side remained constant. The figures given in the text are drawn from the following grouping:

	1919 Wards	1923 Wards
North Side	21–26	42–50
West Side	10–20, 27,28,33–35	20–41
South Side	1–9, 29–32	1–19

See Ward Maps, 1919, 1923, Municipal Reference Library, Chicago. Voting figures are from Official Canvass, Board of Election Commissioners, Mayoral Elections, 1919, 1923.

63. The Polish figures are from Edward R. Kantowicz, *Polish-American Politics in Chicago: 1888–1940* (Chicago and London: University of Chicago Press, 1975), pp. 142–45; the Italian voting is in Humbert S. Nelli, *Italians in Chicago, 1880–1930: A Study in Ethnic Mobility* (New York: Oxford University Press, 1970), pp. 228–31. John M. Allswang examines ten groups: Czechs, Poles, Lithuanians, Yugoslavians, Italians, Germans, Swedes, Jews, blacks, and white "Native Americans" (at least third-generation American residence). His figures are used for the Germans and Swedes, and as confirmation of the Polish and Italian percentages (Allswang's calculations for these latter groups are about the same as the totals reported by Kantowicz and Nelli). See John M. Allswang, *A House for All Peoples: Ethnic Politics in Chicago* (Lexington: University of Kentucky Press, 1971), p. 42.

64. *Chicago Herald and Examiner* (March 17, 1923); *Chicago Tribune* (March 25, 1923); Gosnell, *Negro Politicians*, p. 44; John M. Allswang, "The Chicago Negro Voter and the Democratic Consensus: A Case Study, 1918–1936," *Journal of the Illinois State Historical Society* 60 (Spring 1967): 154–55.

Chapter 5. Taking Charge

1. Charles E. Merriam, *Chicago: A More Intimate View of Urban Politics* (New York: Macmillan Co., 1929), p. 255.

2. *Louisville Post* (April 5, 1923). The resort excursion was a customary junket for Chicago aldermen; Hot Springs, Arkansas, was another favorite spa. The politicos justified their trips by claiming they had to remove their deliberations from the political pressures present in Chicago.

3. *Who's Who in Chicago and Illinois: 1926* (Chicago: A. N. Marquis Co., 1926),

p. 146. Busch was the author of many scholarly works, among them a textbook on courtroom procedures and an analysis of the Sacco-Vanzetti case.

4. Ibid., p. 821.

5. Mary McDowell's career is described in Howard Eugene Wilson, *Mary McDowell, Neighbor* (Chicago: University of Chicago Press, 1928); and in Caroline Hill, *Mary McDowell and Municipal Housekeeping* (Chicago: Millar Publishing Co., 1938).

6. *Who's Who in Chicago: 1926*, pp. 192–93.

7. *Chicago Post* (April 23, 1923).

8. *CDNA: 1924*, p. 796.

9. Merriam, pp. 258–59; *Chicago Tribune* (May 18, 1923, August 23, 1923); *Chicago Post* (May 23, 1923).

10. Barry D. Karl, *Charles B. Merriam and the Study of Politics* (Chicago and London: University of Chicago Press, 1974), p. 142; *Chicago Post* (May 23, 1923); "School Board" (undated memo), Taylor Papers.

11. Hanson was a Thompson appointee but had become an outspoken critic of Big Bill's school policies (*Chicago Daily News* [April 19, 1923]).

12. *Chicago Journal* (April 19, 1923); *Chicago Tribune* (April 21, 1923); Harvey M. Karlen, "Some Political and Administrative Aspects of Municipal Wage Determination in Chicago: 1911–1941" (Ph.D. dissertation, University of Chicago, 1950), pp. 14, 135–39.

13. For details, see Civil Service Commission of Chicago, *Annual Report: 1923*, *passim*.

14. *Chicago Post, Chicago Tribune* (both May 12, 1923).

15. Karlen, pp. 91–96, 117–18; *Chicago Tribune* (May 18, 1923, July 7, 1923). For Chicago budgets during Thompson's administrations (1915–1923), consult the appropriate edition of the annual *Chicago Daily News Almanac*.

16. Karlen, p. 96; *Chicago Post* (July 5, 6, 10, 11, 1923); *Chicago Herald and Examiner* (August 1, 29, 1923, September 11–13, 1923).

17. Karlen, pp. 280–85; *Chicago Post* (May 2, 1923); *Chicago Daily News* (August 28, 1923); E. O. Griffenhagen to WED (November 7, 1923), Dever Papers.

18. Karlen, pp. 285–88; Leonard D. White, *Conditions of Municipal Employment in Chicago: A Study in Morale* (Chicago: City Clerk, 1925), *passim*.

19. Merriam, Chapter 2; John H. Lyle, *The Dry and Lawless Years* (Englewood Cliffs, NJ: Prentice-Hall, 1960), p. 16.

20. *Chicago Daily News* (April 17, 1923); *Chicago Herald and Examiner* (April 18, 1923, June 1, 1923); *Chicago Post* (June 1, 1923).

21. *Chicago Herald and Examiner* (April 23, 1923); *Chicago Journal* (May 8, 9, 1923); William Bottoms to WED (May 11, 1923), Dever Papers.

22. *Chicago Daily News* (July 2, 1923); Harry P. Weber, *An Outline History of Chicago Traction* (Chicago: Chicago Surface Lines, 1936), pp. 184–85.

23. *Chicago Herald and Examiner* (July 16,17, 1923); *Chicago Journal* (November 28, 1923). At the end of 1923, the Chicago traction fund totaled about $37.5 million (*Chicago American* [December 21, 1923]).

24. *Chicago Daily News* (May 16, 1923).

25. The general conduct of Chicago's mayors during labor difficulties is described in Howard Burton Myers, "The Policing of Labor Disputes in Chicago: A Case Study" (Ph.D. dissertation, University of Chicago, 1929); see especially pp. 1137–38. Prior to Dever's term, the most successful mayoral intervention in such a dispute had been Thompson's arbitration in the 1915 streetcar strike; see Lloyd Wendt and Herman Kogan, *Big Bill of Chicago* (Indianapolis: Bobbs-Merrill Co., 1953), pp. 123–27.

26. *Chicago Tribune* (May 28, 29, 30, 1923; June 5, 9, 15, 1923; July 21, 1923); *Chicago Herald and Examiner* (July 23, 1923).

27. *The Union Leader* (June 23, 1923). The CSL electricians' dispute is described in *Chicago Post* (August 2, 1923; September 11, 1923; October 22, 1923). For the gas workers' case, see *Chicago Tribune* (September 7,8, 1923). The ironworkers' dispute is reported in *Chicago Herald and Examiner* (September 18, 1923). The seamstresses' approach to Dever is noted in *Chicago American* (August 29, 1923). For the mayor's actions in the wildcat tracklayers' strike, see *Chicago Tribune* (September 13, 1923); *Chicago Herald and Examiner* (November 4, 1923).

28. *Chicago Tribune* (May 3, 1923); *Chicago Daily News* (May 19, 1923); *Chicago Herald and Examiner* (May 20, 1923; June 2, 1923).

29. Some typical articles on the mayor's golf game are in *Chicago American* (April 30, 1923); *Chicago Journal* (June 11, 1923); *Chicago Herald and Examiner* (July 19, 1923). His devotion to baseball is indicated by his going to see the Cubs' game on his first full day in office. (see *Chicago Post* [April 17, 1923]).

30. For a sample of stories on the Dever trip, see *Chicago Daily News* (August 1, 3, 1923); *Chicago Post* (August 2, 1923); *Chicago American* (August 7, 1923).

31. For Torrio's biography, see John J. McPhaul, *Johnny Torrio: First of the Gang Lords* (New Rochelle, NY: Arlington House, 1970). Other accounts of the formation of the Chicago crime syndicate are John H. Lyle, *The Dry and Lawless Years* (Englewood Cliffs, NJ: Prentice-Hall, 1960); Fred D. Pasley, *Al Capone: The Biography of a Self-Made Man* (London: Faber and Faber Ltd., 1931); and John Kobler, *Capone: The Life and World of Al Capone* (New York: Putnam, 1971).

32. The group under study was called the *South Side O'Donnells* to distinguish them from the *Klondyke O'Donnells*, who operated in the western suburbs.

33. The events of September 7, 1923 are related in Pasley, pp. 27–30.

34. Lincoln Street is now named Wolcott Avenue.

35. "Statement of Mayor Dever" (press release, September 12, 1923), Dever Papers.

36. *Chicago Herald and Examiner* (September 13, 14, 1923); *Chicago Post* (September 14, 15, 1923); *Chicago Daily News* (September 15, 1923); *Chicago Tribune* (September 16, 1923).

37. *Chicago Journal* (September 18, 1923).

38. Ibid.; *Chicago Tribune* (September 19, 1923).

39. *Chicago Tribune* (September 24, 26, 1923); *Chicago American* (September 19, 1923). The police department transfers are reported in *Chicago Herald and Examiner* (September 19, 1923); *Chicago Journal* (September 29, 1923); *Chicago Post* (October 5, 1923).

40. *Chicago Herald and Examiner* (September 18, 22, 1923).

41. *Chicago Journal* (September 23, 1923); *Chicago Tribune* (October 16, 1923).

42. Quoted in *Chicago Tribune* (September 26, 1923).

43. *Chicago Herald and Examiner* (September 23, 26, 29, 1923); *Chicago Journal* (November 3, 1923); *Chicago Daily News* (November 8, 1923).

44. *Chicago Tribune* (September 12, 1923); Francis X. Busch to WED (August 13, 1923); WED to Morgan A. Collins (August 8, 1923); both Dever Papers.

45. *Chicago Tribune* (October 8, 1923).

46. George Brennan's role as a spokesman for the wets is described in Merriam, pp. 183–84. See also Brennan's comments in *Chicago Tribune* (October 26, 1923).

47. *Chicago Herald and Examiner* (October 18, 23, 1923); *Chicago Tribune* (October 21, 1923); *Chicago Post* (October 9, 1923).

48. *Chicago Tribune* (October 20, 1923).

49. The *Chicago Herald and Examiner* ran editorials on September 19, 24, 1923; October 4, 6, 1923. See also *Chicago Post* (December 4, 1923). The Dever Papers contain much material to indicate the scope of support for the mayor's Beer War. Some of the resolutions of praise include Northwesttown Kiwanis Club (October 26, 1923); Cook County Chapter, Women's Christian Temperance League (September 26, 1923); and Joint Council #25 of the Teamsters' Union (October 12, 1923). For samples of the support letters received, see Mr. and Mrs. James Hudson to WED (September 17, 1923); and George S. Parker to WED (October 10, 1923).

50. Examples of favorable out-of-town articles on the Dever clean-up can be found in *Rome* (GA) *Herald-Tribune* (October 30, 1923); *Washington Star* (October 31, 1923); *Sisson* (CA) *Herald* (November 3, 1923); *St. Louis Post-Dispatch* (November 4, 1923); *Albany* (NY) *Knickerbocker Press* (November 11, 1923); all in Dever Scrapbooks.

51. *New York Times* (November 18, 1923); "Drying Up Chicago," *Literary Digest* 79 (December 15, 1923): 16–17.

52. Some of the newspapers publishing Dever's article were *New York Herald, Indianapolis Star, Springfield* (MA) *Republic* (all November 25, 1923).

53. Quoted in *Chicago Tribune* (November 21, 1923).

54. *Chicago Tribune* (November 11, 29, 1923); *Chicago Herald and Examiner* (December 4, 1923).

55. *Chicago Herald and Examiner, Chicago Tribune* (both January 1, 1924).

56. Pasley, p. 32.

Chapter 6. The Strain of Command

1. Carter H. Harrison to WED (April 9, 1923), Dever Papers. Harrison wrote that, although Dever should make up his own mind on appointments (as he had done when mayor), he thought he should "remind" the new mayor about the qualifications of John Traeger, George Schilling, Oscar Mayer, and Frank Danisch. For Harrison's reaction to Brennan's partonage control see Alex Gottfried, *Boss Cermak of Chicago: A Study in Political Leadership* (Seattle: University of Washington Press, 1962), pp. 135, 387 n. The Democratic rift is described in *Chicago Herald and Examiner* (January 12, 1924).

2. The Harrison for Senator boom is reported in *Chicago Herald and Examiner* (June 9, 1923).

3. Arthur W. Thurner, "The Impact of Ethnic Groups on the Democratic Party in Chicago, 1920–1928" (Ph.D. dissertation, University of Chicago, 1966), pp. 168–73; *Chicago Herald and Examiner* (January 12, 1924).

4. *Dziennika Narodowego* (May 12, 1923).

5. *Chicago Herald and Examiner* (May 30, 1923).

6. For details on the "recognition drive," see Edward R. Kantowicz, *Polish-American Politics in Chicago: 1888–1940* (Chicago and London: University of Chicago Press, 1975) Chapters 15–18. Note also the Polish language newspapers quoted in Douglas Bukowski, "William Dever and Prohibition: The Mayoral Elections of 1923 and 1927," *Chicago History* 7 (Summer 1978): 110–11.

7. *Chicago Tribune* (January 4, 1924; March 18, 1924); *Chicago Daily News* (January 24, 1924); *Chicago Herald and Examiner* (February 19, 1924).

8. *Chicago Herald and Examiner* (March 23, 29, 1924) *Chicago Daily News* (June 18, 1924).

9. Dever had earned Adamowski's enmity the previous January. Just after the alderman had been slated as Democratic candidate for clerk of the circuit court,

Mayor Dever made a speech at a testimonial for Adamowski's opponent. Adamowski did not buy the argument that Dever was merely performing a nonpartisan courtesy for a man he had known well during his days as a judge. The alderman resigned from the ticket and was replaced by another Pole (Leo Winiecke). See *Chicago Tribune* (May 20, 1924); Thurner, p. 169.

    10. *Chicago Tribune* (March 17, 19, 22, 1924); *Chicago Journal* (April 11, 1924).

    11. Harvey M. Karlen, "Some Political and Administrative Aspects of Municipal Wage Determination in Chicago: 1911–1941" (Ph.D. dissertation, University of Chicago, 1950), pp. 139–40; *Chicago Post* (July 15, 1924).

    12. *Chicago Daily News* (January 15, 1924); John M. Allswang, *A House for All Peoples: Ethnic Politics in Chicago* (Lexington: University of Kentucky Press, 1971), pp. 174–75.

    13. *Chicago Tribune* (April 9, 1924).

    14. For a variety of viewpoints on the Dever-Brennan relationship, see Gottfried, pp. 134–36; William H. Stuart, *The Twenty Incredible Years* (Chicago and New York: M. A. Donohue and Co., 1935), pp. 188, 453; Fletcher Dobyns, *The Underworld of American Politics* (New York: Fletcher Dobyns, 1932), pp. 55–57; John Bright, *Hizzoner Big Bill Thompson: An Idyll of Chicago* (New York: Jonathan Cape and Harrison Smith, 1930), p. 202; Virgil W. Peterson, *Barbarians in Our Midst* (Boston: Little, Brown and Co., 1952), pp. 122, 135; Charles E. Merriam, "Some Bosses on My List," lecture delivered at the University of Chicago (May 18, 1948), transcript in Charles E. Merriam Papers, University of Chicago, Chicago.

    15. Merriam, ibid.; Parke Brown, "Brennan of Illinois," *Century Magazine* 112 (September 1926): 600; "Senatorial Campaigns," *Time* 9 (August 9, 1928): 9; "Brennan and the Vanishing American Boss," *Literary Digest* 98 (September 1, 1928): 34.

    16. The Dever for Governor talk is reported in *Chicago Post* (July 20, 1923). Discussion of Dever as a possible national candidate is found in *Chicago Herald and Examiner* (November 11, 1923; May 1, 24, 1924); *Chicago American* (January 14, 1924); *Chicago Tribune* (March 15, 1924; April 13, 1924); *Chicago Daily News* (March 15, 1924; April 10, 1924; May 8, 1924).

    17. For an exposition of Dever's strengths on a national ticket, see P. H. Callahan to Oswald Garrison Villard (May 3, 1924), copy in Dever Papers. Villard was the editor of the influential journal *The Nation*.

    18. *Chicago Daily News* (April 28, 1924; May 2, 1924); *Chicago Herald and Examiner* (June 21, 1924); Brown, p. 599.

    19. The 1924 convention is described in R. K. Murray, *The 103rd Ballot* (New York: Harper, 1976). The Dever boom, such as it was, is reported in *Chicago American* (June 21, 23, 1924); *Chicago Post* (June 23, 1924; July 5, 1924); *Chicago Daily News* (June 24, 25, 1924; July 2, 1924); *Chicago Tribune* (June 11, 21, 1924). The first votes cast for Dever as president were two and one-half votes on the twentieth ballot (*Chicago Herald and Examiner* [July 2, 1924]).

    20. Davis's offer of the vice-presidency for Dever is detailed in *Chicago Tribune* (July 11, 1924); this is the only report of the incident. Murray does not mention it. In his account of the vice-presidential selection, Al Smith recalls that "names were suggested from the Middle West," but does not elaborate (Alfred E. Smith, *Up to Now* [New York: Viking Press, 1929], p. 290).

    21. William E. Dever, "The Problems of a Great City," address delivered at the University of Chicago (June 10, 1924), transcript in Dever Papers.

    22. The ultimate example of plaque politics must be the North Clark Street Bridge. Just below the sign commemorating Thompson, dated 1931, there is a

smaller plaque that reads: "Project Completed 1933, Anton J. Cermak, Mayor."

23. Daniel Burnham and Edward H. Bennett, *The Plan of Chicago* (Chicago: Commerical Club, 1909), *passim;* Carl W. Condit, *Chicago 1910–29: Building, Planning, and Urban Technology* (Chicago and London: University of Chicago Press, 1973), Chapter 3.

24. The official city history of the Plan Commission is in Helen Whitehead, ed., *The Chicago Plan Commission: A Historical Sketch* (Chicago: Department of City Planning, 1961). The Plan Commission's school textbook, at one time used by all eighth graders in the city's public schools, is Walter D. Moody, *Wacker's Manual of the Plan of Chicago* (Chicago: Chicago Plan Commission, 1915). See also Perry Duis, *Chicago: Creating New Traditions* (Chicago: Chicago Historical Society, 1976), pp. 49–55.

25. Condit, p. 247; *Chicago Herald and Examiner* (May 27, 1923).

26. William D. Middleton, *Grand Central: The World's Greatest Railway Terminal* (San Marino, CA.: Golden West Books, 1977), Chapter 6; *Chicago Herald and Examiner* (March 7, 1924).

27. *Chicago Daily News* (March 7, 1924; October 10, 1924); Dever, "Problems."

28. *Chicago Daily News* (March 7, 1924); *Chicago Journal* (April 11, 1924); *Chicago Tribune* (March 14, 1924); Dever, "Problems."

29. Harold M. Mayer and Richard C. Wade, *Chicago: Growth of a Metropolis* (Chicago and London: University of Chicago Press, 1969), pp. 314–15.

30. Henry Justin Smith, quoted in ibid., pp. 309–11. See also Glen E. Holt and Dominic Pacyga, *Chicago: A Historical Guide to the Neighborhoods—The Loop and South Side* (Chicago: Chicago Historical Society, 1979), p. 14.

31. Mayer and Wade, pp. 310–11; Condit, p. 250.

32. Francis X. Busch to WED (January 2, 1924), "Outline for Wacker Drive dedication speech" (undated typescript); both in Dever Papers. See also Mayor of Chicago, *Annual Report: 1924* (Chicago: City of Chicago, 1924).

33. *Chicago Tribune* (March 8, 1924).

34. Mayor of Chicago, *Annual Report: 1924; Chicago Daily News* (October 2, 1924); *Chicago Tribune* (August 12, 1926); *Chicago American* (August 13, 1926).

35. Condit, p. 250; Carl W. Condit, *Chicago 1930–70: Building, Planning, and Urban Technology* (Chicago and London: University of Chicago Press, 1974), pp. 232–33.

36. Mayor of Chicago, *Annual Report: 1924.*

37. The inclination of many old Progressives to favor public works over social welfare as an instrument to reform and uplift society is illustrated in the career of long-time New York public works czar Robert Moses. See Robert A. Caro, *The Power Broker: Robert Moses and the Fall of New York* (New York: Alfred A. Knopf, 1974).

38. William H. Tuttle, Jr., *Race Riot: Chicago in the Red Summer of 1919* (New York: Atheneum, 1970), pp.74–107; St. Clair Drake and Horace R. Cayton, *Black Metropolis* (New York: Harcourt, Brace and Company, 1945), Chapter 3; Charles R. Branham, "The Transformation of Black Political Leadership in Chicago, 1864–1942" (Ph.D. dissertation, University of Chicago, 1981), Chapter 4.

39. The most comprehensive treatment of the 1919 riot, its background, and its aftermath, is in Tuttle; see especially pp. 3–66, 157–83.

40. Harold F. Gosnell, *Negro Politicians* (Chicago: University of Chicago Press, 1935) Chapter 3; Drake and Cayton, pp. 346–51.

41. Ibid., pp. 26–27; Dianne M. Pinderhughes, *Race and Ethnicity in Chicago Politics* (Urbana and Chicago: University of Illinois Press, 1987), pp.74–75.

42. Branham, pp. 328–30.

43. Ibid.

44. *Chicago Record-Herald* (November 9, 1906); Thomas Lee Philpott, *The Slum and the Ghetto: Neighbor Deterioration and Middle-Class Reform in Chicago, 1880–1930* (New York: Oxford University Press, 1978), pp. 196–97.

45. Branham, pp. 330–32.

46. For the shift of black voters to the Democratic party in Chicago during the 1930s, consult Branham, Chapters 7–8; Roger Biles, *Big City Boss in Depression and War: Mayor Edward J. Kelly of Chicago* (DeKalb, Northern Illinois University Press, 1984), Chapter 5; John M. Allswang, "The Chicago Negro Voter and the Democratic Consensus: A Case Study, 1918–1936," *Journal of the Illinois State Historical Society* 60 (Spring 1967).

47. George S. Counts, *School and Society in Chicago* (New York: Harcourt, Brace, 1928), p. 71; Mary Herrick, *The Chicago Schools: A Social and Political History* (Beverly Hills, CA: Sage Publications, 1971), p. 143.

48. For reaction to McAndrew's appointment, see *Chicago Tribune* (January 10, 11, 1924); *Chicago Post, Chicago Daily News* (both January 10, 1924).

49. Herrick, p. 144; Counts, pp.72–77; *Chicago Herald and Examiner* (March 18, 1924); *Chicago Daily News* (March 22, 1924).

50. The background of the teacher councils is related in Counts, pp. 110–15; and Herrick, pp. 94–95, 139–41. For 1924 developments, see Counts, pp. 117–25; *Chicago Herald and Examiner* (May 9, 11, 1924); *Chicago Daily News* (September 8, 1924).

51. *Chicago Daily News* (September 15, 1924); *Chicago Post* (September 16, 1924); *Chicago Journal, Chicago Tribune* (both July 27, 1924). Margaret Haley's autobiography, written in the 1930s, was published in 1982. Her account of McAndrew's tenure is in Chapter 9, "The Carpetbagger." See Robert L. Reid, ed., *Battleground: The Autobiography of Margaret A. Haley* (Urbana: University of Illinois Press, 1982).

52. *Chicago Tribune* (September 26, 1924; October 1,4, 1924).

53. *Chicago Daily News* (October 3, 1924), *Chicago Post* (October 4, 1924).

54. Dever's response to Margaret Haley's charges is reported in the *Chicago Herald and Examiner* (October 5, 1924). Technically, the mayor was correct. The Chicago Board of Education was virtually an independent government within the city borders. Although the mayor of Chicago appointed board members, he could not remove them. (Dever's dumping of the Thompson board was a freak occurrence and brought lengthy litigation.) The board made its own budget and collected its own taxes. So separate was it from the City of Chicago government that on one occasion the city sued the board to make it comply with a disputed ordinance. See Charles E. Merriam, Spencer D. Parratt, and Albert Lepawsky, *The Government of the Metropolitan Region of Chicago* (Chicago: University of Chicago Press, 1933), pp.65–66.

55. *Chicago Journal* (October 10, 1924); *Chicago Herald and Examiner* (October 12, 1924); Lloyd Wendt and Herman Kogan, *Big Bill of Chicago* (Indianapolis: Bobbs-Merrill, 1953), p. 236; *Chicago Tribune* (November 14, 1924).

56. John Kobler, *Capone: The Life and World of Al Capone* (New York: Putnam, 1971), p. 111; John H. Lyle, *The Dry and Lawless Years* (Englewood Cliffs, NJ: Prentice-Hall, 1960), p. 16. Kobler reports the $100,000 per month figure; Lyle, a Chicago alderman at the time, says the bribe offered Collins was $1,000 per day. Either way, a substantial sum. Another contemporary source states that a bribe of $100,000 was offered to Mayor Dever himself (see Edward D. Sullivan, *Rattling the Cup on Chicago Crime* [New York: The Vanguard Press, 1929], p. 149).

57. John Landesco, *Organized Crime in Chicago*, reprint (Chicago and London: University of Chicago Press, 1968), pp. 85–86, 178–79.

58. For some assessments of these politicians, see Gottfried, pp. 140–43; Kobler, pp. 166–70, 322; Lyle, p. 75; Stuart, pp. 225–26; Wendt and Kogan, pp. 239–40.

59. There are numerous historical studies of the 1920s. Among the more useful are: Frederick Lewis Allen, *Only Yesterday: An Informal History of the Nineteen-Twenties* (New York and London: Harper and Brothers Publishers, 1931); Paul A. Carter, *Another Part of the Twenties* (New York: Columbia University Press, 1977); William E. Leuchtenberg, *The Perils of Prosperity, 1914–32* (Chicago: University of Chicago Press, 1958); Page Smith, *Redeeming the Time: A Peoples History of the 1920s and the New Deal* (New York: McGraw-Hill Book Co., 1987); Elizabeth Stevenson, *Babbits and Bohemians: The American 1920s* (New York: Macmillan Co., 1967); Mark Sullivan, *Our Times: The United States, 1900–1925*, vol. 6, *The Twenties* (New York: Charles Scribner's Sons, 1935). The cultural clashes of the decade are examined in John Higham, *Strangers in the Land* (New Brunswick, NJ: Rutgers University Press, 1955), Chapter 10.

60. Thurner, Chapter 10. For a study of the saloon's role in ethnic cultures, consult Perry R. Duis, *The Saloon: Public Drinking in Chicago and Boston, 1880–1920* (Urbana and Chicago: University of Illinois Press, 1983).

61. *Chicago Herald and Examiner* (October 7, 1924).

62. *Chicago Tribune* (October 7, 1924).

63. For an example of the out-of-town reporting of Darrow's speech, see *Kansas City Star* (October 7, 1924). The idea that the speech was a staged public flogging of the mayor is reported in *Chicago Herald and Examiner* (October 8, 1924).

64. *Chicago American* (November 5, 1924). The Brennan organization was so overwhelmed at the polls that one writer describes the election as "The Nadir of the Democratic Party" (Thurner, pp. 199–203).

65. The disintegration of the Democratic alliance prompted the Hearst papers to call for Brennan's retirement from power; see editorials in *Chicago American* (November 5, 1924) and *Chicago Herald and Examiner* (November 6, 7, 1924).

Chapter 7. Showdown on Transit

1. The situation of Chicago public transportation, circa 1924, is described in Paul Barrett, *The Automobile and Urban Transit* (Philadelphia: Temple University Press, 1983), pp. 168–83. The Chicago Surface Lines' operations are detailed in Alan R. Lind, *Chicago Surface Lines: An Illustrated History*, 3d. ed. (Park Forest, IL: Transport History Press, 1979), *passim*; and in James D. Johnson, *A Century of Chicago Streetcars, 1858–1958* (Wheaton, IL: Traction Orange Co., 1964), pp. 7–12.

2. *Chicago Rapid Transit: Rolling Stock, 1892–1947* (Chicago: Central Electric Railfans' Assn., 1973), *passim*; Brian J. Cudahy, "Chicago's Early Elevated Lines and Construction of the Union Loop." *Chicago History* 8 (Winter 1979–80): 194–205.

3. Lind, pp. 347–55.

4. In the period from May 1, 1919, to December 31, 1923, Chicago's motor vehicle registration rose from 75,214 to 218,991 (see "Vehicles Licensed by the City of Chicago Since 1908," pamphlet, Municipal Reference Library). However, mass transit ridership also continued to grow, reaching an all-time high of 1,167,941,688 fares in 1927 (Lind, p. 416).

5. Johnson, pp.33–115; Lind, pp.50–127.

6. Cudahy, pp. 197–98, 204; Stephen P. Carlson and Fred W. Schneider, III, *P.C.C.: The Car that Fought Back* (Glendale, CA: Interurban Press, 1980), p. 173

7. Mayor of Chicago, *Special Message of Honorable William E. Dever, Mayor, Concerning Chicago's Local Transportation Problem . . . October 22, 1924*, p. 11; for details on the surface extensions built, see Lind, pp. 221–347. The construction of the elevated lines is described in James Leslie Davis, *The Elevated System and the Growth of*

Northern Chicago, Northwestern University Studies in Geography, No. 10 (Evanston: IL: Northwestern University, 1965), pp. 14–15. After 1908, the only elevated routes opened were new feeder branches.

8. Trip itineraries are drawn from a 1926 Chicago transit map and service guide reproduced in Johnson, pp.24–30. Travel time is computed using CSL's standard schedule speed of 5–7 miles per hour, and from recollections of the author's family members.

9. Lind, p. 452.

10. Richard E. Becker "Edward Dunne: Reform Mayor of Chicago, 1905–07" (Ph.D. dissertation, University of Chicago, 1971), Chapter 4–5.

11. Chicago Traction and Subway Commission, *Report . . . on a Unified System of Surface, Elevated and Subway Lines, passim.*

12. Harry P. Weber, *An Outline History of Chicago Traction* (Chicago: Chicago Surface Lines, 1936), pp.121–27; Ralph Joseph Burton, "Mass Transport in the Chicago Region: A Study of Metropolitan Government" (Ph.D. dissertation, University of Chicago, 1939), p. 179.

13. Burton, pp. 179–81. The final vote was For, 209,682; Against, 243,334 (Weber, p.127).

14. Burton, p. 181; Weber, pp. 127–28.

15. *Chicago Tribune* (June 20, 1921).

16. The various transit proposals are in Weber, pp.167–69.

17. Ibid., pp. 168, 218; see also Chicago City Council, *An Ordinance Providing for a Comprehensive Municipal Local Transportation System . . . February 27, 1925*, pp. 12–22.

18. *Chicago Herald and Examiner* (May 3, 14, 1924); *Chicago Tribune* (September 5, 1924).

19. Forrest McDonald, *Insull* (Chicago: University of Chicago Press, 1962), *passim.*

20. *Chicago Tribune* (September 29, 1924).

21. *Chicago Post* (October 29, 1924); Dever. *Special Message . . . October 22, 1924*, p. 9.

22. *Chicago Herald and Examiner* (September 7, 20, 1924); *Chicago Post* (September 13, 1924).

23. The Detroit municipal takeover is described in Jack E. Schramm and William H. Henning, *Detroit Street Railways: 1863–1922* (Chicago: Central Electric Railfans' Assn., 1978), Chapter 4. The San Francisco muni story is in Anthony Perles, *The People's Railway: A History of the Municipal Railway of San Francisco* (Glendale, CA: Interurban Press, 1981), *passim.* For information on the New York City Independent subway, see Brian J. Cudahy, *Under the Sidewalks of New York* (Brattleboro, VT: Stephen Greene Press, 1979), Chapter 8.

24. Cudahy, *New York*, pp. 84, 89; *Chicago Herald and Examiner* (May 25, 1923); *Chicago American* (July 18, 22, 1924); *Chicago Tribune* (July 19, 1924).

25. Weber, pp. 179–84; *Chicago Tribune* (October 21, 1924).

26. *Chicago Tribune* (October 22, 1924).

27. Dever, *Special Message . . . October 22, 1924*, pp. 15, 23.

28. *Chicago Post* (October 23, 1924); *Chicago American* (October 23, 31, 1924).

29. *Chicago Tribune* (October 23, 24, 1924).

30. *Chicago Herald and Examiner* (September 30, 1924); *Chicago Tribune* (November 21, 1924).

31. *Chicago Journal* (December 5, 1924).

32. *Chicago Herald and Examiner* (December 5, 1924); *Chicago Post* (November

28, 1924); *Chicago Journal* (December 6, 1924).

33. *Chicago Daily News* (November 24, 1924).

34. Purchase agreements were reached with CSL in January, and with CRT in February. Details are in *Chicago Daily News* (January 26, 1925); and *Chicago Herald and Examiner* (February 24, 1925).

35. *Chicago Journal* (December 6, 1924); *Chicago American* (December 11, 1924). The traction interests did not help the appearance of an unbiased appraisal by some of their actions. Initially, they rejected two lists of appraisers submitted by the city. Then, they refused to accept Major Kelker, the city council's traction engineer, on the appraisal committee. The city and the financiers finally reached a compromise. The city appointed Kelker, the traction interests appointed William Hanegan, and both men together chose a third appraiser. The man they agreed on was William Barclay Parsons, a member of the New York City Transit Commission. See *Chicago Herald and Examiner* (December 3, 12, 1924); and *Chicago Tribune* (January 1, 1925).

36. Quoted in *Chicago Tribune* (January 10, 1925).

37. *Chicago Post* (January 6, 1925); *Chicago American* (January 7, 1925).

38. *Chicago Herald and Examiner* (January 7, 1925); *Chicago Post* (January 8, 1925).

39. *Chicago Tribune* (January 9, 1925).

40. *Chicago Post* (January 9, 1925); *Chicago Tribune* (February 1, 1925). Chicago required that its aldermen be elected with an absolute majority. If no candidate attained the necessary figure in the regular election, then the two top vote getters faced each other in a special run-off election six weeks later. Most contests were settled in the first heat; 1925 was unusual in that fourteen run-offs were required.

41. *Chicago American* (January 2, 1925).

42. Dever's plan called for the Municipal Railway Board to be reduced to seven members at the time 51 percent of the Schwartz certificates had been amortized, with the mayor then having independent appointment power over four members. The financiers wished to continue the 3-3-3 ratio on the board until all the certificates had been retired, but Dever prevailed. See *Chicago Tribune* (January 17, 20, 1925).

43. Edward F. Dunne, *Illinois: The Heart of a Nation*, 5 vols. (Chicago and New York: Lewis Publishing Co., 1933), 2:464–67.

44. *Chicago Herald and Examiner* (February 13, 1925).

45. *Chicago Herald and Examiner, Chicago Tribune* (both February 12, 1925); *Chicago American* (January 17, 30, 1925).

46. *Chicago Journal* (February 28, 1925). Among the "Nay" voters was Bathhouse John Coughlin, who said that he voted against the ordinance because "nobody asked me to vote for it."

47. *Chicago Daily News* (February 28, 1925; March 10, 14, 1925); *Chicago Post* (March 12, 1925).

48. *Chicago Herald and Examiner, Chicago Journal* (both March 24, 1925).

49. George Sikes's first article appeared in *Chicago American* (March 12, 1925). For a typical Dunne essay analyzing the traction ordinance, see *Chicago Journal* (March 14, 1925). The Harrison interview is in *Chicago Daily News* (March 30, 1925).

50. *Chicago Herald and Examiner* (March 2, 15, 24, 1925).

51. *Chicago Tribune* (January 10, 1925); *Chicago American* (February 18, 1925).

52. Ickes is quoted at length in *Chicago Daily News* (March 28, 1925); Haley in *Chicago Daily News* (April 1, 1925). The coolness of some old Progressives and Independents to Dever's ordinance is detailed in *Chicago Journal* (March 31, 1925; April 6, 1925). Since the *Journal* vigorously opposed the plan, its analysis is somewhat overblown. Merriam's advice to Dever on campaign strategy and Dever's response

are found in Charles E. Merriam to WED (March 22, 1925), and WED to Charles E. Merriam (March 24, 1925), both in Merriam Papers.

53. *Chicago Daily News* (February 28, 1925; March 3, 1925).

54. For the "men only" controversy, see *Chicago Journal* (March 9, 10, 12, 1925), with Mrs. Fairbank's response to the charge quoted in *Chicago Daily News* (March 20, 1925). Hearst press propaganda against the ordinance is voluminous: see any edition of the *Chicago American* or the *Chicago Herald and Examiner* from March 1 through April 7, 1925. The proordinance forces published a counterattack to the Hearst charges in an article titled "Twenty Lies Circulated and Answered About the Traction Plan" (*Chicago Daily News* [April 3, 1925]).

55. *Chicago Tribune* (April 6, 1925); *Chicago Journal* (April 4, 1925).

56. *Chicago Journal* (March 28, 1925; April 3, 1925); *Chicago Herald and Examiner* (April 2, 1925).

57. *Chicago Tribune* (April 4, 1925).

58. Official Canvass, Board of Election Commissioners (Propositions of April 7, 1925), Municipal Reference Library.

59. On September 30, 1947, the new Chicago Transit Authority purchased the properties of the Chicago Surface Lines for $75 million, and those of Chicago Rapid Transit for $12.1 million. By that time, both companies were in receivership and their physical assets had greatly depreciated. Although transit ridership had been stimulated temporarily by World War II, the patronage trend was a downward spiral. See Roderick K. deCamp, "The Chicago Transit Authority: A Study in Responsibility" (Ph.D. dissertation, University of Chicago, 1958), pp. 47–49.

60. For an opposite view, see Barrett, p. 201–205.

61. Opponents of the transit package were careful not to portray the matter in partisan terms. In far outlying, transit-starved districts, where the voters would be naturally inclined to support efforts at improving service, the antiordinance forces advertised the Dever ordinance as simply another way of aiding downtown businessmen with neighborhood dollars. See Barrett, p. 558.

62. Figures for the 1922 Prohibition referendum are in *CDNA: 1924*, pp. 753–54.

63. *Chicago Tribune* (April 8, 1923).

64. *Chicago Herald and Examiner* (April 10, 1925).

65. Ibid.

Chapter 8. Hanging On

1. *Chicago Daily News, Chicago Post* (both April 8, 1925).

2. *Chicago Journal* (June 1, 1926).

3. Neil McCullough Clark, *Mayor Dever and Prohibition: The Story of a Dramatic Fight to Enforce the Law.* (Westerville, OH: American Issue Publishing Co., 1925), *passim.* The copy of the booklet in the Harvard University library is identified as "Gift of Intercollegiate Prohibition Assn.; October 5, 1931."

4. *New York Times* (January 9, 1925); Raymond B. Fosdick, *John D. Rockefeller, Jr.: A Portrait* (New York: Harper and Bros., 1956), p. 253.

5. *Chicago Tribune* (January 7, 1925); William E. Dever, "Speech Before Committee of One Thousand," address delivered at the Waldorf-Astoria Hotel, New York City (January 6, 1925), transcript in Dever Papers.

6. *Chicago Tribune* (January 8, 15, 1925).

7. Elmer Davis, "Portrait of an Elected Person," *Harper's Magazine* 155 (July 1927): 180.

8. Ibid.; Lloyd Wendt and Herman Kogan, *Big Bill of Chicago* (Indianapolis: Bobbs-Merrill Co., 1953), pp. 239–40.

9. John Kobler, *Capone: The Life and World of Al Capone* (New York: Putnam, 1971), Chapter 9.

10. *Chicago Journal* (November 10, 1924); *Chicago Herald and Examiner* (November 14, 1924).

11. Fred D. Pasley, *Al Capone: The Biography of a Self-Made Man* (London: Faber and Faber Ltd., 1931), pp. 45–48; *Chicago American, Chicago Journal* (both November 19, 1924). Hughes eventually returned to the force in 1927 as Mayor Thompson's police commissioner.

12. Kobler, Chapter 9.

13. *Chicago Tribune* (April 12, 29, 1925; June 15, 1925); *Chicago Herald and Examiner* (July 30, 31, 1925).

14. *Chicago Tribune* (August 8, 25, 1925); *Chicago Daily News* (January 16, 1925).

15. *Chicago Tribune* (April 12, 1925).

16. For Hearst press editorials on crime conditions, see *Chicago Herald and Examiner* (July 30, 31, 1925; August 3, 6, 1925); see also *Chicago Tribune* (October 6, 8, 1925). The city council resolution is reported in *Chicago Tribune* (November 20, 1925).

17. *Chicago Daily News* (March 3, 1926; April 3, 1926); U.S. Congress, Senate Subcommittee of the Committee of the Judiciary, *The National Prohibition Law*. Hearings on bills to amend the National Prohibition Act (April 5–24, 1926), 69th Cong., 1st sess., 1926, pp.652–59. (Hereafter cited as *Prohibition Hearings, 1926*.)

18. *Prohibition Hearings, 1926*, pp. 1228–37.

19. Ibid., pp. 1365–66, 1390–91. Olson later claimed that his own efforts forced Dever and Chief Collins into enforcing the Volstead Act. For both sides of the controversy, see *Chicago Journal* (April 26, 1926); *Chicago Daily News, Chicago Herald and Examiner* (both April 27, 1926).

20. *Prohibition Hearings, 1926*, pp. 1377–78, 1384–85.

21. Ibid., pp. 1383–84.

22. *Chicago Journal, Chicago Post* (both April 24, 1926). For an out-of-town reaction, see *Manchester* (CT) *Herald* (April 24, 1926).

23. *Chicago Tribune* (April 29, 1926).

24. Pasley, pp. 114–17; William H. Stuart, *The Twenty Incredible Years* (Chicago and New York: M. A. Donohue and Co., 1935), pp. 271–73.

25. Stuart, pp. 273–74.

26. Kobler, Chapter 13.

27. *Chicago Herald and Examiner* (October 3, 1926).

28. William E. Dever, "Get at the Facts," *Atlantic Monthly* 138 (October 1926): 518–24.

29. Finley Peter Dunne, *Observations by Mr. Dooley* (New York: Robert Howard Russell, 1902), p. 168.

30. Edmund Morris, *The Rise of Theodore Roosevelt* (New York: Coward, McCann, and Geoghegan, 1979), pp. 496–512.

31. Carl W. Condit, *Chicago, 1910–29: Building, Planning, and Urban Technology* (Chicago and London: University of Chicago Press, 1973), pp. 149, 250–51, 269.

32. *Chicago Tribune* (December 7, 1924); *Chicago Herald and Examiner* (December 24, 1924; May 9, 1926). In later years, Municipal Airport was renamed Midway Airport.

33. *Chicago Daily News* (December 9, 1925, February 5, 1926); *Chicago Journal* (April 8, 1926; May 20, 1926).

34. *Chicago Tribune* (April 17, 18, 1925; May 27, 1925); Alan R. Lind, *Chicago Surface Lines: An Illustrated History*, 3d ed. (Park Forest, IL: Transport History Press, 1979), pp. 453–73; William Booth Philip, "Chicago and the Down State, A Study of Their Conflicts: 1870–1934" (unpublished Ph.D. dissertation, University of Chicago, 1940), pp. 196–97.

35. *Chicago Post* (July 15, 1925); *Chicago Tribune* (July 16, 1925); Harvey M. Karlen, "Some Political and Administrative Aspects of Municipal Wage Determination in Chicago, 1911–1941" (Ph.D. dissertation, University of Chicago, 1950), pp. 98–99, 106–107; *CDNA: 1928*, p. 818.

36. *Chicago Tribune* (August 4, 1926); Howard Eugene Wilson, *Mary McDowell, Neighbor* (Chicago: University of Chicago Press, 1928), pp. 206–208; Thomas Lee Philpott, *The Slum and the Ghetto: Neighborhood Deterioration and Middle-Class Reform in Chicago, 1880–1930* (New York: Oxford University Press, 1978), pp. 251–69. Philpott notes that real estate interests dominated the housing commission: the state law discussed was actually drafted by the Chicago Real Estate Board, then sold in the name of the Chicago Housing Commission. It was enacted in June 1927, shortly after Dever left office.

37. Details of the events mentioned: WED and Tom Mix, *Chicago Daily News* (March 31, 1925); WED and Jackie Coogan, *Chicago Daily News* (August 6, 1924); WED and Al Jolson, *Chicago Herald and Examiner* (December 24, 1925); WED and Queen Marie, *Chicago Herald and Examiner* (November 14, 1926); WED opening the bowling tournament, *Chicago Post* (February 23, 1924); WED at Eucharistic Conference, *Chicago Post* (June 18, 1926).

38. Arvey's observations are reported in Arthur W. Thurner, "The Impact of Ethnic Groups on the Democratic Party in Chicago, 1920–1928" (Ph.D. dissertation, University of Chicago, 1966), p. 281. Other details on Dever's home life are noted in *Chicago American* (October 22, 1924); *Chicago Herald and Examiner* (April 20, 1923; September 16, 1923; June 29, 1925; April 26, 1926); *Chicago Tribune* (January 25, 1926).

39. *Chicago American* (April 17, 1925).

40. *Chicago Tribune* (September 1, 1925).

41. Stuart, p. 271; Fletcher Dobyns, *The Underworld of American Politics* (New York: Fletcher Dobyns, 1932), pp. 57–67; Carroll Hill Wooddy, *The Chicago Primary of 1926* (Chicago: University of Chicago Press, 1926), Chapter 4.

42. *Chicago Tribune* (September 1, 1925); Wooddy, pp. 34, 164.

43. *Chicago Tribune* (October 9, 1925); *Chicago Post* (January 23, 1926).

44. This scenario is developed in Paul M. Green, "Irish Chicago," in *Ethnic Chicago*, ed. Peter d'A. Jones and Melvin G. Holli (Grand Rapids, MI: William B. Eerdmans Publishing Co., 1981), pp. 234–41.

45. Wooddy, pp. 160–61. Thurner quotes Michael Igoe as saying Brennan ran for the senate because nobody else wanted to (Thurner, pp. 168–69). Brennan himself said he became a candidate because "I think somebody ought to be in the race with the Volstead Law as his issue in order to make a test of Prohibition sentiment"; see "Brennan and the Vanishing American Boss," *Literary Digest* 98 (September 1, 1928): 36.

46. Wooddy, pp. 160–64.

47. *Chicago Tribune* (March 3, 6, 1926). Brennan's campaign is described in Parke Brown, "Brennan of Illinois," *Century Magazine* 112 (September 1926): 593–601; Wooddy, pp. 160–64; "Senatorial Campaigns," *Time* 9 (August 9, 1926), p. 9.

48. *Chicago Herald and Examiner* (September 15, 29, 1926).

49. *Chicago Daily News, Chicago Tribune* (both November 3, 1926). Because of various

campaign irregularities, the U.S. Senate refused to seat Smith, necessitating a special election in 1928; details are in Carroll Hill Wooddy, *The Case of Frank L. Smith: A Study in Representative Government* (Chicago: University of Chicago Press, 1931).

Chapter 9. The Unmaking of the Mayor: 1927

1. *Chicago American* (November 9, 1926); *Chicago Daily News* (November 10, 1926); John Bright, *Hizzoner Big Bill Thompson: An Idyll of Chicago* (New York: Jonathan Cape and Harrison Smith, 1930), p. 250; *Chicago Herald and Examiner* (December 14, 1926).

2. *Chicago Herald and Examiner* (July 12, 1923, November 7, 1926); *Chicago Tribune* (October 16, 19, 1925); *Chicago Post* (November 14, 1926); *Chicago American* (December 1, 1926).

3. *Chicago American* (December 10, 1926); *Chicago Journal* (November 13, 1926).

4. *Chicago Tribune* (November 4, 1926); *Chicago Herald and Examiner* (November 4, 7, 1926).

5. Carr was reported to be the "logical standard-bearer next spring" (if Dever retired) by the *Chicago Daily News* (November 3, 1926). For a discussion of Carr's strengths as a possible candidate, see Green, "Irish Chicago," in *Ethnic Chicago*, ed. Peter d'A. Jones and Melvin G. Holli: (Grand Rapids, MI: William B. Eerdmans Publishing Co., 1981), p. 236.

6. M. James Flynn to WED (December 22, 1926), Dever papers; *Prohibition Hearings, 1926*, pp. 1384–85.

7. *Chicago Herald and Examiner* (December 23, 1926).

8. *Chicago Herald and Examiner* (December 18, 1926).

9. *Chicago Daily News* (December 28, 1926).

10. Bright, p. 204; Lloyd Wendt and Herman Kogan, *Big Bill of Chicago* (Indianapolis: Bobbs-Merrill Co., 1953), p. 214.

11. Carroll Hill Wooddy, *The Chicago Primary of 1926* (Chicago: University of Chicago Press, 1926), pp. 18–33, 286–87.

12. Ibid., pp. 20–21.

13. Wendt and Kogan, pp. 216–18.

14. Ibid., p. 222; William H. Stuart, *The Twenty Incredible Years* (Chicago and New York: M. A. Donohue and Co., 1935), p. 227.

15. Stuart, pp. 267–68. Wooddy suggests that Harding was slated on his own merits, and Thompson was brought in only afterward (Wooddy, *Chicago Primary*, pp. 30–31).

16. Stuart, pp. 250–51; Wooddy, Chapter 3; *Chicago Tribune* (April 7, 1926).

17. Wendt and Kogan, pp. 231–32.

18. Ibid., p. 233.

19. *Chicago American, Chicago Journal, Chicago Tribune* (all December 11, 1926).

20. *Chicago Journal* (December 30, 1926); *Chicago Daily News* (January 28, 1927; February 12, 1927). Dever's nominal opponent in the primary was Martin Walsh, a West Side attorney.

21. *Chicago Daily News* (January 24, 1927, February 7, 1927).

22. Bright, p. 250; *Chicago Daily News* (February 7, 1927).

23. George S. Counts, *School and Society in Chicago* (New York: Harcourt, Brace, 1928), pp. 266–68; Mary Herrick, *The Chicago Schools: A Social and Political History* (Beverly Hills, CA: Sage Publications, 1971), p. 167.

24. Stuart, pp. 292–97. It was revealed during the campaign that the offending

history texts had actually been adopted during Thompson's administration, but that information seems to have made little impact on the story. For a British viewpoint on Thompson's Anglophobic campaign, see S. K. Ratcliffe, "King George in Chicago," *The New Statesman* 29 (April 23, 1927): 34–36.

25. *Chicago Herald and Examiner* (January 5, 1927); Wendt and Kogan, pp. 262–63; Fred D. Pasley, *Al Capone: The Biography of a Self-Made Man* (London: Faber and Faber, 1931), p. 142.

26. Harold Ickes to WED (March 4, 1927), Ickes Papers; Arthur W. Thurner, "The Impact of Ethnic Groups on the Democratic Party in Chicago, 1920–1928" (Ph.D. dissertation, University of Chicago, 1966), p. 267; Albert Brunker to Julius Rosenwald (February 14, 1927), Julius Rosenwald Papers, University of Chicago, Chicago; "Mud-slinger v. 'Rats'," *Time* 9 (February 21, 1927): 8–9.

27. *Chicago Daily News, Chicago Tribune* (both January 26, 1927).

28. *Chicago Daily News* (February 4, 1927); *Chicago Post* (February 19, 1927); *Chicago Herald and Examiner* (February 21, 1927).

29. *Chicago Tribune* (February 23, 1927).

30. *Chicago Daily News, Chicago Tribune* (both February 23, 1927).

31. John M. Allswang, *A House for All Peoples: Ethnic Politics in Chicago* (Lexington: University of Kentucky Press, 1971), p. 57; "What 'Big Bill's' Victory Means," *Literary Digest* 93 (April 16, 1927): 6.

32. *Chicago Tribune* (February 23, 1927).

33. Harold Ickes to WED (March 4, 1927), Ickes Papers.

34. Some writers have incorrectly combined these two committees in their accounts of the 1927 election. For information on the Independent Republicans for Dever Committee, see *Chicago Tribune* (March 2, 1927); and David R. Johnson, "Crime Fighting Reform in Chicago: An Analysis of Its Leadership, 1919–1927" (M.A. thesis, University of Chicago, 1966), pp. 83–84. The Independent Republicans' campaign methods are described (and taken to task) in a letter by attorney Carl V. Wisner. Wisner felt the committee should spend less money on newspaper ads and more on precinct organizing (Carl V. Wisner to Graham Taylor [March 18, 1927], Taylor Papers). For an example of one of the ads, see *Chicago Tribune* (March 24, 1927).

35. *Chicago Daily News* (March 7, 1927); Clayton F. Smith to Raymond Robins (March 30, 1927), Robins Papers.

36. *Chicago Tribune* (March 8, 1927).

37. *Chicago Daily News, Chicago Herald and Examiner* (both February 23, 1927).

38. Bright, pp. 250–51.

39. Thompson originally hurled the slur at both Dever and Brennan. The party leader chose not to reply (see *Chicago Herald and Examiner* [March 1, 1927]; *Chicago Tribune* [March 3, 17, 1927]).

40. Wendt and Kogan, p. 254; *Chicago Tribune* (March 16, 24, 1927).

41. *Chicago Tribune* (March 11, 12, 14, 1927).

42. "Equal Rights to All, Special Privileges to None" (undated typescript), Dever Papers. This document was a proposal of campaign strategy submitted to the mayor; the author is unknown.

43. Ibid.; *Chicago Post* (January 14, 1927); *Chicago Daily News* (March 4, 8, 1927); *Chicago Tribune* (March 10, 1927).

44. *Chicago Tribune* (April 3, 1927); Harold F. Gosnell, *Negro Politicians* (Chicago: University of Chicago Press, 1935), p. 369; Stuart, pp. 304–305.

45. *Chicago Daily News* (March 4, 1927); *Chicago Tribune* (March 24, 1927).

46. See Thomas Lee Philpott, *The Slum and the Ghetto: Neighborhood Deterioration and Middle-Class Reform in Chicago, 1880–1930* (New York: Oxford University Press,

1987), especially Chapter 13.

47. Bright, p. 256: Wendt and Kogan, p. 267; *Chicago Tribune* (March 21, 1927).

48. Wendt and Kogan, pp. 266–67; *Chicago Tribune* (February 18, 1927).

49. George C. Hoffman, "Big Bill Thompson: His Mayoral Campaigns and Voting Strength" (M.A. thesis, University of Chicago, 1956), p. 40: *Chicago Tribune* (February 26, 1927). Thompson also had the support of what was left of the Cook County Democrats, the old Bobbie Burke political club of the early 1900s (*Chicago Herald and Examiner* [March 2, 1927]).

50. For examples, see *Chicago Tribune* (March 21, 1927); *Chicago Herald and Examiner* (March 12, 28, 1927).

51. Pasley, p. 136; Wendt and Kogan, pp. 257, 268–69.

52. *Chicago Tribune* (March 29, 30, 1927); *Chicago American* (April 4, 1927).

53. Stuart, pp. 316–17.

54. *Chicago Herald and Examiner, Chicago Tribune* (both April 6, 1927); Wendt and Kogan, p. 271.

55. Official Canvass, Board of Election Commissioners (April 5, 1927), Municipal Reference Library.

56. Ibid.; *Chicago Tribune* (April 6, 1927) gives a detailed, ward-by-ward analysis.

57. *Chicago Tribune* (April 6, 1927).

58. Allswang, p. 42.

59. John D. Buenker, "The Progressive Era: A Search for a Synthesis," *Mid-America* 51 (July 1969): 190–91.

60. Allswang, p. 42.

61. Humbert S. Nelli, *Italians in Chicago, 1880–1930: A Study in Ethnic Mobility* (New York: Oxford University Press, 1970), pp. 224–31. See also Dianne Marie Pinderhughes, "Interpretations of Racial and Ethnic Participation in American Politics: The Cases of Black, Italian, and Polish Communitites in Chicago, 1910–1940" (Ph.D. dissertation, University of Chicago, 1977), pp. 204–207.

62. Edward R. Kantowicz, *Polish-American Politics in Chicago: 1888–1940* (Chicago and London: University of Chicago Press, 1975), pp. 142–50.

63. Edward Herbert Mazur, "Minyans for a Prairie City: The Politics of Chicago Jewry, 1850–1940" (Ph.D. dissertation, University of Chicago, 1974), pp. 274, 280–83.

64. David Dolnick, "The Role of Labor in Chicago Politics since 1919" (M.A. thesis, University of Chicago, 1939), pp. 30–33.

65. Among the contemporary national magazine commentaries on Dever's loss to Thompson: Nels Anderson, "Democracy in Chicago," *Century Magazine* 116 (November 1927): 71–78; Elmer Davis, "Portrait of an Elected Person," *Harper's Magazine* 155 (July 1927): 171–85; Kate Sargent, "Chicago, Hands Down!" *The Forum* 78 (November 1927): 708–24; William Allen White, "They Can't Beat My Big Boy!" *Collier's* 129 (June 18, 1927):. 8–9, 46–47; "What 'Big Bill's' Victory Means," *Literary Digest* 93 (April 6, 1927): 5–7; "Why Chicago Did It," *The New Republic* 50 (April 20, 1927), pp. 234–36. The *St. Louis Star* observation is quoted in the *Literary Digest* article, p. 7. Will Rogers is quoted in Elmer Davis, p. 172.

66. Alex Gottfried, *Boss Cermak of Chicago: A Study of Political Leadership* (Seattle: University of Washington Press, 1962), pp. 151–52, 388; Donald Richberg, "Gold-Plated Anarchy: An Interpretation of the Fall of the Giants," *The Nation* 136 (April 5, 1933): 369. Richberg claims that he was preparing a series of exposés for the *Chicago Daily News* on the Thompson-Insull connection, and that the articles were not published because of Insull's threat to Brennan. See also Fletcher Dobyns, *The*

Underworld of American Politics (New York: Fletcher Dobyns, 1932), pp. 71–72; Lloyd Lewis and Henry Justin Smith, *Chicago: The History of Its Reputation* (New York: Harcourt, Brace and Co., 1929), p. 454.

67. Dever himself scoffed at reports that Brennan had knifed him, saying that the party leader had done "all he could" to help his reelection. See press release (October 15, 1928), Dever Papers.

68. *Chicago Tribune* (April 6, 1927); Charles E. Merriam to Carroll H. Wooddy (May 9, 1927), Merriam Papers. Dever recognized the importance of the Prohibition issue as the campaign progressed. The *Chicago Herald and Examiner* (February 27, 1927) quotes an interview with the mayor: "If they beat me in April, it will be purely and simply because I have enforced the law. Had I been satisfied to wink at evasion, there would be no contest."

69. Elmer Davis, pp. 172, 182–83. See also David R. Johnson, Chapter 3.

70. "Why Chicago Did It," pp. 234–36.

71. Anderson, p. 72.

72. Quoted in Elmer Davis, p. 183.

Chapter 10. The Least-Known Chicago Mayor

1. *Chicago Post* (April 7, 1927); *Chicago Herald and Examiner* (April 13, 1927).

2. *Chicago Herald and Examiner* (April 7, 1927). WED to Charles S. Cutting (May 18, 1927); WED to Silus Strawn (May 18, 1927); both Dever Papers.

3. WED to Graham Taylor (May 18, 1927), Dever Papers.

4. Harold Ickes to Raymond Robins (May 16, 1927), Ickes Papers. The most thorough coverage of the Dever banquet appeared a thousand miles away, in the *Woburn Daily Times* (May 16, 1927).

5. *Chicago Tribune* (February 7, 1928).

6. WED to Raymond and Whitcomb Company (September 22, 1927); Margaret and Raymond Robins to WED (December 8, 1927); WED to Margaret and Raymond Robins (December 8, 1927); all Dever Papers.

7. A sampling of Dever's speaking schedule: December 3, 1927, Chicago Bar Association; December 15, 1927, Rock Island Railroad Club of Chicago; January 26, 1928, Milwaukee Businessman Club; February 28, 1928, Louisville Credit Men's Association. The quotation is from an uncredited newspaper clipping (dated January 27, 1928), Dever Scrapbooks.

8. *Chicago Daily News* (August 5, 1927). Edward H. Levi to WED (March 28, 1928); WED to Edward H. Levi (March 31, 1928); both Dever Papers. (Although high-school editor Levi was not able to benefit from Dever's views on public affairs, he still went on to become attorney general of the United States.) See also WED to W. H. Stayton (March 27, 1928), Dever Papers.

9. WED to E. W. Rossiter (November 17, 1927); A. P. Sandles to WED (March 19, 1928); both Dever Papers.

10. Franklin D. Roosevelt to WED (December 3, 1928), Dever Papers.

11. WED to Martin J. O'Brien (October 24, 1928); WED to James Michael Curley (February 6, 1929); both Dever Papers. *Chicago Herald and Examiner* (September 4, 1929).

12. Raymond Robins to WED (March 6, 1929); WED to M. J. Collins (July 12, 1929); both Dever Papers. *Chicago Herald and Examiner, Chicago Tribune* (both September 4, 1929).

13. *Chicago Herald and Examiner, Chicago Journal of Commerce* (both September 4,

1929); *Chicago American* (September 6, 1929).

14. Thompson, Dunne, and O'Brien are quoted in *Chicago Post* (September 4, 1929); the Cermak statement is in *Chicago Tribune* (September 4, 1929); Arvey's speech is reported in the Proceedings of Chicago City Council, Special Meeting (September 5, 1929), copy in Dever Papers.

15. The editorials cited are *Chicago Times* (September 5, 1929); *Chicago Post* (September 4, 1929); *New York Times* (September 7, 1929); *Brooklyn Tablet* (September 14, 1929); "Editorially," *The Chicagoan* 7 (September 28, 1929): 7. The McCutcheon cartoon is in *Chicago Tribune* (September 5, 1929).

16. *Chicago Post* (September 5, 6, 1929); *Chicago American*, *Chicago Daily News* (both September 6, 1929).

17. Dever's death postponed the scheduled party slatemaking sessions to select candidates for the superior court (*Chicago Post* [September 5, 1929]).

18. Paul M. Green, "Irish Chicago," in *Ethnic Chicago* ed. Peter d'A. Jones and Melvin Holli (Grand Rapids, MI: William B. Eerdmans Publishing Co., 1981), p. 238.

19. Connie Fletcher, "Big Ideas that Went Bust," *Chicago* 30 (February 1981): 112. Used with permission.

20. New York City fusion politics, particularly in the classic campaign of 1933, is described in Arthur Mann, *LaGuardia Comes to Power: 1933* (Philadelphia: J. B. Lippincott Co., 1965).

21. Reform Democrat Robert Merriam, the professor's son, ran as a Republican fusionist against Richard J. Daley in 1955; Daley won the close contest. Independents and reform Democrats united to elect Jane Byrne to the mayoralty in 1979, but long-time party regular Byrne governed in traditional organization style. Harold Washington's 1983 election marked the first clear victory of a reform mayor over the Democratic machine.

22. Green, "Irish Chicago," *passim*.

23. John Hopkins became Chicago's first Roman Catholic mayor in 1893. However, he was not elected to a full term and merely filled out what was left of the assassinated Carter Harrison, I's, tenure.

24. Becker's study of Dunne concentrates on his years as mayor (1905–1907). For details on the rest of Dunne's career, particularly his term as governor, see John D. Buenker, "Edward F. Dunne: The Urban New Stock Democrat as Progressive," *Mid-America* 50 (January 1968): 3–21.

25. *Chicago Herald and Examiner* (March 18, 1924); Arthur W. Thurner, "The Impact of Ethnic Groups on the Democratic Party in Chicago, 1920–1928" (Ph.D. dissertation, University of Chicago, 1966), pp. 263–64.

26. Charles E. Merriam, *Chicago: A More Intimate View of Urban Politics* (New York: Macmillan Co., 1929), p. 259.

27. Edward R. Kantowicz, *Polish-American Politics in Chicago: 1888–1940* (Chicago and London: University of Chicago Press, 1975), p. 146.

28. See Paul M. Green, "The Chicago Democratic Party, 1840–1920: From Factionalism to Political Organization" (Ph.D. dissertation, University of Chicago, 1975), *passim*.

29. The only recent scholarly articles on Dever have been the Bukowski essay in *Chicago History,* and the author's "William E. Dever: A Chicago Political Fable," in Paul M. Green and Melvin G. Holli, eds., *The Mayors: The Chicago Political Tradition* (Carbondale: Southern Illinois University Press, 1987), pp. 82–98.

Bibliography

Books

Abbott, Edith. *The Tenements of Chicago: 1908–35*. Chicago: University of Chicago Press, 1936.

Allen, Frederick Lewis. *Only Yesterday: An Informal History of the Nineteen-Twenties*. New York and London: Harper and Bros., 1931.

Allswang, John M. *Bosses, Machines, and Urban Voters: An American Symbiosis*. Port Washington, NY and London: National University Publications, Kennikat Press, 1977.

————. *A House for All Peoples: Ethnic Politics in Chicago*. Lexington: University of Kentucky Press, 1971.

Andrews, Wayne. *Battle for Chicago*. New York: Harcourt, Brace and Co., 1946.

Asbury, Herbert. *Gem of the Prairie: An Informal History of the Chicago Underworld*. New York: Alfred A. Knopf, 1940.

Asinof, Eliot. *Eight Men Out*. New York: Holt, Rinehart, and Winston, 1963.

Barrett, Paul. *The Automobile and Urban Transit*. Philadelphia: Temple University Press, 1983.

Biles, Roger. *Big City Boss in Depression and War: Mayor Edward J. Kelly of Chicago*. DeKalb: Northern Illinois University Press, 1984.

Bingay, Malcolm W. *Of Me I Sing*. Indianapolis: Bobbs-Merrill Co., 1949.

The Book of Chicagoans [later *Who's Who in Chicago and Illinois*]. Chicago: A. N. Marquis, 1905–50.

Boston Directory. . . . Boston: Adams, Sampson, and Co., 1850–90.

Bright, John. *Hizzoner Big Bill Thompson: An Idyll of Chicago*. New York: Jonathan Cape and Harrison Smith, 1930.

Bryce, James. *The American Commonwealth*, 2 vols. 3d ed. New York and London: Macmillan Co., 1895.

Buder, Stanley. *Pullman: An Experiment in Industrial Order and Community Planning, 1880–1930*. New York: Oxford University Press, 1967.

Buenker, John D. *Urban Liberalism and Progressive Reform*. New York: Charles Scribner's Sons, 1973.

Burnham, Daniel, and Edward H. Bennett. *The Plan of Chicago*. Chicago: Commerical Club, 1909.

Carlson, Stephen P., and Fred W. Schneider, III. *P.C.C.: The Car that Fought Back*. Glendale, CA: Interurban Press, 1980.

Caro, Robert A. *The Power Broker: Robert Moses and the Fall of New York*. New York: Alfred A. Knopf, 1974.

Carter, Paul A. *Another Part of the Twenties*. New York: Columbia University Press, 1977.

Chicago Daily News Almanac. Chicago: Chicago Daily News, 1900–31.

Chicago Public Works: A History. Chicago: Rand McNally and Co., 1973.

Chicago Rapid Transit: Rolling Stock, 1892–1947. Chicago: Central Electric Railfans' Association, 1973.

Clark, Neil McCullough. *Mayor Dever and Prohibition: The Story of a Dramatic Fight to Enforce the Law*. Westerville, OH: American Issue Publishing Co., 1925.

Clayton, John, ed. *The Illinois Fact Book and Historical Almanac, 1673–1968*. Carbondale and Edwardsville: Southern Illinois University Press, 1970.

Condit, Carl W. *Chicago 1910–29: Building, Planning, and Urban Technology*. Chicago and London: University of Chicago Press, 1973.

———. *Chicago 1930–70: Building, Planning, and Urban Technology*. Chicago and London: University of Chicago Press, 1974.

Counts, George S. *School and Society in Chicago*. New York: Harcourt, Brace, 1928.

Cudahy, Brian J. *Destination: Loop*. Brattleboro, VT: Stephen Greene Press, 1982.

———. *Under the Sidewalks of New York*. Brattleboro, VT: Stephen Greene Press, 1979.

Davis, Allen F. *Spearheads of Reform: The Social Settlements and the Progressive Movement, 1890–1914*. New York: Oxford University Press, 1971.

Davis, James Leslie. *The Elevated System and the Growth of Northern Chicago*. Northwestern University Studies in Geography No. 10. Evanston, IL: Northwestern University, 1965.

Dedmon, Emmett. *Fabulous Chicago*, 2d ed. New York: Atheneum, 1981.

Demaris, Ovid. *Captive City*. New York: Lyle Stuart, 1969.

DeWitt, Benjamin Parke. *The Progressive Movement*. New York: Macmillan Co., 1915.

Dobyns, Fletcher. *The Underworld of American Politics*. New York: Fletcher Dobyns, 1932.

Drake, St. Clair, and Horace R. Cayton. *Black Metropolis*. New York: Harcourt, Brace and Company, 1945.

Duis, Perry. *Chicago: Creating New Traditions*. Chicago: Chicago Historical Society, 1976.

———. *The Saloon: Public Drinking in Chicago and Boston, 1880–1920*. Urbana and Chicago: University of Illinois Press, 1983.

Dunne, Edward F. *Illinois: The Heart of a Nation*, 5 vols. Chicago and New York: Lewis Publishing Co., 1933.

Dunne, Finley Peter. *Observations by Mr. Dooley*. New York: Robert Howard Russell, 1902.

Forthal, Sonya. *Cogwheels of Democracy: A Study of the Precinct Captain*. Westport, CT: Greenwood Press, 1972.

Forty-four Cities in the City of Chicago. Chicago: Chicago Plan Commission, 1942.

Fosdick, Raymond B. *John D. Rockefeller, Jr.: A Portrait*. New York: Harper and Bros., 1956.

Ginger, Ray. *Altgeld's America*, reprint ed. New York: New Viewpoints, 1973.

Gosnell, Harold F. *Machine Politics, Chicago Model*. Chicago: University of Chicago Press, 1937.

————.*Negro Politicians*. Chicago: University of Chicago Press, 1935.

Gottfried, Alex. *Boss Cermak of Chicago: A Study of Political Leadership*. Seattle: University of Washington Press, 1962.

Gould, Louis L., ed. *The Progressive Era*. Syracuse, NY: Syracuse University Press, 1974.

Grant, Madison. *The Passing of the Great Race*, rev. ed. New York: Charles Scribner's Sons, 1919.

Green, Paul M. and Melvin G. Holli, eds. *The Mayors: The Chicago Political Tradition*. Carbondale: Southern Illinois University Press, 1987.

Handlin, Oscar. *Boston's Immigrants*, rev. ed. Cambridge, MA: Belknap Press of Harvard University Press, 1959.

————. *The Uprooted*, 2d. ed. Boston: Little, Brown, and Co., 1973.

Harrison, Carter H. *Growing Up with Chicago*. Chicago: Ralph Fletcher Seymour, 1944.

————. *Stormy Years: The Autobiography of Carter H. Harrison*. Indianapolis: Bobbs-Merrill Co., 1935.

Hays, Samuel P. *The Response to Industrialism, 1885–1914*. Chicago: University of Chicago Press, 1957.

Hermann, Charles H. *Recollections of Life and Doings in Chicago*. Chicago: Normandie House, 1945.

Herrick, Mary. *The Chicago Schools: A Social and Political History*. Beverly Hills, CA: Sage Publications, 1971.

Higham, John. *Strangers in the Land*. New Brunswick, NJ: Rutgers University Press, 1955.

Hill, Caroline. *Mary McDowell and Municipal Housekeeping*. Chicago: Millar Publishing Co., 1938.

Historic City: The Settlement of Chicago. Chicago, City of Chicago, 1976.

Hofstadter, Richard. *The Age of Reform: From Bryan to F.D.R.* New York: Alfred A. Knopf, 1955.

Holli, Melvin G. *Reform in Detroit: Hazen S. Pingree and Urban Politics*. New York: Oxford University Press, 1969.

Holli, Melvin G., and Peter d'A. Jones, eds. *Biographical Dictionary of American Mayors, 1820–1980: Big City Mayors*. Westport, CT: Greenwood Press, 1981.

Holt, Glen E., and Dominic Pacyga. *Chicago: A Historical Guide to the Neighborhoods— The Loop and South Side*. Chicago: Chicago Historical Society, 1979.

Hoyt, Homer. *One Hundred Years of Land Values in Chicago*. Chicago: University of Chicago Press, 1933.

Ickes, Harold L. *The Autobiography of a Curmudgeon*. New York: Reynal and Hitchcock, 1943.

Jackson, Kenneth T. *The Ku Klux Klan in the City: 1915–1930*. New York: Oxford University Press, 1967.

Jewell, Frank. *An Annotated Bibliography of Chicago History*. Chicago: Chicago Historical Society, 1979.

Johnson, Claudius O. *Carter Henry Harrison I, Political Leader*. Chicago: University of Chicago Press, 1928.

Johnson, James D. *A Century of Chicago Streetcars, 1858–1958*. Wheaton, IL: Traction Orange Co., 1964.

Jones, Peter d'A., and Melvin G. Holli, eds. *Ethnic Chicago*. Grand Rapids, MI: William B. Eerdmans Publishing Co., 1981.

Kantowicz, Edward R. *Polish-American Politics in Chicago: 1888–1940*. Chicago and London: University of Chicago Press, 1975.

Karl, Barry D. *Charles E. Merriam and the Study of Politics*. Chicago and London: University of Chicago Press, 1974.

Karlen, Harvey M. *The Governments of Chicago*. Chicago: Courier Publishing Co., 1958.

Kennedy, Eugene. *Himself! The Life and Times of Mayor Richard J. Daley*. New York: Viking Press, 1978.

King, Hoyt. *Citizen Cole of Chicago*. Chicago: Horder's Inc., 1931.

Kobler, John. *Capone: The Life and World of Al Capone*. New York: Putnam, 1971.

Kolko, Gabriel. *The Triumph of Conservatism*. New York: Macmillan Company, 1963.

Lakeside Annual Directory of the City of Chicago. Chicago: Chicago Directory Co., 1889–1916.

Landesco, John. *Organized Crime in Chicago*, reprint. Chicago and London: University of Chicago Press, 1968.

Lepawsky, Albert. *The Judicial System of Metropolitan Chicago*. Chicago: University of Chicago Press, 1932.

Leuchtenberg, William E. *The Perils of Prosperity, 1914–32*. Chicago: University of Chicago Press, 1958.

Levine, Edward M. *The Irish and Irish Politicians*. Notre Dame, IN: University of Notre Dame Press, 1966.

Lewis, Lloyd, and Henry Justin Smith. *Chicago: The History of Its Reputation*. New York: Harcourt, Brace and Co., 1929.

Lind, Alan R. *Chicago Surface Lines: An Illustrated History*, 3d ed. Park Forest, IL: Transport History Press, 1979.

Link, Arthur S., and Richard L. McCormick. *Progressivism*. Arlington Heights, IL: Harlan Davidson, 1983.

Local Community Fact Book: Chicago Metropolitan Area. Chicago: Chicago Fact Book Consortium, University of Illinois at Chicago, 1984.

Lyle, John H. *The Dry and Lawless Years*. Englewood Cliffs, NJ: Prentice-Hall, 1960.

Mann, Arthur. *LaGuardia: A Fighter against His Times, 1882–1933*. Philadelphia: J. B. Lippincott Co., 1959.

———. *LaGuardia Comes to Power: 1933*. Philadelphia: J. B. Lippincott Co., 1965.

———, ed. *The Progressive Era: Liberal Renaissance or Liberal Failure*. New York: Holt, Rinehart and Winston, 1963.

———, ed. *The Progressive Era: Major Issues of Interpretation*, 2d ed. Hinsdale, IL: Dryden Press, 1975.

Martin, Edward M. *The Role of the Bar in Electing the Bench in Chicago*. Chicago: University of Chicago Press, 1936.

Mayer, Harold M., and Richard C. Wade. *Chicago: Growth of a Metropolis*. Chicago and London: University of Chicago Press, 1969.

McDonald, Forrest. *Insull*. Chicago: University of Chicago Press, 1962.

McPhaul, John J. *Johnny Torrio: First of the Gang Lords*. New Rochelle, NY: Arlington House, 1970.

Merriam, Charles E. *Chicago: A More Intimate View of Urban Politics*. New York: Macmillan Co., 1929.

Merriam, Charles E., Spencer D. Parratt, and Albert Lepawsky. *The Government of the Metropolitan Region of Chicago*. Chicago : University of Chicago Press, 1933.

Middleton, William D. *Grand Central: The World's Greatest Railway Terminal*. San Marino, CA: Golden West Books, 1977.

Montgomery, Royal E. *Industrial Relations in the Chicago Building Trades*. Chicago: University of Chicago Press, 1927.

Moody, Walter D. *Wacker's Manual of the Plan of Chicago*. Chicago: Chicago Plan Commission, 1915.

Morris, Edmund. *The Rise of Theodore Roosevelt*. New York: Coward, McCann and Geoghegan, 1979.

Murray, R. K. *The 103rd Ballot*. New York: Harper, 1976.

Nelli, Humbert S. *Italians in Chicago, 1880–1930: A Study in Ethnic Mobility*. New York: Oxford University Press, 1970.

Ostrogorski, M. *Democracy and the Organization of Political Parties*, 2 vols. New York and London: Macmillan Co., 1902.

Pacyga, Dominic A., and Ellen Skerrett. *Chicago: City of Neighborhoods*. Chicago: Loyola University Press, 1986.

Pasley, Fred D. *Al Capone: The Biography of a Self-Made Man*. London: Faber and Faber Ltd., 1931.

Perles, Anthony. *The People's Railway: A History of the Municipal Railway of San Francisco*. Glendale, CA: Interurban Press, 1981.

Peterson, Virgil W. *Barbarians in Our Midst*. Boston: Little, Brown and Co., 1952.

Philpott, Thomas Lee. *The Slum and the Ghetto: Neighborhood Deterioration and Middle-Class Reform in Chicago, 1880–1930*. New York: Oxford University Press, 1978.

Pierce, Bessie Louise, ed. *A History of Chicago*, 3 vols. New York: Alfred A. Knopf, 1937–1957.

———, ed. *As Others See Chicago: Impressions of Visitors, 1673–1933*. Chicago: University of Chicago Press, 1933.

Pinderhughes, Dianne M. *Race and Ethnicity in Chicago*. Urbana and Chicago: University of Illinois Press, 1987.

Poles of Chicago: 1837–1937. Chicago: Polish Pageant, 1937.

Reid, Robert L., ed. *Battleground: The Autobiography of Margaret A. Haley*. Urbana: University of Illinois Press, 1982.

Riordan, William L., ed. *Plunkitt of Tammany Hall*, paperback ed. New York: E. P. Dutton and Co., 1963.

Royko, Mike. *Boss: Richard J. Daley of Chicago*. New York: E. P. Dutton and Co., 1971.

Schramm, Jack E., and William H. Henning. *Detroit's Street Railways: 1863–1922*. Chicago: Central Electric Railfans' Association, 1978.

Sewall, Samuel. *The History of Woburn, Middlesex County, Massachusetts*. Boston: Wiggins and Lunt, 1868.

Smith, Alfred E. *Up to Now*. New York: Viking Press, 1929.

Smith, Page. *Redeeming the Time: A Peoples History of the 1920s and the New Deal*. New York: McGraw-Hill Book Co., 1987.

Stead, William T. *If Christ Came to Chicago!* Chicago: Laird and Lee, 1894.

Steffens, Lincoln. *The Autobiography of Lincoln Steffens*. New York: Harcourt, Brace and Co., 1936.

Stehman, J. Warren. *The Financial History of the American Telephone and Telegraph Company*. Boston and New York: Houghton Mifflin Co., 1925.

Stevenson, Elizabeth. *Babbits and Bohemians: The American 1920s*. New York: Macmillan Company, 1967.

Stuart, William H. *The Twenty Incredible Years*. Chicago and New York: M. A. Donohue and Co., 1935.

Sullivan, Edward D. *Rattling the Cup on Chicago Crime*. New York: Vanguard Press, 1929.

Sullivan, Mark. *Our Times: The United States, 1900–1925*, 6 vols. New York: Charles Scribner's Sons, 1926–1935.

Tarr, Joel Arthur. *A Study of Boss Politics: William Lorimer of Chicago*. Urbana: University of Illinois Press, 1971.

Taylor, Graham. *Chicago Commons through Forty Years*. Chicago: Chicago Commons Association, 1936.

————. *Pioneering on Social Frontiers*. Chicago: University of Chicago Press, 1930.

Thernstrom, Stephan. *Poverty and Progress: Social Mobility in a Nineteenth Century City.* Cambridge, MA: Harvard University Press, 1964.

Timberlake, James H. *Prohibition and the Progressive Movement*. New York: Atheneum, 1970.

Townsend, Walter A. *Illinois Democracy*, 5 vols. Springfield, IL: Democratic Historical Association, 1935.

Tuttle, William H., Jr. *Race Riot: Chicago in the Red Summer of 1919*. New York: Atheneum, 1970.

Vieg, John A. *The Government of Education in Metropolitan Chicago*. Chicago: University of Chicago Press, 1939.

Von der Rhoer, Edward. *Master Spy.* New York: Charles Scribner's Sons, 1981.

Wade, Louise C. *Graham Taylor, Pioneer for Social Justice: 1851–1938*. Chicago: University of Chicago Press, 1964.

Weber, Harry P. *An Outline History of Chicago Traction*. Chicago: Chicago Surface Lines, 1936.

Weiss, Nancy Joan. *Charles Francis Murphy, 1858–1924: Respectability and Responsibility in Tammany Politics*. Northampton, MA: Smith College, 1968.

Wendt, Lloyd. *Chicago Tribune: The Rise of a Great American Newspaper.* Chicago: Rand McNally and Co., 1979.

Wendt, Lloyd, and Herman Kogan. *Big Bill of Chicago*. Indianapolis: Bobbs-Merrill Co., 1953.

Wendt, Lloyd, and Herman Kogan. *Lords of the Levee: The Story of Bathhouse John and Hinky Dink*. Indianapolis: Bobbs-Merrill Co., 1943.

Werner, M. R. *Julius Rosenwald: The Life of a Practical Humanitarian*. New York: Harper and Brothers, 1939.

White, Leonard D. *Conditions of Municipal Employment in Chicago: A Study in Morale*. Chicago: City Clerk, 1925.

Whitehead, Helen, ed. *The Chicago Plan Commission: A Historical Sketch*. Chicago: Department of City Planning, 1961.

Wiebe, Robert H. *The Search for Order, 1877–1920*. New York: Hill and Wang, 1967.

Wik, Reynold M. *Henry Ford and Grass-Roots America*. Ann Arbor: University of Michigan Press, 1972.

Wilson, Howard Eugene. *Mary McDowell, Neighbor.* Chicago: University of Chicago Press, 1928.

Woburn. Boston: Edison Electric Illuminating Co., 1909.

Wooddy, Carroll Hill. *The Case of Frank L. Smith: A Study in Representative Government*. Chicago: University of Chicago Press, 1931.

————. *The Chicago Primary of 1926*. Chicago: University of Chicago Press, 1926.

Zink, Harold. *City Bosses in the United States*. Durham, NC: Duke University Press, 1930.

Articles

"Ad Nauseam." *Time* 9 (April 11, 1927), p. 12.

Addams, Jane. "Why the Ward Boss Rules." *The Outlook* 58 (April 2, 1898), pp. 879–82.

Allswang, John M. "The Chicago Negro Voter and the Democratic Consensus: A Case Study, 1918–1936." *Journal of the Illinois State Historical Society* 60 (Spring 1967): 154–55.

Anderson, Nels. "Democracy in Chicago." *Century Magazine* 116 (November 1927), pp. 71–78.

"Brennan and the Vanishing American Boss." *Literary Digest* 98 (September 1, 1928), pp. 34–36.

Brown, Parke. "Brennan of Illinois." *Century Magazine* 112 (September 1, 1926), pp. 593–601.

Buenker, John D. "Dynamics of Chicago Ethnic Politics, 1900–1930." *Journal of the Illinois State Historical Society* 67 (April 1974), pp. 175–99.

———. "The Progressive Era: A Search for a Synthesis." *Mid-America* 51 (July 1969), pp. 175–93.

———. "Edward R. Dunne: The Urban New Stock Democrat as Progressive." *Mid-America* 50 (January 1968), pp. 3–21.

Bukowski, Douglas. "William Dever and Prohibition: The Mayoral Elections of 1923 and 1927." *Chicago History* 7 (Summer 1978): 109–18.

Bunche, Ralph J. "The Thompson-Negro Alliance." *Opportunity* 7 (March 1929), pp. 78–80.

"Chicago's New Mayor." *The Outlook* 133 (April 18, 1923), pp. 693–94.

"Chicago's Political Circus." *World's Work* 54 (June 1927), pp. 122–24.

Cudahy, Brian J. "Chicago's Early Elevated Lines and Construction of the Union Loop." *Chicago History* 8 (Winter 1979–80): 194–205.

Davis, Allen F. "Raymond Robins: The Settlement Worker as Municipal Reformer." *Social Services Review* 33 (June 1959), pp. 131–41.

Davis, Elmer. "Portrait of an Elected Person." *Harper's Magazine* 155 (July 1927), pp. 171–85.

Dever, William E. "Get at the Facts." *Atlantic Monthly* 138 (October 1926), pp. 518–24.

"Drying Up Chicago." *Literary Digest* 79 (December 15, 1923), pp. 16–17.

Duis, Perry, and Glen E. Holt. "Chicago as It Was: Big Bill's Pageant of Progress." *Chicago* 29 (September 1980), pp. 112–14, 116.

"Editorially." *The Chicagoan* 7 (September 28, 1929), p. 7.

Fletcher, Connie. "Big Ideas that Went Bust." *Chicago* 30 (February 1981), p. 112.

Flynn, William J. "Thompson the Cowboy Rides In." *The Nation* 124 (April 20, 1927), pp. 421–22.

Griffenhagen, Edwin O. "The Merit System in Chicago and Cook County." *National Municipal Review* 18 (November 1929), pp. 691–93.

Haller, Mark H. "Organized Crime in Urban Society: Chicago in the Twentieth Century." *Journal of Social History* 41 (Winter 1971–72): 210–34.

Hays, Samuel P. "The Politics of Reform in Municipal Government in the Progressive Era." *Pacific Northwest Quarterly* 55 (October 1964), pp. 159–69.

Hoyt, Homer. "Inventory Gives Low-Down on Near Northwest." *Real Estate* 16 (April 26, 1941), pp. 11–14.

"In Chicago." *Time* 9 (April 18, 1927), p. 13.

"Last of the Bosses." *The Outlook* 149 (August 29, 1928), pp. 693–94.

McCormick, Richard L. "The Discovery that 'Business Corrupts Politics': A Reappraisal of the Origins of Progressivism." *American Historical Review* 86 (April 1981), pp. 247–74.

Merriam, Robert E. "Why Reformers Fail." *Chicago* 1 (May 1954), pp. 20–25, 69.

"Mud-Slinger v. 'Rats.'" *Time* 9 (February 21, 1927), pp. 8–9.

Ratcliffe, S. K. "King George in Chicago." *The New Statesman* 29 (April 23, 1927), pp. 34–36.

Richberg, Donald. "Gold-Plated Anarchy: An Interpretation of the Fall of the Giants." *The Nation* 136 (April 5, 1933), pp. 368–69.

Sargent, Kate. "Chicago, Hands Down!" *The Forum* 58 (November 1927), pp. 708–24.
———. "Chicago, Hands Up!" *The Forum* 58 (October 1927), pp. 522–31.
Schottenhamel, George. "How Big Bill Thompson Won Control of Chicago." *Journal of the Illinois State Historical Society* 45 (Spring 1952): 30–49.
"Senatorial Campaigns." *Time* 9 (August 9, 1926), p. 9.
"Settling Chicago's Traction Question." *The Outlook* 85 (March 1907), p. 537.
Tarr, Joel A. "William Kent to Lincoln Steffens: Origins of Progressive Reform in Chicago." *Mid-America* 47 (January 1965), pp. 48–57.
Taylor, Graham. "New Hope in Our Ward Politics." *The Commons* 6 (April 1901), p. 15.
"What 'Big Bill's' Victory Means." *Literary Digest* 93 (April 20, 1927), pp. 5–7.
White, William Allen. "They Can't Beat My Big Boy." *Collier's* 129 (June 18, 1927), pp. 8–9, 46–47.
"Why Chicago Did It." *The New Republic* 50 (April 20, 1927), pp. 234–36.
Yarros, Victory S. "Sketches of American Mayors: William E. Dever of Chicago." *National Municipal Review* 15 (July 1926), pp. 390–94.

Newspapers

Boston Globe, 1923–1925.
Boston Post, 1904, 1923–1927
Chicago American, 1900–1929.
Chicago Chronicle, 1905.
Chicago Daily News, 1900–1929.
Chicago Examiner, 1900–1914.
Chicago Herald and Examiner, 1914–1929.
Chicago Inter-Ocean, 1905–1911.
Chicago Journal, 1904–1929.
Chicago Post, 1900–1929.
Chicago Record-Herald, 1902–1910.
Chicago Tribune, 1900–1929.
Lightnin' (Chicago), 1928–1929.
New York Times, 1923–1929.
Woburn Daily Times, 1923–1929, 1976.

Unpublished Materials

Becker, Richard E. "Edward Dunne: Reform Mayor of Chicago, 1905–07." Ph.D. dissertation, University of Chicago, 1971.
Beckman, Ellen Josephine. "The Relationship of the Government of the City of Chicago to Cook County from 1893 to 1916." M.A. thesis, University of Chicago, 1940.
Branham, Charles R. "The Transformation of Black Political Leadership in Chicago, 1864–1942." Ph.D. dissertation, University of Chicago, 1981.
Burton, Ralph Joseph. "Mass Transport in the Chicago Region: A Study of Metropolitan Government." Ph.D. dissertation, University of Chicago, 1939.
Camitta, Hugh D. "Raymond Robins: Study of a Progressive, 1901–1917." Honors thesis, Williams College, 1965.
Cressey, Paul F. "The Succession of Cultural Groups in the City of Chicago." Ph.D. dissertation, University of Chicago, 1930.

DeCamp, Roderick. "The Chicago Transit Authority: A Study in Responsibility." Ph.D. dissertation, University of Chicago, 1958.

Dolnick, David. "The Role of Labor in Chicago Politics since 1919." M.A. thesis, University of Chicago, 1939.

Green, Paul M. "The Chicago Democratic Party, 1840–1920: From Factionalism to Political Organization." Ph.D. dissertation, University of Chicago, 1975.

Hoffman, George C. "Big Bill Thompson: His Mayoral Campaigns and Voting Strength." M.A. thesis, University of Chicago, 1956.

Johnson, David R. "Crime Fighting Reform in Chicago: An Analysis of Its Leadership, 1919–1927." M.A. thesis, University of Chicago, 1966.

Karlen, Harvey M. "Some Political and Administrative Aspects of Municipal Wage Determination in Chicago, 1911–1941." Ph.D. dissertation, University of Chicago, 1950.

Mazur, Edward Herbert. "Minyans for a Prairie City: The Politics of Chicago Jewry, 1850–1940." Ph.D. dissertation, University of Chicago, 1974.

Miller, Joan S. "The Politics of Municipal Reform in Chicago during the Progressive Era: The Municipal Voters' League as a Test Case, 1896–1920." M.A. thesis, Roosevelt University, 1966.

Myers, Howard Barton. "The Policing of Labor Disputes in Chicago: A Case Study." Ph.D. dissertation, University of Chicago, 1929.

Perlstein, Eugene. "The Progressive Movement in Chicago: 1919–1924." M.A. thesis, University of Chicago, 1948.

Philip, William Booth. "Chicago and the Down State, A Study in Their Conflicts: 1870–1934." Ph.D. dissertation, University of Chicago, 1940.

Pinderhughes, Dianne Marie. "Interpretations of Racial and Ethnic Participation in American Politics: The Cases of Black, Italian, and Polish Communities in Chicago, 1910–1940." Ph.D. dissertation, University of Chicago, 1977.

Rex, Frederick. "The Mayors of the City of Chicago from March 4, 1837 to April 13, 1933." Typescript, Municipal Reference Library, Chicago.

Thurner, Arthur W. "The Impact of Ethnic Groups on the Democratic Party in Chicago, 1920–1928." Ph.D. dissertation, University of Chicago, 1966.

Tingley, Ralph R. "From Carter Harrison II to Fred Busse: A Study of Political Parties and Personages from 1896 to 1907." Ph.D. dissertation, University of Chicago, 1950.

Manuscript Collections

Chicago Historical Society, William E. Dever Papers, Chicago.

Chicago Historical Society, William E. Dever Scrapbooks, Chicago.

Library of Congress, Walter L. Fisher Papers, Washington, D.C.

Newberry Library, Carter Harrison II Papers, Chicago.

Library of Congress, Harold L. Ickes Papers, Washington D.C.

Chicago Historical Society, Mary McDowell Papers, Chicago.

University of Chicago, Charles E. Merriam Papers, Chicago.

Chicago Historical Society, Agnes Nestor Papers, Chicago.

State Historical Society of Wisconsin, Raymond Robins Papers, Madison.

University of Chicago, Julius Rosenwald Papers, Chicago.

American Jewish Archives, Adolph Sabath Papers, Cincinnati.

Newberry Library, Graham Taylor Papers, Chicago.

Public Documents and Reports

Chicago Board of Education. Proceedings.

Chicago Board of Education. Reports of the General Superintendent of Schools.

Chicago City Council. *An Ordinance Providing for a Comprehensive Municipal Local Transportation System . . . February 27, 1925.*

Chicago City Council. Proceedings.

Chicago Civil Service Commission. Annual Reports.

Chicago Traction and Subway Commission. *Report . . . on a Unified System of Surface, Elevated, and Subway Lines: 1916.*

Cook County Appellate Court. Reports.

Cook County Superior Court. Reports.

Mayor of Chicago (William E. Dever). Annual Reports.

Mayor of Chicago (William E. Dever). *Special Message of Honorable William E. Dever, Mayor, Concerning Chicago's Local Transportation Problem . . . October 22, 1924.*

Mayor of Chicago (William Hale Thompson). *Eight Years of Progress* (1923).

Tax List of the Town of Woburn (Massachusetts) *1861.*

U.S. Congress, Senate, Subcommittee of the Committee on the Judiciary. *The National Prohibition Law.* Hearings on bills to amend the National Prohibition Act (April 5–24, 1926), 69th Cong., 1st sess., 1926.

U.S. Department of Commerce, Bureau of the Census. *Ninth Census of the United States, 1870. Population.*

U.S. Department of Commerce, Bureau of the Census. *Tenth Census of the United States, 1880. Population.*

U.S. Department of Commerce, Bureau of the Census. *Twelfth Census of the United States, 1900. Population.*

Index

EVANSTON TOWNSHIP HS
EVANSTON, IL 60204

101 111918

Central Library

DATE DUE

A